Introduction to Watershed Development

To those aquatic ecologists, watershed managers, and land-use planners who have struggled—sometimes against great odds and with varied success—to preserve the limnological quality and aesthetic beauty of those world heritage lakes that I have grown so to love: Walden Pond (United States), Windermere (United Kingdom), Lago Como (Italy), Sea of Galilee (Israel), Dal Lake (India), Xi Hu (China), and Biwako (Japan). And to the philosopher Thales, who over two and a half millennia ago was one of the first to recognize water's true worth; "Everything is water, water is all," he stated simply with conviction and accuracy.

Introduction to Watershed Development

Understanding and Managing the Impacts of Sprawl

Robert L. France

ROWMAN & LITTLEFIELD PUBLISHERS, INC.
Lanham • Boulder • New York • Toronto • Oxford

ROWMAN & LITTLEFIELD PUBLISHERS, INC.

Published in the United States of America
by Rowman & Littlefield Publishers, Inc.
A wholly owned subsidiary of The Rowman & Littlefield Publishing Group, Inc.
4501 Forbes Boulevard, Suite 200, Lanham, Maryland 20706
www.rowmanlittlefield.com

PO Box 317
Oxford
OX2 9RU, UK

British Library Cataloguing in Publication Information Available
Library of Congress Cataloging-in-Publication Data

France, R. L. (Robert Lawrence)
   Introduction to watershed development : understanding and managing the impacts of
sprawl / Robert L. France.
      p. cm.
   Includes bibliographical references and index.
   ISBN 0-7425-4208-4 (cloth : alk. paper)—ISBN 0-7425-4209-2 (pbk. : alk. paper)
   1. Watershed management. 2. Cities and towns—Growth—Environmental aspects.
I. Title.
   TC409.F73 2006
   333.91—dc22

                                                                    2005017106

Printed in the United States of America

♾ ™ The paper used in this publication meets the minimum requirements of American
National Standard for Information Sciences—Permanence of Paper for Printed Library
Materials, ANSI/NISO Z39.48–1992.

Contents

PART III. PROBLEM MITIGATION

PART IV. PROBLEM MANAGEMENT

Preface

Anecdotes of Sprawl . . .

. . . IN HISTORY

The detrimental transformation of landscapes by development has long been recognized, in both the ancient world (e.g., R. L. France, *Back to the Garden: Searching for Eden in the Mesopotamian Marshes,* 2006) as well as within North America (e.g., C. Merchant, *Reinventing Eden: The Fate of Nature in Western Culture,* 2004), from where the following anecdote is taken. While exploring the once Edenic Mississippi River valley to collect bird specimens almost two hundred years ago, the noted painter John James Audubon bemoaned the loss of natural purity in the area:

> When I think of those times, and call back to my mind the grandeur and beauty of those almost uninhabited shores; when I picture to myself the dense and lofty summits of the forest, that everywhere spread along the hills, and overhung the margins of the stream, unmolested by the axe of the settler. . . . When I see that . . . the vast herds of elks, deer and buffaloes . . . have ceased to exist; when I reflect that all this grand portion of our Union, instead of being in a state of nature, is now more or less covered with villages, farms, and towns, where the din of hammers and machinery is constantly heard; that the woods are fast disappearing under the axe by day, and the fire by night; . . . when I see the surplus of Europe coming to assist in the destruction of the forest, and transplanting civilization into its darkest recesses;—when I remember that these extraordinary changes have all taken place in the short period of twenty years, I pause, wonder, and although I know all to be fact, can scarcely believe its reality. (Audubon's *Delineations of American Scenery and Character,* cited in Merchant 2004).

... IN RECENT NEWS

In the lead "Land Matters" column in the February 2005 issue of *Landscape Architecture* magazine, editor J. William Thompson examined the "deeply ambivalent" response of landscape architects to sprawl and began the article by recounting one of the most newsworthy events concerning rampant development from the previous year:

> One morning in December, Hunters Brooke, a seemingly ordinary new subdivision in Charles County, Maryland, made national news: Arsonists [it was believed at the time] had struck during the night, torching 10 houses priced between $400,00 and $500,00. Given the history of the subdivision, ecoterrorism was immediately suspected.
>
> For at least five years, local environmentalists had bitterly opposed Hunters Brooke. In 2000, the Sierra Club singled it out as "quintessential sprawl" that "threatens a fragile wetland and important historical sites near the Chesapeake Bay." Environmental groups sued the U.S. Environmental Protection Agency and the Corps of Engineers for allowing Hunters Brooke to be built. They charged that runoff and other impacts would damage Araby Bog, an adjacent wetland that filters rain before it flows into the Potomac River and is home to such rare plants as the halberd-leaved greenbrier and red milkweed.
>
> Yet home building at Hunters Brooke plowed ahead despite these challenges. Frustrated with the unresponsiveness of legal channels, had environmental outlaws such as the Earth Liberation Fund taken matters into their own hands? (Thompson 2005)

... IN FILM

Sunshine State, directed by John Sayles, is the best film that has been made about the social and environmental ramifications of sprawl. There are wonderful, humorous, and unsettling scenes involving competing real estate developers, corrupt city planning officials, Visigoth-like land clearers, an ethically challenged landscaper architect, and many opposing or supporting locals, all focused around the issues of development of an attractive and historic beachfront area in Florida. The film begins with a group of retirees on a golf course, where one—a former developer played by comedian Alan King—lectures about the benefits of development:

"In the beginning there was nothing."

"Wilderness."

"Worse than wilderness. Endless swamp acreage. A land filled with crocodiles."

"Alligators."

"Alligators . . . Crocodiles . . . If you're talking about retirement bungalows, that's not a selling point. Mosquitoes that would strip you to the bone."

"Swampland."

"Swamplands. They were asking ten cents an acre for. This was worse. The old name in Seminole means 'You shouldn't go there.'"

"But we bought it."

"We bought it because we knew. We weren't selling land. What's land? A patch of dirt; a tree. Who cares?"

"Farmers care."

"Farmers! Farmers are for TV adds. People with tractors; amber waves of grain. They shoot it all in Canada. I'm talking about certified public accountants from Toledo with a fixed pension and a little nest egg who don't want to spend their Golden Years trekking through slush. Dreams are what you sell. A concept. You sell sunshine. You sell orange groves. You sell gentle breezes wafting through the palm trees."

"There were palm trees?"

"In the brochures there were palm trees; stately ones."

"Then, when they came down and saw it . . . ?"

"As long as the dredges stayed three lots ahead of the buyers we were in like Flint. This was the end of the Earth populated by people who ate catfish. And almost overnight, out of the muck and mangroves, we created this!"

"Golf courses?"

"'Nature . . . On a leach!"

And in another scene, a developer explains their land acquisition strategy to an apprentice as they spy on locals going about their business in an area that the real estate company has designs on:

"HQ says that this is where we establish our beachhead, and then spread out to take the rest of it. The other side has the end of the island locked up and they're infiltrating into the beach area."

"We're not opposing?"

"Zoned residential. Hostile native population. It's a minefield. Whereas here is the soft underbelly of the island."

"A key property?"

"Point of weakest defense. You make the frontal assault. I'll go behind the lines."

"Somebody's on the inside?"

"Working on it."

... IN FICTION

A Flash of Green by John D. MacDonald was published in 1962 and is one of the first works of fiction to touch upon the environmental consequences of watershed development. In this respect, what the book may lack in terms of subtlety or quality of writing (i.e., it is really in the genre of pulp fiction) it makes up for in terms of prescience. Once again the scene is Florida where a team of land developers pounces upon a coastal town to advance their development scheme through backroom and back alley deals with local corrupt politicians and greedy businesspeople and against the wishes of a few citizens rallying to block the project, which would involve filling in part of their estuarine bay to build a new subdivision. As MacDonald pessimistically writes:

> Once you had consistently eliminated most of the environmental features which had initially attracted a large tourist trade, the unalterable climate still made it a good place to live. New permanent residents would bolster the economy. And so, up and down the coast, the locals leaned over backward to make everything as easy and profitable as possible for the speculative land developers. . . . And so a hundred operators converged on the "sun coast," platting the swamps and sloughs, clearing the palmetto scrub lands, laying out and constructing the suburban slums of the future. (MacDonald 1962)

The development plans and model are eventually presented to the community in a scene reminiscent of the thousands of such public meetings that occur daily throughout the country:

> The second exhibit was considerably more impressive. It was a detailed table-top miniature of how the entire development would look after it was completed and all the houses had been built. There was a landscaped entrance, a serpentine wall, a tiny sign that read *Palmland Isles—A Planned Community—Styled for the Best of Tropical Living*. Bright cars speckled the blue curves of asphalt roads and made a herringbone pattern in the parking area of a shopping center. Indigo canals wound through the filled land, with cruisers at miniature docks. (MacDonald 1962)

The development moves ahead despite the opposition of the Save Our Bay environmentalists (referred to pejoratively by the developers as "that group of S.O.B.'ers") due to the overall abstracted view that most people have of the value of nature in addition to a short collective memory and general apathy, as explained by one of the land speculators:

> All the damn bird watchers and do-gooders and nature boys, they got an abstraction they're in love with. But the average man, you tell him that bay is a mess of mud flats likely to make his kids sick, he won't see anything pretty in it, and he won't want to save it. When the average man goes to look at nature, he wants something going on, like a porpoise coming ten feet up out of the water to eat a fish. . . . There's nothing going on in that bay they can look at. But the [expletive] do-gooders got this abstraction they look at. They like the idea of nature being left the hell alone. Boy, it is never left alone. Never. Not when there's a dollar you can make out of it. Now, what I'm saying is that money in hand is a lot more persuasive than the abstraction of leaving it like it was when the Indians first found it. So it's easier to chase a man off an abstraction than it is to chase him away from meat and potatoes. . . .
>
> Once it's filled, the ones who were against it won't give a damn either. Maybe they'll feel regretful they lost, and maybe they'll scowl when they look out onto that fill and the houses going up on it, but after they've seen it fifty times they won't notice it any more, and they won't miss the bay unless they stop and remember how it used to be. The only thing left of that bay will be some memories and some old photographs hanging around. And after it's filled there'll be thousands and thousands of folks coming down here who won't even realize it was open bay water, and they'll be bored if you try to tell them it was. . . . What the common man wants is television, air conditioning, a backyard barbecue, healthy kids and a normal sex life. If it was the last bay left in the world, he might get agitated. But there's always more bays. . . . If he sees one pelican and one blue heron a week, he's glad there's wild water birds around for him to look at. If they don't look at him, he'll yell and wave his arms to make sure they do. He likes nature to notice him. And that bay doesn't notice him worth a damn. It just sits there, and when it's gone he won't miss it. (MacDonald 1962)

THE PRESENT BOOK

Purpose and Structure

Environmental scholars have informed us (e.g., Gewertz 2005) that finally at the beginning of the twenty-first century we have reached a point in time where our collective appetite for resources exceeds that which the planet can continue to sustainably provide. Also, there is no place on the Earth, it appears, that is free from the by-products of human society (e.g., France 1992c; France and Blais 1998). And nowhere has the intersection between human culture and nature been felt more intensely than within or around our growing cities (e.g., Abbott and Holland 2006). More and more of us live in or adjacent to such cities, and more and more of these are clustered into small strips that hug our coastlines. The reality is that for three-quarters of the people who will read this book, the dominant landscape feature that they can observe if they stand up and look out their windows is rooftops and a sea of concrete.

"Sprawl" as it has become known—the cancerlike spread of development from urban centers out into the countryside—is coming to be realized as one of our most serious and influential environmental concerns (e.g., EPA 2001). Indeed, there is one study, published by the National Resources Defense Council (NRDC), that focuses particularly on the effects of sprawl on water resources (NRDC 2002). An Internet search on the admittedly pejorative term "sprawl" reveals more than eight hundred thousand items, and a search through the Harvard library system and through a major Internet bookseller indicates a corpus of between 160 and 280 titles that exist on the subject. Approaches such as "smart growth" or "new urbanism" are often heralded as means to adapt to sprawl. Interestingly, given the serious impact that development can inflict upon watershed functionality and health (France 2002a), with the exception of a few documents (e.g., Richman et al. 1999; USDH 2003; EPA 2004), most of the literature on watershed management (reviewed in France 2005) has been strangely silent on the topic.

The present book makes no attempt to review the voluminous literature on either sprawl or watershed management. Instead, a logical framework is presented of a small subset of the total number of the various perspectives that exist in which to measure, minimize, and manage the problem of development from a viewpoint of understanding the responses of watersheds and their inhabitants to this stress.

The first ten chapters are arranged to address the following sequence of questions and their corresponding subject areas provoked by those queries:

Part I. Problem Measurement
  1. How are things linked?
     • Chapter 1, "Seeking the Connection," deals with land-water ecotonal coupling through examples of large woody debris in streams and beaver lodges in lakes.
  2. What is wrong?
     • Chapter 2, "Setting the Agenda," gives an overview of horizon issues in water resources management and provides an overview of watershed management concerns.

3. How bad is it?
   - Chapter 3, "Surveying the Effects," examines the development of biomonitoring indices to assess the extent of environmental degradation as well as to promote communication among watershed stakeholders.

Part II. Problem Minimization
4. How can development be planned?
   - Chapter 4, "Exploring Choice," introduces a strategy protocol for laying out the options available for water-sensitive environmental management.
5. What is the ultimate development cap?
   - Chapter 5, "Establishing 'Enough,'" reviews empirical approaches that have been used to determine the limits of growth.
6. What locations can be developed?
   - Chapter 6, "Examining Sites," describes methods to assess the development potential of sites based on their environmental sensitivity.
7. What will the future look like?
   - Chapter 7, "Engaging Time," presents examples of alternative futures models to predict the consequences of various scenarios of land-use development.

Part III. Problem Mitigation
8. How can damage be fixed?
   - Chapter 8, "Framing Sites," describes several example strategies for protecting water quality from stormwater runoff.
9. Can public parks help?
   - Chapter 9, "Functioning Art," reviews the landscape architecture of creating wetland parks to treat stormwater runoff.
10. What about private and public waterside areas?
    - Chapter 10, "Fixing Home(scapes)," summarizes several documents designed to educate residents about the benefits of waterfront buffer gardens and greenways.

Chapter 11, "Annotation," summarizes the take-home lessons of the previous chapters. And chapter 12, "Application," shows how all these perspectives can be applied to a particularly illustrative case study, which also been previously used as the reference system in the companion book published by Rowman & Littlefield, R. France, ed., *Facilitating Watershed Management: Fostering Awareness and Stewardship* (2005).

Sources of Material

The material for this book has been assembled from a diversity of sources including my own scientific research (chapter 1), environmental scholarship (chapters 3, 4, 5, and 9), professional consulting (chapter 12), and academic teaching (chapters 1 and 6). Chapters 2, 7, 8, and 10 contain material originally presented (but subsequently reworked and updated substantially herein) at an international conference at Harvard University that also provided the material for my previous books *Handbook of Water Sensitive Planning and Design* (Lewis Publications, 2002), *Deep Immersion: The Experience of Water* (Green Frigate Books, 2003), and *Facilitating Watershed Management: Fostering Awareness and Stewardship* (Rowman & Littlefield, 2005).

Some of the present material has been previously published (albeit in very different forms) as the article "The Importance of Beaver Lodges in Structuring Littoral Communities in Boreal Headwater Lakes," *Canadian Journal of Zoology* (75): 1009–1013, for part of chapter 1; as the chapter "Theoretical Framework for Developing and Operationalizing and Index of Zoobenthos Community Integrity: Application to Biomonitoring with Zoobenthos Communities in the Great Lakes" in the gray literature (and thus difficult to obtain) publication *An Ecosystem Approach to the Integrity of the Great Lakes in Turbulent Times,* Great Lakes Fishery Commission Special Publication 90–4, pp. 169–194, for chapter 3; and as the article "Green World, Gray Heart? The Promise and the Reality of Landscape Architecture in Sustaining Nature," *Harvard Design Magazine: Building Nature's Ruin?* 18 (Spring/Summer 2003), for chapter 9.

ACKNOWLEDGMENTS

I wish to particularly thank those individuals whose work and words appear in these pages for the first time; first, those whose presentations at the original Harvard water conference that inspired the chapters that have been written around their informative talks: Robert Zimmerman, Peter Rogers, Timothy Ford, Richard Forman, and Timothy Weiskel in chapter 2; Carl Steinitz and Kathy Freemark in chapter 7; Bruce Ferguson, David Nichols, Scott Weinberg, and William Wenk in chapter 8; and Becka Roolf, Betty Lambright, Julia O'Brien, and Daniel Driscoll in chapter 10 (if any mistakes exist in these chapters it is due to my own misinterpretations); and second, those from whom I solicited the thoughtful responses shown in chapter 4: Robert Abbott, Kathy Freemark, Leslie Zucker, and Sarah Michaels. For chapter 4, I'd also like to acknowledge Henry Regier's work in categorizing the various perspectives of ecological integrity, Carl Steinitz for introducing me to the escaped tigers framework, and Amir Mueller for combining these two concepts. Conversations with Robert Steedman were instrumental in formulating the ideas in chapters 3 and 5, and my reflections about the case study presented in chapter 12 benefited from discussions with Nick Pouder, Duke Bitsko, Cynthia Jensen, Simone Krieger, and especially Dan Driscoll during the master planning process. I am very grateful to have been able to have learnt from my Harvard colleague, Carl Steinitz, whose ideas and work inform not only chapters 4 and 7 as mentioned above but also the student framework used for site assessments described in chapter 6. I also thank Mina France for help with manuscript preparation, Brian Romer for facilitating this publication, and Alan Berger for use of his compelling photograph as the cover image.

Part I

PROBLEM MEASUREMENT

Chapter One

Seeking the Connection
Land-Water Ecotonal Coupling

The students were running transect lines up and down both sides of the small stream, obtaining measurements of the sinuosity and pool and riffle sequencing. We were at a decommissioned air force base in southern New Hampshire and were surveying various morphological features of an artificially created stream that had at one time been interred in a large underground pipe. Then, with redevelopment of the old base as a new corporate office campus, the stream had been "daylighted" and brought back up to the surface as one of the ecological restoration projects being undertaken on the large property. The students were measuring the stream to determine just how realistic its contrived morphology was to that characteristic of several nearby natural streams they had examined earlier. Analysis would later show that the newly created stream was not quite in line with the geomorphological patterns of natural streams, our conclusions being that the process of dynamic equilibrium under which all natural streams function would be unlikely to be met in the long term for this particular stream. The implication of this inaccurate design would be that either the forces of erosion or those of deposition would eventually transfigure the new stream away from what the designer had intended and toward that which the laws of nature regulated. At the time of the survey, however, I was immediately struck by the overt unnaturalness of the stream in terms of a complete absence of woody debris within the constructed channel. The sequence of pools and riffles seemed to be created solely by small boulders that had been added here and there to the channel. How did such artifice compare to the pattern of natural streams? And how could one believe such a stream to be "restored" without attention paid to the presence of woody debris? Several months later, I returned to the former air force base, this time with another group of students as part of a regional tour of wetlands

and ponds constructed for both stormwater treatment and as compensatory
mitigation for natural wetlands that had been "lost" during site development.
The pond we visited was at the time six months old, and although filled with
water and no doubt functioning ably in terms of runoff detention and flooding
abatement, it seemed to be a sterile desert in terms of pond life. Even though
the pond had been constructed within a forested parcel of land, the site had
been cleared of all trees within dozens of meters of the new shoreline. How
important was it, I wondered, to provide a renewable supply of woody debris
to the shallow water for the small fishes that had been stocked in the pond or
for the aquatic insects that would naturally make their way there? Should
more effort have been spent on shoreline plantings to provide this? Or could
perhaps the purposeful insertion of woody debris into the water as part of the
design process have provided a habitat resource in the pond, just as it might
have helped the morphological evolution of the previously visited stream?

INTRODUCTION

There are two truisms in aquatic science and sprawl development germane to
the present book. The first is that scientists love to divide up the world in order
to (in their minds) better study it, one of the most convenient of these divisions
being based on those individuals who study either (but rarely both) aquatic or
terrestrial ecosystems. The second truism is that planners and developers are
themselves affected by this dichotomization of the world, believing that lakes
and rivers are somehow immune to the effects of forest clearance and site construction. It is important, therefore, to take every opportunity possible to demonstrate the tight intercoupling that exists between land and water.

In particular, the shallow water littoral zones of lakes, once thought to be
components of isolated systems (Forbes 1887), are now considered to be intermediate stages or ecotones in a dynamic continuum from the land to the water
(e.g., Likens 1984). And increasingly rivers have become recognized to be integral parts of functioning watersheds (e.g., Leopold 1994). The real possibility
exists, therefore, for aquatic systems to be adversely affected by landscape modifications associated with urbanization. In this regard, one of the most overt of
all the effects of sprawl development is a corresponding decrease in the number
of shoreline riparian trees and their supply of wood to waters (Christensen et al.
1996; Schueler and Holland 2000). This chapter presents two research projects
that demonstrate the importance of accumulations of large woody debris provided by such trees for structuring river geomorphology and lake ecology.
Through repeatedly documenting such findings, it is hoped that planners and
developers will follow the evolution that has taken place in ecological thinking

wherein it is now accepted that aquatic systems are very much dependent upon terrestrial ones, thereby behooving caution in our development of the latter if we are at all concerned about preserving the health of the former.

CHARACTERIZATION OF WOODY DEBRIS AND ITS INFLUENCE ON STREAM POOL FORMATION: IMPLICATIONS FOR RESTORATION DESIGN

Introduction

The input of large woody debris (LWD) from riparian shore vegetation to streams and rivers is a natural process and one that is necessary for maintaining dynamic geomorphological functioning in flowing waters through, among other roles, its dramatic influence on pool formation (Keller and Swanson 1979; Andrus, Long, and Froehlich 1988; Carlson, Andrus, and Froehlich 1990). Over the last several decades, a major paradigmatic shift has occurred in the way LWD in water bodies has become viewed by forest managers and landscape ecologists. At one time, accumulations of LWD were naively thought to be detrimental to the health of streams, and attempts were made to "clean" waters of their presumed deleterious influence. Now, however, LWD is regarded as being essential to maintaining a high biological integrity of rivers (see chapters 3 and 4). In many respects this can be attributed to the indirect role of LWD in impeding current flow and providing pool habitats for fish (Swanson et al. 1984) and also in entrapping leaves and providing a food and habitat resource for invertebrates (O'Connor 1991). It should be no surprise, then, that numerous studies exist documenting that removal of LWD almost invariably results in decreases in both the abundance and diversity of stream fauna (Elliott 1986; Bragg and Kershner 1997). Of interest for stream restoration is the observation that the reciprocal seems to hold true as well; i.e., that the artificial placement of LWD into stream courses (Angermeier and Karr 1984; House and Boehne 1986) will result in positive benefits through returning a dynamism to fluvial processes hitherto absent due to the inevitable cleaning of (sub)urban and agricultural waterways of all obstructions by hydroengineers in their misguided attempt to move water through our sprawlscapes as quickly as possible. Such habitat improvement procedures (the installation of logs and branches, the construction of deflectors, etc.) are therefore designed to mimic the effects of naturally occurring LWD.

Streams of decreased ecological integrity are often in serious need of repair (Steedman 2005; Riley 1998). The field of stream restoration and bioengineering is a rapidly growing and increasingly important occupation in which landscape designers play prominent and important roles (Hackl 1983; Ryder and Swoope 1997; Manning 1997). Re-creation of habitat through the in-stream placement of LWD is often a requirement for successful project resolution (Riley 1998). However, lack of strategic planning in the designed placement of such structures has been criticized (Hilderbrand et al. 1997). As Bilby and Ward (1989) state, "Although the role played by woody debris in streams has been well defined qualitatively, relatively little information is available on the variability in the characteristics, amount, or function of woody debris with changes in stream size." In particular, as urbanization and agricultural development become prevalent, it is increasingly difficult to find natural undisturbed streams in comparable physiographic terrain upon which to model restoration activities (FISRWG 1998). Therefore, unless we pattern our in-stream restorative additions of LWD in relation to what occurs naturally, these actions will ultimately meet with only limited success.

In general, "data on the size and spatial distribution of debris in undisturbed streams and rivers is largely unknown" (Robinson and Beschta 1990). And unfortunately, almost all the information we have about characterizing in-stream accumulations of LWD comes from forestry-related studies in the Pacific Northwest (e.g., Bilby and Ward 1989) and other regions of North America (Angermeier and Karr 1984; Monzyk, Kelso, and Rutherford 1997; Lehtinen, Mundahl, and Madejczyk 1997) that have little applicability to concerns about urbanization in New England (although Bilby and Likens's [1980] study of coniferous forested streams in Vermont and New Hampshire provides some limited guidance). Because of this data impediment, in-stream restoration projects in the northeastern United States are forced by default to begin on tenuous ground. The purpose of this study was to document the size, shape, abundance, orientation, stability, and influence on pool formation of LWD in New England streams remote from overt human activity. It is hoped that such knowledge could serve as a foundation upon which to plan later stream restoration projects.

Methods

Over a period of three years, groups of landscape architecture students visited the Harvard Forest for the first of several such trips there to foster ecological understanding prior to undertaking land-use planning exercises (Ahern et al. 2002). The Harvard Forest is located in the Central Uplands region of Massachusetts and is now covered by a transition hardwood-hemlock-white pine forest following agricultural abandonment in the late nineteenth century (Fuller et al. 1998; Foster, Motzkin, and Slater 1998). Periodic climatic disturbances have played a major role in structuring patterns of forest succession in the region.

Students undertook surveys of LWD in four streams at two locations: several first-order channels joining into a second-order stream that feeds into Harvard Pond, which is a small beaver impoundment near the town of Petersham, and a nearby third-order stream that enters the Swift River, itself a fourth-order stream supporting an important salmonid sport fishery. Thirteen numerical variables of demonstrated utility from studies on the West Coast (Triska and Cromack 1979; Andrus, Long, and Froehlich 1988; Robinson and Beschta 1990) were selected to characterize these New England streams and their LWD:

Streams: bankfull width and thalweg depth

Pools: length, width, depth, and number of pools in 30-meter (m) transects, and whether their formation was due to geologic processes (bedrock ledges and boulders) or could be attributed to LWD

LWD: length, diameter, and number of pieces in 30-m transects, their decay class (from I = early to V = late), their orientation with respect to streamflow ($0°$ = rootwad situated upstream, $90°$ = crosscurrent position, and $180°$ = aligned with rootwad pointed downstream), and their contact influence to the streambed and bankside (Zone 1 = streambed surface in water at low flow, Zone 2 = streambed surface at bankfull height, Zone 3 = edge between streambed and streambank channel at bankfull height, and Zone 4 = shoreline above bankfull height)

At least five groups of students over the three years independently surveyed different reaches for each of the four stream types to enable calculation of averages for all characteristics.

Results and Discussion

In the present study, surveyed fourth-order stream reaches were twice as deep and three times as wide as surveyed first-order stream reaches. As with the case for West Coast streams (Bilby and Ward 1989), those in New England displayed a similar relationship of LWD to channel morphology across the four stream-order categories, differing from the Pacific situation only in the actual values of the measurement characteristics. The numerical density of pools decreased with progressive stream order at the same time as their size/volume increased. In first-order reaches, about half of all the pools were formed through the actions of LWD; this decreased to less than a fifth of all such pools in fourth-order reaches. The numerical density of LWD decreased and the size increased with progressive stream order. LWD in low-order stream reaches was predominantly composed of old material, whereas that in third- and fourth-order reaches was made up more substantially by newer pieces of earlier decay classes. In fourth-order reaches, most LWD was orientated downstream and in contact with the streambanks. In contrast, most LWD in first- and second-order reaches was situated within the stream channel with no particular favored direction of orientation.

Together these results reflect a role of decreasing morphological importance of LWD as stream order increases in New England. As streams get larger, the coincident increase in water current discharge and velocity removes much LWD, leaving behind only those newly imported pieces having greater stability in terms of their size, orientation, and secure anchoring to the streambank. In contrast, in low-order reaches with lower water velocities, less stable LWD of smaller size can remain behind to a greater age, regardless of either anchoring or orientation with respect to flow. The lingering presence of LWD in low-order reaches enables it to play a much more significant role there in pool formation than is the case in higher-order reaches.

Design Restoration Implications

Urbanization increases the rate of flow and volume discharge of streams due to accelerated runoff caused by impervious surfaces (Schueler 1995; Riley 1998). In such situations, it may be unwise to simply attempt to mimic conditions characteristic of streams of an equivalent order found in more natural settings, as would be the case for restoring agriculturally degraded rural streams. Instead, a more appropriate strategy for design is one that is roughly based on a hydrological equivalency to natural streams of a higher order and therefore greater current velocity and volume discharge.

Restoration of first-order streams in suburban New England settings with low to moderate levels of watershed imperviousness should be roughly based on the following design guidelines: plan to create ten pools of about 6 m^2 each per 30 m of stream reach, half of which to arise from accumulations of LWD. These accumulations should be comprised of about twenty-eight pieces of LWD in moderate to late stages of decay and of a size of 3 m in length and 0.2 m in diameter. About one-fifth of these LWD pieces should be anchored to the streambank, and a quarter should be oriented in relation to downstream flow.

Restoration of first-order streams in New England urban settings of moderate to high levels of watershed imperviousness should be roughly based on the following design guidelines: plan to create about five pools of about 20 m^2 each per 30 m of stream reach, a third to a half of which to arise from accumulations of LWD. These accumulations should be comprised of about twelve pieces of LWD in new to moderate stages of decay and of a size of 4 m in length and 0.3 m in diameter. About a third of these LWD pieces should be anchored to the streambank, and a third should be orientated in relation to downstream flow.

It is important to recognize that the design pattern for assembling accumulations of LWD for purposes of recreating in-stream habitat is only one process in comprehensive stream corridor restoration, together with streambank erosion treatment, possible channel reconstruction, riparian replanting, and watershed management (see chapters 2 and 10; see also Schueler 1995; Herson-Jones, Heraty, and Jordan 1995; Riley 1998; FISRWG 1998). Further, the artificial placement of natural assemblages of LWD is only one of many options available for in-stream habitat restoration (Newbury, Gaboury, and Watson 1995), though it is often an attractive one due to being relatively inexpensive and easily adaptable to a wide variety of situations (FISRWG 1998). The design guidelines provided in this chapter should nevertheless prove useful as one aspect needed for the successful restoration of urban streams in future planned daylighting projects (Pinkham 1999).

THE IMPORTANCE OF BEAVER LODGES IN STRUCTURING LAKE LITTORAL COMMUNITIES

Large woody debris in lakes provides an important habitat for benthic macroinvertebrates and littoral fishes (Vogele and Rainwater 1975; Moring, Rooling, and Sante, 1986; Moring et al. 1990). Beaver (*Castor canadensis*) are prominent vectors in importing allochthonous (terrestrial-derived) organic matter to fresh waters (e.g., Naiman, McDowell, and Farr 1984; Johnson and Naiman 1987, 1990). Several investigations have measured the effects of beaver dam impoundments on riverine ecology, but no study previous to France (1997a) had assessed the role of beaver lodges on the abundance and richness of littoral organisms in boreal forest lakes.

Methods

Benthic (bottom) and epibenthic organisms were sampled within the littoral zones of four small headwater lakes in northwestern Ontario that were surrounded by a dense coniferous forest (see details in France 1997a). Each lake contained two to seven abandoned beaver lodges of an average size of $7 \times 5 \times 2$ m composed of birch (*Betula payrifera*) and aspen (*Populus tremuloides*) branches and saplings (5–15 cm diameter). All lodges surveyed in the study were located along straight shorelines in areas of bare rock and sand substrate.

Benthic macroinvertebrates (shrimps, worms, and various larval insects; France 1997a) were sampled with a handheld corer at wading depths. The first survey sampled three habitat types characteristic of these littoral zones: (1) a dense mulch of wood fragments associated with previous feeding activity located near the lodges, (2) thick organic sediments situated in bays, and (3) sand accumulations found between rocks and boulders. In the second survey, samples were collected along transects 1 to 21 m from the lodges within all four study lakes. Epibenthic organisms (small fishes, crayfish, diving beetles, tadpoles, leeches, etc.; France 1997a) were first sampled with baited minnow traps placed in water up to 3 m deep around the perimeters of the lakes in three habitat types: (1) LWD near the beaver lodges, (2) LWD from submerged windthrow trees, and (3) bare rocks or boulders. For the second survey, traps were placed along transects from 2 to 47 m from the beaver lodges.

Results and Discussion

Animal abundance was greatly elevated in proximity to beaver lodges to distances of about 9 m (France 1997a). Total densities of benthic marcoinvertebrates were, on average, almost three times higher in LWD near beaver lodges than in sand near rocks. Likewise, densities of epibenthic organisms were more than three times higher near lodges and windthrow LWD than above rocks. There were no significant differences in abundance of marcoinvertebrates between lodges and distant bays where terrestrial organic sediment had accumulated or in the abundance of epibenthic animals between lodges and distant groupings of submerged windthrow trees. In twelve cases, a particular macroinvertebrate taxon was found in the beaver lodge habitat and not in the sand-rock habitat, but in only three cases did the reverse situation occur. In twelve cases, a particular fish species was found near beaver lodges and not above rocks, but in only four cases did the reverse situation occur. And in six cases, a particular amphibian species was found near beaver lodges and not above rocks, but in only a single case did the reverse situation occur.

Ecological Significance

The results indicate that beaver lodges play an important role as habitat oases (*sensu* France 1993) in low productivity, headwater lakes in the boreal forest, where the rocky littoral zone precludes extensive growth of aquatic plants. In such situations, accumulations of LWD occurring through the activity of beaver serve to strongly influence the distribution of benthic and epibenthic organisms along the otherwise marginally hospitable shoreline consisting of sand and rocks. As a result, both richness and density are elevated in proximity to beaver lodges.

The similarity of animal densities between lodges and accumulations of organic debris or windthrow LWD indicates that there is nothing particularly unique about beaver lodges themselves apart from their role as centers for large accumulations of terrestrial wood and organic debris. Macroinvertebrates are probably attracted to accumulations of LWD due to their role as a food resource, a substrate for biofilm growth, an entrapping agent of organic silt and sediment, and as refuge from predation (Dudley and Anderson 1982). Similarly, littoral fishes are probably attracted to LWD by elevated concentrations of food there as well as by the physical structures themselves that can be used for shelter (Negus 1987; Everett and Ruiz 1993).

Wildlife Management

In this study, data on lodge frequency and the distribution and abundance patterns of littoral animals suggest that as much as 10 percent of the total standing crop of macroinvertebrates, 15 percent of the total standing crop of littoral fishes, and almost 100 percent of the standing crop of large diving beetles and newts were associated with beaver lodges in the study lakes (France 1997a).

Although often regarded as either pests (e.g., Ingle-Sidorowicz 1982; Hacker and Coblentz 1995) or as simply fur producers (Novak 1976), beaver are really a valuable habitat resource for littoral communities in boreal forest lakes through their role as importers of allochthonous material across ecotonal boundaries. As a result, calls for increased trapping of this original "landscape architect" and keystone species may be shortsighted.

CONCLUSION

It is wrong to envision aquatic systems as being uncoupled from their surrounding landscape. The example described in this chapter—showing how large woody debris can regulate both the structural form of streams as well as the biological integrity of lakes—represents only one of the myriad of ways in which forests can influence water bodies (see chapter 6 for other linkages). Obviously, then, what transpires on the land can, and indeed often will, have a dramatic effect on how lakes and streams function. The particular lesson for regulating watershed development in terms of ensuring a long-term supply of woody debris to waters should be clear.

Chapter Two

Setting the Agenda

Issues and Challenges in Integrated Watershed Education and Management for the Public Palate

The shoreline crowds already numbered in the many thousands by the time I arrived at my first Head of the Charles rowing regatta, the largest public participatory event on an urban river in the world. It was wonderful to see so many rowers whiz by and so many more observers there to cheer them on. And all this in a river I well knew to have been, until recently, sorely suffering from the effects of watershed development in terms of discharges of stormwater runoff and occasionally combined sewage overflows. Now, however, though far from back to its predevelopment level of quality, the Charles River had rebounded to a much more healthy state through the combined actions of many governmental, private, and nonprofit environmental groups. In between races, I found myself speculating on how much the general public knew about the hard-fought battles won and lost to bring the river to its present state, where the risk of infection from direct water contact was negligible. And how much did those now reveling in the enjoyment of this unique sporting event know about the sorry state of water elsewhere in the world: issues of paucity and of disease, and of the need to manage the precious resource from a landscape perspective supported by an ethical responsibility to protect it? Several years later, I was kayaking my way upstream in the Charles River at the edge of Boston and couldn't help but notice the striking difference between where I was in the suburbs and the urbanized landscape near the Harvard and MIT campuses where the rowing regatta had taken place in the artificially regulated waters of the Lower Basin. Here in the suburbs, the lushly forested banks with their few scattered homes gave, I knew, a false impression about the health of the river. Soon, almost unbelievably, my shallow-draft kayak began to hit the bottom. Again and again, I tried to make my way farther upstream in the hot August weather until, frustrated, I had to step out of the boat and, standing in foot-deep water in the middle of the wide river, swing the kayak around toward the city before hopping back in. The lack of water depth and current in such a large river channel was truly astonishing. How much was this due to the massive suburban sprawl in the area, visually screened from where I was on the river by the presence of riparian trees, but still possibly making its presence felt in terms of an altered hydrology?

INTRODUCTION

For many, water is no longer regarded as "water" but rather as a substance called "H_2O." The philosopher Ivan Illich pessimistically reflected on the sad fact that what was once a fluid that "drenches the inner and outer spaces of imagination" has now become an industrial and technical utility often corrosive to the skin (Illich 1986). As a culture, we have lost our collective memory of water as being the archetypal source of our dreams (Bachelard 1999), replacing it with a water regarded as only "stuff." Instead, argues Robert Wetzel, general secretary of the International Society of Limnology, we need to regard freshwater as a common trust of humanity, requiring civilization "to move united, assertively, and with dispatch to save the element, and thus us all" (France 2003a). Many have suggested that we therefore need nothing short of the development of a new water culture (e.g., Schwenk 1989). The core of the problem is that for most of us—and this really means the majority of the world's population that now live in cities—water flows by unappreciated and occasionally even unrecognized. The disheartening truth is that as a civilization we have become effectively blind to both the inherent beauty (Dreiseitl, Grau, and Ludwig 2001) and the experiential delight (France 2003a) of water.

How then do we go about altering the course of our collective water consciousness? How do we begin to (re)instill an ethos of stewardship in our actions and thoughts about the watersheds in which we all reside? How can fostering this paradigm shift be used for pragmatically facilitating environmentally sensitive and even supportive watershed management—in other words, the treatment of our landscapes as places instead of mere spaces, of our ecosystems as homes rather than houses? In short, in order to plan our common future, what are some pressing issues of water resource management today, and how we have gone about managing watersheds in the past?

HORIZON ISSUES IN WATER RESOURCES MANAGEMENT: HARVARD PERSPECTIVES (ROGERS ET AL. 2000)

In spring 2000, a symposium entitled "Water Sensitive Planning and Design" was hosted by the Graduate School of Design at Harvard University. The gathering began with an introductory plenary lecture by myself providing a ten thousand-year, postmodern overview of human culture and water nature relationships, which has since formed the core of the book *Deep Immersion: The Experience of Water* (France 2003a). At the end of the symposium, following two intense days of detailed technical presentations (compiled in France 2002a, 2005), I asked four prominent Harvard professors, representing diverse professional backgrounds, to offer a few summary comments about topics in water resource management from their own disciplines. In a sense, this was an attempt to bring the audience back out to big-picture issues. The following synopsis reviews some of the key points raised by Professors Peter Rogers (Faculty of Arts and Sciences), Timothy Ford (School of Public Health), Richard Forman (Design School), and Timothy Weiskel (Divinity School):

- The World Commission on Water for the Twenty-first Century meeting in The Hague in March 2000 was attended by more than 150 water or environmental ministers and more than 10,000 conference participants. The commission had been working for over a year with the World Bank and the United Nations (UN) to study and report on the conditions and future of the world's water resources. The results of these 1,700 meetings and $14 million will generate a vision for water in the twenty-first century.
- Water is the resource that is most likely to cause us trouble. The major reason is the organization of the world's population such that major portions of it are faced with dire water shortages for drinking or sanitation, making disease a major problem. The second reason is that 70 percent of the water is used in agriculture, with 40 percent of the world's food being produced by irrigation. Given the rapid increase in the world's population, the demands on our already stressed water resources will become serious; in short, the arithmetic simply doesn't add up. Predictions are that in twenty years, unless we do something serious about it, we will be in a devastating situation. This is not pessimism; it is realism. What can we do to ensure that the next several generations have an adequate water supply?
- The environmental damage from irrigation agriculture is just as dire. For example, if you take water out of the stream for crops, you will seriously impact the aquatic ecosystem.
- The recommendations to deal with all this are somewhat disappointing in light of the $14 million spent to come up with the World Water Vision tenet that "Every human being should have access to safe water for drinking, appropriate sanitation, and enough food and energy at reasonable cost. Providing adequate water to meet these basic needs must be done in a manner that works in harmony with nature."
- The point is that there are things you can do to achieve this recommenda-

tion. And for the first time in UN history, they come out very strongly in favor of having to pay for water's use. The meeting will therefore bring forth the recommendation of full-cost pricing for water. Although it might be argued that this is a long way from noble social programs, the point is that unless humans understand the value of water, they will never do anything sensible in terms of its conservation. The United States is a prime example in the underpricing of the true worth of water, except for perhaps Boston. Here, we have found that since the prices increased (though still below real cost), water use decreased by 20 percent. The situation for agriculture is even more dramatic. In those areas where pricing is more in line with true value, farmers are making far more rational decisions in their use of water.

- The School of Public Health is engaged in a program to look at the different environmental risks associated with water in Russia, bring Russian water resource engineers and regulators to the United States to see the diversity of water treatment facilities that are available, and send them back home with the information to run workshops in their own cities to explore the different options.

- Images of beautiful water-sensitive designs in Europe and America contrast markedly with what one finds in many Russian cities where water is treated very much like a waste product, not a design element. There, the health burden is very high due to the additive effects of polluted air and contaminated food, which predispose the population to dangers from water pollution. The source waters that many Russian cities use for their drinking water are probably some of the most contaminated that exist anywhere, making the Mississippi River seem quite clean by comparison. For example, many Russian cities use water treatment plants that are forty years old and built for populations that are many times smaller than they are today.

- It would be wrong to suggest that this is just a Russian problem, as many American cities also rely upon antiquated water distribution technologies that are falling apart and thus creating diseases such as hepatitis and various types of dysentery. The problem with showing many American state-of-the-art treatment systems to the Russians is that here we are starting with relatively clean source water. In the Russian case, much of this advanced technology is not really applicable until they remove the serious contamination in their source waters.

- The American Society of Microbiology is actively researching the options about what can be done with respect to monitoring the quality of drinking water. Some of the pathogens are very difficult to measure. Viruses, for example, are thought to cause a large portion of disease, but we don't have appropriate techniques to measure them in our facilities. The 1993 outbreak of crytosporidia parasites in Milwaukee, in which four hundred thousand people got sick, was the largest waterborne disease infection that has ever occurred in the United States.

- Much research is now being focused on cancer-producing elements in water and on endocrine disrupters, polychlorinated biphenyls (PCBs), and other chemicals that can change infant growth.
- Boston's Water Authority is currently being sued by the Environmental Protection Agency because the Water Authority refuses to put in place expensive filtration treatment systems, believing that they can rely on watershed protection of source waters.
- Many of the patterns on the landscape have been and are being created by flowing water. This leads to a changing mosaic on the land with water—like wildlife, pollination, and fires—moving across the surface from one place to another. This has implications for us as designers. Most of what we do as designers is to focus on and arrange objects in the world. An alternative view is to first find out where the flows are and then to locate the static objects. The result is that we can create designs that won't be fighting the floods or the elk migration routes in our backyards.
- One societal objective of any watershed association is to focus on the thin blue strip running down the middle of the land. But that is only one of the goals in managing a watershed. Both aesthetics and biodiversity are equally valid watershed design goals. We can be surprised when we look at things at different site scales. One study has shown, for example, that the site-specific effects on a river of a handful of cottages are more severe than the large clear-cut on the opposite shore. If, however, we look at the river and all its tributaries from the watershed perspective, it is probable that the clear-cut's influence would be more strongly felt than that of the few dwellings.
- Conclusions may also vary as to which particular stress is the most serious in light of different temporal scales. If we look at things from the horizon of sustainability—something that most designers fail to do—we may come up with completely divergent assessments of whether, for example, it is the cottages or the clear-cut that is the threat about which we should be most concerned.
- Landscape ecology as a profession has for the most part ignored urban issues and stormwater or watershed foci. The first rule of ecology seems to be to get as far away from houses and roads as possible. The result is that there are really two different cultures of environmental researchers, neither of which reads the other's literature. One of the exciting challenges is to get conservation and urban planners together. And we need to search for integrative general principles, some of which almost certainly will involve water.
- Site-specific designers dealing with water need to tell society that their cre-

ated landscapes can become the null model about how environmentally sound development should happen. Everything else should then be judged against this background. This can only be accomplished with a set of emerging principles. That is the challenge, and it is currently not being met.

- Road system ecology may very well be the next big environmental design topic. If you add a rectilinear road network overtop a dendritic stream network in a watershed, a lot of things change such as peak flow from the headwaters. The important finding is that it is not just the density of roads on the landscape that is of significance, it is the shape or form of the network of those roads. The influence of roads on wetlands and small streams is particularly important. Overall, we estimate that about one-fifth of the surface area of the United States is affected by roads.
- The basic truth is that humans live in embedded systems yet make up fictions about how they are in control, which of course they are not, as they discover every once in a while. The reality is that we live in a system we did not create and cannot control, so illusions of control are just that.
- More of us are moving to cities, and more of those cities are moving to the margins of our continents. By 2020, 70 percent of the human population is expected to be living within fifty kilometers (km) of the sea. As a result, water will be considered a problem in terms of source and of waste. So it is here that designers will need to focus. Urban water problems will become the major environmental concern.
- There are general design principles that are so simple they are almost insulting in that they do not call for any great insight. Water flows downhill. As a result, we all live downstream. The sociological application of this is that if you get pissed on, you get pissed off. The result is that water is going to become more and more a political issue as more and more people realize they are being pissed on. As people become more and more outraged, the systems are not yet available to contain that outrage. Full cost accounting of freshwater will have to become more important.
- We like to approach problems in the hydrological cycle as if they were engineering problems. Our last best chance is to realize that engineering solutions to the hydrological cycle will not work. Our best chance is not to dominate and control but to reinsert ourselves as individuals, as collectivities, as cities, as civilizations within the strictures of the hydrological cycle. Theologians have been writing about this, but no one really pays attention to them, and for good reason: most have ignored contemporary issues, going on and on about the history of religious belief and not about the nature of our religious commitments in the modern world.
- Unfortunately, our religious beliefs are governed more and more by the fiction that we are in charge of the hydrological cycle. We need to learn to

accept, to celebrate, and to design within the limits of the hydrological cycle if we wish to situate humans and natural systems in a sustainable concert.

• We live in what can be called the Terminal Mesozoic, where species are being lost at a rate not seen since earlier geologic periods. We have a choice to proceed to the Technozoic or to the Ecozoic. The engineering imperative is to push us toward the Technozoic as if a part of the system can control the whole. We need to go over to the Ecozoic and insert the human back within the natural biogeochemical cycle, or we're not going to make it. That's an engineering problem, but its an engineering problem informed by a sense of place within an ecosystem.

IDEAS AND CONCERNS IN ENVIRONMENTAL EDUCATION: A LITERATURE REVIEW

We desperately need a new reawakening of humanity. Such a "conscious evolution" can be brought about through the innovative redesign of our relationship to the natural world (Hubbard 1998). We have to find ways in which to inspire our dreams, motivate our visions, and actualize our restorative projects. We need to rediscover our connectivity to our nonhuman brethren (Wilson 1984) at the same time as remembering our forgotten rootedness to the places we inhabit. We need to design minds by fusing feeling with knowledge, and subject with object, toward an end of building environmentally sustainable and just societies. And to design minds, we need to redesign how we shape them through education.

Our way into and *out of* the next century can only be accomplished through a collective reeducation of our species (Kennedy 1993). It can be argued that we are in our present ecological crisis largely through a failure of our present educational system (Orr 1994). This has occurred because conventional education has been a celebration of the human potential, often at the expense of the environment. As a result, people are devoid of a sense of both place and of stewardship for that place. "Stewardship" here should not be confused with an antiquated Judeo-Christian form of anthropocentrism. Instead, environmental stewardship (*sensu* France 2005) should be looked upon as a form of caretaking or benign governance by those (i.e., us) who have been the instigator and who have wrought the most damage to natural systems.

"One of the penalties of an ecological education is that one lives alone in a world of wounds," wrote the naturalist Aldo Leopold (France 2006). Education should return to its ancient roots in instilling truth rather than its modern preoccupation with facts and reasons. A spiritual perspective in teaching about the natural world would promote a goal of knowledge that arises from love and aids in the "reunification and reconstruction of broken selves and worlds" (Palmer 1993). Through adopting such a lifelong syllabus—learning about ourselves in solitude, about our world in silence, and about our mutual relationship in some form of ritual—we can enable our survival by being true *environmental* stewards rather than by being mere *deck* stewards rearranging the chairs on our planetary *Titanic* before its fateful demise (see chapter 9).

There are four books that provide solid introductions to educators struggling with creating a new pedagogy for fostering environmental consciousness, respect, and corrective action.

Ecological Literacy: Education and the Transition to a Postmodern World (Orr 1992) is perhaps the seminal work on environmental education. Its premise is that we need to develop and foster a literacy of the natural world, allowing us to read our landscapes and thereby to understand our roles in shaping those landscapes:

- Environmental issues are complex and cannot be understood through a single discipline. Thus, education must be firmly based in postmodernism, requiring a new agenda that integrates scientific, ethical, aesthetic, and religious perspectives designed to "heal, connect, liberate, empower, create, and celebrate." At the same time, we must recognize the potential subversive nature of such an educational system, for "to see things in their wholeness is politically threatening."
- Ecological literacy is based on facilitating a sense of wonder and joy about the natural world and, as such, flourishes through direct experience with nature rather than simply from reading about it.
- We need to reeducate our eyes and hearts into rejecting the notion that ugliness is the normal and the sole solution (i.e., consider, for example, multifunctional stormwater wetland parks rather than sterile engineered stormwater detention basins, as outlined in chapter 9 of this volume).
- Environmental education should alter the way people behave, not merely just how they talk. To this end, we need to develop a pedagogy of place using Thoreau as the model. Thoreau "lived his subject" in such a way that *Walden* is "an antidote to the idea that education is a passive, indoor activity occurring between the ages of six and twenty-one" (France 2003b). In short, we need education to promote the reinhabitation of our landscapes and to foster an attitude of care and stewardship of those places.

The book by Palmer (1998), *Environmental Education in the 21st Century: Theory, Practice, Progress and Promise,* is important in its comprehensive review of different educational strategies needed for closing the rhetoric and reality gap.

- Although there are no instant recipes for ensuring success in environmental education, there is a consensus developing that progress requires some combination of formal programs with significant experiences involving informal engagement with the environment. In fact, survey results clearly demonstrate that fully six times more people identify outdoor experiences (particularly during childhood) as inspiring environmental consciousness compared to knowledge gained from books.
- Individual holistic development arises from the integration of education about, for, and from/in the environment. Outdoor experiences can foster aesthetic or spiritual appreciation of the environment, one part of which is motivated by beauty. Therefore, the use of art (paintings, music, etc.) as instructional examples to inspire environmental consciousness is to be recommended.
- "Stewardship grows from a fundamental reorientation of perception wherein the natural world becomes vested with the same values as the built world."
- The linear model in which increased knowledge about the environment will somehow lead to favorable attitudes and actions to promote better environmental quality needs to be abandoned.
- The point is strongly made that environmental education is "about 'empowerment' and developing a sense of 'ownership' improving the capacity of people to address environment and development issues in their own communities." By dealing with beliefs and attitudes, individuals can be given information to help them support those beliefs and therefore to translate attitudes into actions.
- Clearly, "education and communication are inseparable processes that impact upon people's thinking and actions." Environmental education therefore builds the motivations and skills essential to enable individuals to become environmental citizens.
- People need to feel ownership of not only the problems but also the solutions, and to be able to see the practical benefits that arise from becoming more environmentally literate. As a result, designed and built demonstration projects are great ways to "translate concepts and messages into action." In other words, because information alone does not necessarily lead to changed behavior, education therefore needs to offer the prospect of direct improvement in people's lives by informing, empowering, and inspiring action (France 2005).

Education for the Environment: Stimulating Practice (Plant 1998) is based on tackling the educational quandary voiced more than two millennia ago by Euripides that "we know the good, we apprehend it clearly, but we can't bring it to achievement," through offering a collection of suggestions toward operationalizing education:

- We need to develop students' sensitivities toward the natural world through the purposeful recollection of their personal experiences of communicating with nature. This can be married with the use of testimonials from established nature writers to develop a "disclosure discourse." In this respect, we must move from the tendency in environmental education to view nature as "something out there" to viewing nature as being something that is internalized and thus shaping of our identities (France 2003a).
- Much of what passes for environmental education is cosmetic and veils underlying political, economic, and practical realities.
- A postmodern focus is needed that questions old assumptions and develops new connections. This must be tempered with understanding of the danger implicit in such an approach that fragmentation may ensue with no reference to any universal truths.
- Above all, we must face the reality that knowledge about the natural world without fostering a drive to care for it is of only limited value. Learning in this respect is about the process of developing capacities for intelligent action rather than merely transmitting and regurgitating discrete elements of information.

The twelve chapters in *Ecological Education in Action: On Weaving Education, Culture, and the Environment* (Smith and Williams 1999) focus on emphasizing the inseparable embeddedness of humans in natural systems and on the ways to foster this through both formal classroom curricula and nonformal experiential education.

- There is a need to develop a sense of place as well as a sense of community living within that place. Understanding of watersheds allows people to become rooted in their location and thereby provides the framework for fostering community. A feeling of community in turn develops through actions that help watershed neighbors. In one humorous yet pointed example, a teacher made young students memorize the tributaries of their local large river as opposed to memorizing the capital cities of states and countries.
- It is erroneous and limiting to cling to the belief that environmental education is really only about science and technology. Instead, we must find ways to fuse emotion and intellect and to understand the aesthetic, moral, functional, and economic underpinnings of our inhabited landscapes. One such approach is to study, understand, and embrace the form and function involved in the design of ecologically sustainable buildings: "The curriculum embedded in any building instructs as fully and as powerfully as any course taught in it."

- We can learn about our watersheds through nontraditional means and from nontechnical sources, as one particularly integrative example showed: "Besides studying their own watersheds, students picked a river in the United States and conducted historical research on the impact of that river on humans and also ways in which humans had changed the course and nature of the river. They read novels in which rivers play a significant role, did art projects and painted murals, sang songs about rivers, conducted experiments and studied water properties, learned about water conservation in their own homes, and monitored steams as they participated in streamwalks. Students wrote poems, which were compiled in a book, *A River of Words*. The culminating activity of this unit was a "River Festival" at the school, where students displayed their art and writing" (see France 2003a).
- Environmental education works best when it recognizes the truism that we need experience "to shape our understanding of the world, its capacity for healing, and the role of humans in the process" (Smith and Williams 1999). In this respect, projects such as designing and tending gardens or planting trees link people with water, soil, air, and plants, allowing them to become active participants in shaping their own environments. The apogee of this approach is to engage people in the educational and transformative art and science of ecological restoration, which can "contribute in a potentially profound manner to the shift in consciousness that must accompany the formation of an ecologically sustainable culture" (France 2006). A simple way to affect this, for example, is to have people disconnect all the downspouts in the buildings they live or work in.

WATERSHED MANAGEMENT: THE CHARLES RIVER WATERSHED EXPERIENCE (ZIMMERMAN 2000)

In Boston as elsewhere, it appears that most citizens are only dimly aware of the watershed concept. The key to watershed stewardship is education about watershed processes (France 2005). Therefore, as effective watershed managers we need to be efficient environmental educators, repeatedly delivering the message that we all live in a watershed and must learn how to live within it.

Robert Zimmerman, director of the Charles River Watershed Association (CRWA), one of the most successful such organizations in the United States, likes to quip that his previous background in Medieval literature was a good precursor to working with watersheds: "One needs to know a lot about feudalism and being able to interpret Middle English helps a good deal with reading engineering documents" (Zimmerman 2000).

The Charles River watershed occupies 308 square miles in eastern Massachusetts and is the longest river contained within the state. From the headwaters in the town of Hopkinton, which is also the start of the famous Boston Marathon, what takes marathoners twenty-six miles to reach downtown Boston takes the river takes eighty miles, in the process dropping 318 feet. It is thus a reluctant river, not really wanting to get to the harbor. The river also borders thirty-five towns, making consensus-building and effective management a challenge.

The watershed is besieged by arguments among different environmental agencies, each believing its own set of particular problems to be those most worthy of attention. The overreaching problem, however, is one of scale and a limited view held by many of the players. For example, a developer might want to site a new fifty-acre shopping mall, and the consultants hired to assess the feasibility of this plan will likely study only four hundred feet of a single reach of the river. From this, the consultants will determine that the impacts on that reach of the river from the proposed shopping mall will be essentially nonexistent, and therefore they will advise to go ahead and allow for the development to proceed. In the end, Zimmerman (2000) came to the conclusion that what the watershed was really suffering from was "death by a thousand studies." What was not being done was for anyone to start looking at the watershed as a whole, as an ecosystem, as something to think about and understand as an operating and living system. So in 1994, the CRWA began an integrated modeling, monitoring, and management project that involved monthly sampling of 37 sites located along the river and an additional 102 sites on the ten largest tributaries, which were monitored twice a summer. With such a program in place, the CRWA began to learn about how their watershed behaved and what the most pressing environmental concerns were that affected the health of the river.

Problems with Imperviousness

In rural and forested New England, about 35 percent of the rain penetrates the ground and starts to move through and collect in underground aquifers that eventually serve as a source of recharge to rivers and streams (Zimmerman 2000). In fact, about 65 percent of the flow for New England rivers comes from groundwater seepage. Unfortunately, in urban, suburban, and exurban areas, this natural water cycle no longer exists. In its place, a new entity has been created in the form of an impacted and human-made water cycle. Now the rain hits the pavement that covers the ground as driveways, parking lots, and roadways and also hits front lawns that are really little better in terms of their permeability. This runoff then collects in storm drains whereupon its release into rivers will often cause both physical and biological problems (France 2002a).

Today in urban centers such as Boston, the situation exists that if one lives miles from a river but has a storm drain nearby, every action on the property will have an influence on the river as if the lot were right on its banks. Much less water penetrates the ground, most of it instead accelerating off. Rivers in such situations suffer from feast or famine in terms of their flow (i.e., at several times during the year there is too much water from runoff and flooding results, whereas during the rest of the year there is barely any baseflow due to the absence of groundwater recharge). Now all of a sudden we are turning one-inch rainstorms into 5-year floods, and 5-year rainstorms into 20-year floods. Around Boston, for example, a 50- to a 100-year rainstorm in 1996 resulted in a 150–200-year flood that caused serious damage (Zimmerman 2000).

Another result of paving over the ground is that we are forced to demand more and more water from out of the ground to supply us with drinking water. In Massachusetts, more than half the population get their drinking water from groundwater sources. And like all good citizens, "we know that water comes from the tap and goes down the drain" (Zimmerman 2000). But when it goes down the drain, the preferred method for the last fifty years for treating that wastewater has been to capture it in big pipes and send it off to another location: a surface discharge wastewater treatment plant where it is cleaned and then discharged at the outer edge of Boston Harbor. What this means is that a system has been created that is not sustainable. You can't cut rainwater off from the ground, expect to pump more and more water out of the ground and then send that water to some third location to get cleaned up, and expect to have water in the ground upon which to draw. For the first time in history, we have actually taken ourselves out of the natural water cycle.

Massive growth on the outskirts of Boston makes the "job" of a raindrop harder in terms of making a soft landing on permeable terrain. Underneath are large aquifers used for public drinking water supply wells that are not being replenished. Problems exist with combined sewer overflows, low in-stream baseflow, and massive amounts of stormwater runoff. But these are really the symptoms of the fundamental problem of the way we engineer towns to treat rain as if it were trash, a liability we want to get rid of it as quickly as possible (Zimmerman 2000). And when we do this, the runoff tends to be heavily polluted by what it has picked up from the streets. The CRWA, therefore, began to think of ways in which to fundamentally address the problem. It is not good enough to merely figure out what the problem is. You need to figure out what the solutions are, test them, and continue to monitor them. In short, many of us who live on sewer systems are looking at some of the finest engineering known to man of effectively dewatering entire regions. In Massachusetts, for example, about 60 percent of the water treated as wastewater is otherwise potable water that has leaked into the system as it made its way out to the harbor. And across the nation, those sewer systems that operate at about 50 percent of the water being treated as otherwise potable water leaking in are considered to be well-run systems.

Environmental Zoning in Watershed Management

Rivers suffering from "feast or famine" in terms of flow are like canaries in the coal mine, warning us that something wrong is going on with groundwater and that we had better pay attention. The CRWA has adopted several strategies to understand and manage development in their watershed.

The components of environmental zoning include comprehensive wastewater management, geographic information systems (GIS) and hydrologic analysis, stormwater management, land-use changes, and adoption and implementation of recommendations. We need to think about wastewater when it was just water: where it came from, where it is going, and what we can do with it along the way. We have a suite of options to treat wastewater, from on-site septic systems all the way up to large regional centralized endpoints. GIS analysis is used to determine how land and water work together, particularly in examining environmental functions and finding ways in which to connect rainwater to groundwater. Rather than zone our cities based on demographics and transportation corridors, we should determine how the towns function as environmental areas and then determine where to put people and transportation in order to protect those environmental functions now and well into the future (Zimmerman 2000).

The goal of environmental zoning is to sustain all our water resources (quality and quantity, stormwater, wastewater, and drinking water). And it is not just adequate to sustain water resources for the next 20 years. We have to get around the misconception held by planners that two decades is geologic time, after which it is somebody else's responsibility. Instead, we should adopt the Native American point of view that one must protect something for seven generations, or about 150 years (Zimmerman 2000). We need to think in that sort of time frame, because the decisions we make today have far-reaching repercussions. Bostonians, for example, are now paying $20 billion to correct transportation mistakes made in the 1950s and 1950s. We need to prioritize open-space acquisition, the idea being that if you are going to protect land it makes sense to protect the land that protects and sustains environmental functions. And finally, we need to be clever about regulating growth. Land-use regulation in the United States is not very good, but there are terrific water regulations. So, we ought to be able to apply our water regulation laws to control land use, thus getting at the whole notion of sprawl (Zimmerman 2000).

Soil maps are essential in developing environmental zoning, because it is important to prioritize and protect those sandy soils that allow rainwater to recharge aquifers. Next of importance are all the areas around vernal pools, wetlands, and other water bodies (see chapter 6).

The CRWA used GIS analysis to map development over the last decade in order to get the attention of citizens who had hitherto not really thought they had a problem with growth. For one town that learned it was in the midst of a decade-long 40 percent growth increase, the CRWA provided them with a map that prioritized which land would be most useful to purchase development rights in order to protect those specific areas that were critically important for protecting its groundwater supply for drinking as well as for stream baseflow. In particular, the CRWA suggested to the town to put a moratorium on further development of an industrial park that had been planned to sit right atop an important aquifer. The suggestion was made to trade development rights (as described in chapter 8), moving future development to another office park that was situated above impermeable soil and thus was not nearly as critical in terms of watershed function. Other recommendations involved a plan to increase density (see chapter 8) and produce affordable housing in areas not affecting the aquifer.

The CRWA started modeling the amount of aquifer water based on various simple scenarios of development and policy implementation. The exercise showed that if the aquifers could be filled up by directed and treated wastewater, the streams would return to their historic norms of baseflows that had not been seen in decades. There is a need, therefore, to get towns to think about wastewater differently (i.e., it is only wastewater if you "waste" it), because if they don't and simply continue to send their wastewater away, the regional aquifer will run dry within forty years. Modeling indicated the amount of water presently being lost as recharge and predicted that at maximum build-out the aquifers would irreparably suffer from actually being mined to complete depletion (for another example of this sort of problem, see chapter 7). Even under current situations where only 15 percent of the homes have on-site septic systems, the models found that unless these were situated directly above where water was being drawn from (i.e., a public water supply), their discharge into the ground may contribute little toward slowing down the rate of aquifer disappearance as a result of the entire region experiencing recurring droughts due to climate warming. Futures modeling (chapter 7) thus needs to start thinking about what the impacts of development will be as evapotranspiration increases, because the growing season is being extended and problems could develop even if the amount of rainfall does happen to increase (Zimmerman 2000).

In addition to implementing transferable development rights to protect recharge areas, other land-use tools include improved cluster and multihousing zoning and density development bylaws (some of these are discussed in chapter 8). And communities need to seriously consider the options of recycling postindustrial brownfields as an obvious means of reducing greenfield sprawl.

In the end, by applying water regulation to regulate land use, environmental zoning products include priorities for open-space acquisition, water budget analysis, recommendations for townwide stormwater management, and new growth (sprawl) bylaws or overlay districts. Environmental zoning benefits include improved surface and groundwater quality and sustained groundwater quantity, growth that recognizes water resources, and up-front environmental review (see chapter 8). In terms of the latter, developers are often favorably inclined to this approach because they see it as environmental streamlining. At present, developers can get caught in a prolonged spiral of review at many government levels. In contrast, when this type of analysis from environmental zoning is undertaken, more than half of the environmental requirements that are needed to locate any new development are accomplished from the start, enabling a savings of time and money invested.

Zimmerman (2000) strongly believes that society needs to develop a complete new way of thinking about how our towns and cities develop, considering the environment first rather than last in terms of remediation. It is wise to remember in this light that land remediation or restoration, just like product recycling, is really what you do after you sin (France 2006). It is far better in the long run to have not committed the sin at all.

Chapter Three

Surveying the Effects

Developing Biomonitoring Indices to Facilitate Communication among Watershed Stakeholders

Leaning over the side of the boat, I raised the dredge upward and, holding the sampling device over a screen perched atop an empty bucket, opened the jaws, allowing the light-colored, sandy sediments and water to pour out. After a brief rinsing of the screen and the sediment oozing through, I bent down to examine the small invertebrates that remained behind. They were a variety of shapes and sizes, and it didn't take a taxonomist to realize that the collection was extremely diverse. It was easy to recognize and identify the many small snails and clams present, as it was the much larger and more dynamic mayfly larvae, the latter's delicate gills waving away beautifully. Other insect larvae were represented also, from the savage-looking and relatively enormous dragonflies to the tiny, multicolored mites and beetles. It was the rapid-moving small crustacean shrimps and baby crayfish that were most interesting to watch as they scuttled about on the screen trying to seek cover amid the broken stalks of the many varied plants that had also been scooped up from the bottom with them. After a few minutes of observation and enumeration of the fauna, I reached back over the side of the small boat, poured the creatures back into the water, and looked at the shoreline. Only a few buildings interrupted the continuous green buffer that went right down to the water's edge, wrapping its way around the entire small bay. In the distance, if I strained my ears, I could just make out the sound of traffic on the small country roads set far back inland. I couldn't help but reflect on how different this site was, along with its resident lake-bottom invertebrates, from the one I had visited just a few hours before at another location along the Lake Ontario shoreline. There, at a site within the developed harbor of the city of Hamilton (not far from Toronto), the conditions had been remarkably different. Gone were the shoreline trees and small collection of housefronts, replaced instead by large industrial complexes that sprawled along the shoreline, separated only by parking lots between the buildings whose drainage pipes poured out their cocktail of runoff contaminants directly into the area where I was sampling. Lifting up the dredge at that location and examining its contents had revealed a completely different sample despite being part of the same lake as the more pristine site that I had just completed. At the developed site, the sediments had been a rich organic mud that stank as it was poured through the sieve. No plant parts were present. And the diversity of invertebrates was reduced to only a single type of organism in great abundance that resembled small, red threads. Given the remarkable difference between the invertebrate communities from the two sites, was it possible, I wondered, to somehow use these overt differences to assess the relative state of aquatic health between the two locations?

INTRODUCTION

Water contamination at developed sites is often ephemeral, associated with short, intense rainfall events and consequent runoff pulses or combined sewer overflow discharges (France 2002a). Continuous chemical monitoring devices are expensive and inform only about water quality in the immediate area. Obviously, there is a need for measures that can somehow characterize an entire watershed's response to the effects of sprawl.

Living organisms provide convenient full-time, integrative monitors of environmental perturbations because they are not affected by temporary amelioration or usually by transient activity that degrades habitat (France 1990). Further, the use of living organisms as early warning indicators is an important means for reducing the degree of surprise as new problems emerge. Biological monitoring, or biomonitoring, is based on exploiting the sensitivities of sentinel organisms to pollution and dates back to the use of caged canaries taken underground by miners to warn them of poisonous gases (e.g., Karr and Chu 1999). And the idea that organisms sampled in nature could reflect the ambient environmental conditions dates back to Aristotle, who commented on the "small, red threads" (i.e., pollution-tolerant tubificid worms) inhabiting the developed harbor of Athens.

Bioassessment consists of both bioassay-toxicology (laboratory) studies and biomonitoring (field surveillance) and has received increasing recognition as a means of identifying, understanding, and even ultimately predicting perturbation stress (Levin and Kimball 1984; Herricks and Cairns 1982). As a result, there is a need to mesh new concepts for maintaining biological integrity with the established, diverse tradition of biomonitoring.

The integrated toxicity test design (Buikema and Benfield 1979; Lehmkuhl 1979; France 1986), although heralded as the most valuable tool in ecotoxicological research, is still little used. The approach is very important, however, because the relationships between life histories and environmental disturbances are usually subtle and difficult to interpret. Laboratory studies provide precise dose-effect information concerning the effects of single pollutants but can never successfully duplicate all the interacting variables characteristic of natural environments. On the other hand, field studies often cannot provide the sensitivity necessary to detect adverse effects before they reach crisis proportions. The failure to assimilate both laboratory and field information in concert produces studies that may have limited utility in solving contaminant problems. Combining field monitoring and laboratory bioassays is necessary for understanding whether legislative criteria are overproductive or underproductive in mitigating environmental disturbance. A method is needed for integrating laboratory and field data based on reciprocal objectives of increasing or decreasing relevance (prediction) and identification (understanding) of mechanisms (France 1990).

In this hierarchical framework (ordered from molecules to cells to organs to individuals to populations to biotic communities to ecosystems), mechanistic understanding of the influences of environmental stress brought about by watershed development will increase by looking at progressively smaller organismic levels, whereas the relevance predicted for humans will increase from examination of progressively higher levels of biological organization. Unfortunately, most environmental studies operate at only the lower levels yet attempt to make predictions about top-level processes. For example, take the statement from a scientific paper that an understanding of physiological response is needed to predict how far degradative activities have to be lowered to avoid ecosystem damage. This is not only overoptimistic, it is erroneous. It can only be hoped, at best, to use one level's understanding to predict the next level's behavior. The problem is, therefore, that because few environmental scientists have studied attributes about aquatic communities, we still have relatively little power in terms of being able to predict the environmental consequences of rampant sprawl at the level of ecosystem dysfunction. It is also important to note that to be identified at all, certain system responses must be observed or sought at the community level and that these responses may not be predictable from a synthesis of research on lower-level (i.e., single organism or physiological) components (France 1990). Achieving an appropriate study program is a matter of proper definition and bounding before research is undertaken. There is a need to integrate applied research with basic research to avoid what Vallentyne (1978) has referred to as "band-aid, fire-fighting efforts" in watershed management.

Dilution and dispersion of contaminants in the natural environment and the resultant chronic exposure of organisms to sublethal concentrations of such substances is likely to affect a much greater biomass than exposure to lethal concentrations (France 1986). The affected community may continue to exist, but usually in some modified or crippled form. As the Food and Agriculture Organization (FAO), stated, "Not very sophisticated indices will be required to diagnose acute continuing stress. Death is easily recognized. It is of more interest to determine where the boundary lies between acute and chronic and between chronic and no significant practical effect" (FAO 1976).

INDEX OF BIOTIC INTEGRITY

Great emphasis was placed in the 1978 Great Lakes Water Quality Agreement on not just reaffirming the determination of the two countries to restore and enhance the water quality but also on assuring that the "biological integrity of these waters is maintained." Philosophically, the term "integrity" is central to the land ethic of the pioneer American conservationist Aldo Leopold (1947): "A thing is right when it tends to preserve the integrity, stability, and beauty of the biotic community. It is wrong when it tends otherwise." This chapter addresses the objective scientific meaning of integrity; the subjective ethical implications of this precept are discussed in France (1992a).

In the broadest sense, integrity refers to the wholeness, diversity, or degree of connectiveness within a biotic community and can be viewed as an emergent property of ecosystems. In this respect, ecosytems are only a special example of general systems, which Paul Weiss has defined as "a complex unit in space and time whose subunits cooperate to preserve its integrity and its structure and its behavior and tend to restore them after a nondestructive disturbance" (Goldsmith 1988). As Fisher (1990) stated, "ecological integrity is currently described by its collective parts or attributes."

Obviously, as Kay (1990) identified, "the concept of integrity must be seen as multidimensional and encompassing a number of ecosystem behaviors." Integrity terms are also not value-free. Although Leopold (1947) never explicitly defined exactly what he meant by integrity, he did provide some clues concerning the mutual interrelatedness of biological communities (France 1990). Integrity, therefore can be defined in many ways, be it a property either intrinsically or latently applied to ecosystems by humans (Serafin 1990), with no sole definition being solely accurate.

In 1988, a workshop sponsored by the Great Lakes Fishery Commission and the Science Advisory Board of the International Joint Commission gathered together two dozen theoretical and practical scientists and other researchers to explore the meanings and implications of the word "integrity" in joint U.S. and Canadian law. Not surprisingly, given the historic murkiness behind the word and concept (Regier and France 1990), workshop participants generated a complicated, and not terribly useful, argot about what it was they thought "integrity" means (France 1990; but see chapter 4 for a pragmatic distillation of this discussion).

Problems may arise, therefore, in developing techniques for operationally defining and practically applying concepts for gauging environmental quality within impacted locations such as the designated Areas of Concern within the Great Lakes (Ryder and Edwards 1985). The ambiguous interpretations that frequently characterize assessments of ecosystem status and thereby hamper progress in biological monitoring prompted the National Academy of Science as early as 1975 to explicitly affirm that "indices are needed for such goals as the integrity of ecosystems" (CEQ 1975). Despite this, it was not until a half decade later that Karr (1981) developed the Index of Biotic Integrity (IBI) as a tool to help managers, through the interpretation of biological data, to quantify river health or integrity.

Because human uses can affect the biota in many ways, such a measure of biotic integrity must incorporate a broad array of ecological characteristics that are sensitive to various (both chemical and physical) forms of degradation. Karr developed a series of parameters (called metrics) that reflect individual, population, community, and ecosystem attributes in an integrated framework. The five types of metrics are:

• Species richness and abundance
• Local indicator species
• Trophic composition
• Fish abundance
• Fish health condition

Together these metrics provide information about a range of structural and organizational aspects of the ecosystem. Individually, each metric explains a specific attribute of the sampling site. It is important to note that although no single metric is always a reliable indicator of degradation, in aggregate they appear responsive both to changes of relatively small magnitude and to broad ranges of perturbation. Some metrics are sensitive across the entire range of investigation, others to only a portion of that range of environmental conditions. Later testing by Karr and associates (e.g., Miller, Karr, and Steedman 1988) revealed that no single metric appeared redundant with respect to another. Indeed, the great strength of the IBI is its multiparameter assessment ability (Karr and Chu 1999).

Measuring the biotic integrity of a body of water is analogous to measuring human health from a suite of different techniques (cardiograms, x-rays, blood pressure, blood and urine chemistry, etc.). The major aim, therefore, is to construct an agglomerate index that summarizes this diversity of biological information into a single value considered synonymous with community health (Steedman 2005; France 1990). Communities lacking integrity in this respect are often already degraded and when further perturbed, are likely to change rapidly and often unpredictably—either linearly or though a catastrophic flip (Kay 1990)—to even less desirable states (Frey 1975). And in some cases integrity may be evident more from its absence than its presence.

INDEX THEORY AND CONCERNS

There is a need for a catholic biological scale of water quality that compares and contrasts the biotic communities in all locations and habitats under all circumstances (Truett et al. 1975). Section 102(2) of the 1969 U.S. National Environmental Policy Act directed all federal government agencies to "identify and develop methods and procedures . . . which will ensure that presently unquantified environment amenities and values may be given appropriate consideration in decision-making." This was reaffirmed in 1975 by the National Academy of Science, which at that time concluded that the efforts of federal agencies to develop and use environmental indices had been inadequate. An index (such as the IBI) is a number, usually dimensionless, whose value expresses (in a linear or simple curvilinear function) a measure or estimate of the relative magnitude of some condition such as the pollution load of a body of water or the estimated effectiveness of a proposed pollution abatement program. Such a system for rating water quality offers promise as a useful tool in the administration of water pollution abatement programs and has a number of benefits (France 1990; Karr and Chu 1999). The Council on Environmental Quality (CEQ) (1975) distinguishes between two types of indices:

- Goal indices that measure progress toward broad societal reforms.
- Programmatic indices that relate to a specific progress designed to maintain or change some aspect of an immediate environment under consideration.

The nature and complexity of an index is dependent upon its subject, the purpose it is designed for, and the rigor of the requirements it should have in order to be scientifically defensible. Several biological indicators may be integrated into one index for complex problems. There are precedents for such techniques with respect to the well-known and accepted use of indices by economists to communicate trends in the cost of living, unemployment, and gross national product (GNP).

Once defined, understood, and accepted, indices can be quickly grasped and compared in many cases where assimilating and comparing a complicated set of data would be too time-consuming and confusing to be practical or useful (Truett et al. 1975). By providing a convenient format for summarizing and handling data, indices allow for direct analysis of biotic communities without the need for referring to cumbersome tables, curves, or multivariate outputs. By depicting trends through time in relation to pollution abatement and by comparing environmental quality among geographic areas, indices are one of the most effective ways to communicate information to policy makers and the general public (Landwehr and Deininger 1976).

The selection of indices can be regarded as a two-stage process involving, first, the selection of stimulus-response factors appropriate to the problem and, second, the selection of appropriate measures of these factors (FAO 1976). The major end point in development of any index should be the translation of a scientifically defensible analysis of many components of the environment into an optimum number of terms with maximum information content. To do this, we must accept some reduction in precision but in turn gain the ability to communicate. In current times of strict funding, public accountability, and increased concern by all with regard to pollution problems, watershed scientists and policy makers must develop techniques, such as indices of biotic integrity, to express complex concepts to laypeople in as uncomplicated a fashion as possible (France 1990).

An important concern is the need to examine the use of any index of biotic integrity in light of the extensive and diverse literature on the theoretical rationale for developing environmental indices in general. Such an examination should be based on a comprehensive understanding of the causal mechanisms that relate response type to stimulus type. For example, the following stages suggested by the FAO (1976) need to be addressed in the development and application of biotic indices:

- Marshaling of insights concerning the stimulus-response system under study.
- Application of preexisting indices that are sufficiently general in their nature that immediate application can be made.
- Rapid development of new indices on an ad hoc basis.
- Empirical observation of new community responses or properties, including initiation of statistical studies to develop correlations and causal hypotheses.
- Synthesis of the hypotheses into a larger conceptual framework; that is, modeling with use of computer simulations.

- Formulation of new indices from the models based on abstracting the results of the simulations.
- Use of computer simulation models to test the new indices.
- Field testing new indices developed through conceptual processes.

By adopting this framework, the following questions can be addressed:

- What are the trade-offs between communication facilitation and ecological acumen?
- Is biotic community integrity the best means of abstracting and communicating changes in environmental quality?
- How can the a priori selection of parameters be best undertaken to form an effectual monitor of health in relation to both recognized/expected stresses and as yet unconceived/unanticipated surprises?

As the CEQ (1975) identified, the utility and shortcomings of indices should be examined by laypeople and specialists alike. Attention should be directed toward identifying and accepting some point of balance between the accredited managerial advantages in using agglomerative indices (Thomas 1972; CEQ 1975) and the noted, and perhaps not insignificant, weaknesses in such indices (FAO 1976).

The managerial advantages in using indices include:

- Communication ease among those segments of society concerned with environmental quality. In this respect, indices serve a vital educational function.
- Resulting increased public sensitivity and participation in decision making. For example, environmental impact statements are prime candidates for application of such indices.
- Encouraged accountability of public officials. For example, the use of indices summarizing changes in the economy has raised the whole level of political discussion about such concerns since these indices have achieved widespread recognition.
- Distillation and standardization of voluminous data in an objective format so that the efforts of special interest groups (e.g., the Sierra Club, Greenpeace, etc.) can become more efficient, to the benefit of all concerned.

The weaknesses in use of indices include:

- Lack of transparency in discrimination of the sensitivity of reactant components of the index. For example, during aggregation, the primary measurement data need not and should not be lost. The information conveyed by indices should be accessible for more detailed examination if the need arises; that is, indices should be capable of being disaggregated as well as aggregated.

- Difficulty in identifying the agents of perturbation (an important concern in areas characterized by a complex milieu of pollutants). For example, recognition that index answers are at best largely correlative and that cause-and-effect relations, although often indicated, should not be referred without further testing.

- Practical questions relating to the spatial bounds and temporal variability (including seasonal effects) that must be considered. For example, because no biological measure remains constant in a turbulent environment, the concept of a baseline is misleadingly oversimplified. We must therefore recognize that there exists a spectra of values that encompass the normal range of responses.

- Mathematical naivete and possible statistical artifice at best, or obfuscation at worst, between environmental variables and biotic responses. For example, the lack of logical methodology in constructing of some agglomerative indices is almost legendary; that is, solving problems of scale by converting each separate factor into a dimensionless index number often does not solve the problem of assigning subjective weights to each of those component metrics due to the existence of multiplicative effects (e.g., synergisms) and dependence on human values.

Emphasis should be placed on recognizing all these concerns during the screening of potential parameters for measuring the effects of stress upon any assemblage of biological monitors (France 1990). Finally, it must always be remembered that the credibility of any index is only as good as the supporting data base.

As Karr (1981) identified, a long-term goal in the use of the IBI and related biomonitoring tools should be the treatment of the index as a statistic that has sampling and other sources of variability. The distributional properties of biotic indices must therefore be documented, perhaps using sensitivity or uncertainty analysis (Fontaine and Stewart 1990). Once this is done, such indices can be used in the design of research programs (as in Jackson and Resh 1988) and as functional vehicles for predicting the effects of anthropogenic perturbation (such as sprawl) on natural systems through extrapolation, rather than through subjective retrogressive assessment on a system-by-system basis of damage that is already manifest (Rosenberg, Schindler, and Nero 1981). Further, using index information to calculate the cost-effectiveness of different management decisions should be investigated through use of gaming approaches via computer simulations (FAO 1976).

Questions of interest might include time to stress detection, financial cost of index application, level of pollutant reached before affirmative action, and the full degree of degradation that has occurred at the time the decision was made. By undertaking such analyses, some of the trial and error can be removed before the biomonitoring program is applied in the field.

Still, the major worry some justifiably have about indices is fear of information loss through oversimplification (France 1990). In fact, by definition, an index represents a condensed form of understanding, a stripped-down model, in which factors of secondary importance are intentionally deleted (FAO 1976). Patrick (1975), drawing upon the analogy of an environmental physician, stated, "Just as in medical treatment, you get what you pay for. The more thorough and competent the examination, the better the diagnosis. The more you try to reduce things to a single number, the more you lose in the measurement. . . . In other words, you ought to have different degrees of information just as we do for medical examinations, depending on your questions." To continue with this analogy, consider the Canadian physician Norman Bethune, who was exalted in China for his efforts during the second Sino-Japanese War, when at one point he was the only qualified doctor among 13 million people and once operated without thought to himself on 115 cases in sixty-nine hours while constantly under heavy artillery fire. Obviously, in such a situation, considerable hedging was required. The number of environmentally diseased areas affiliated with rampant development and warranting our attention as "environmental physicians" (*sensu* Schaeffer, Herricks, and Kerser 1988; Rapport 1989) is increasing at an alarming rate. As in Bethune's dilemma, however, often detailed diagnoses are possible on only a limited number of these systems. Ignoring others because of lack of time or money is tantamount to euthanasia. Trade-offs in the form of integrity indices are therefore required in the interim. By design, then, such empirical biomonitoring procedures can compensate for recognized sacrifices in descriptive precision and detail by greatly expanding the frame of reference from which general inferences can be drawn (Peters 1986).

It is important to remember that use of biotic integrity indices is neither the panacea that some would believe or the spreading cancer that others would suggest (France 1990). Such indices are designed as managerial, not ecological, tools (Steedman 2005). This is an important distinction worth keeping in mind. Facile and naive use of biotic index procedures by government managers continues to be a problem. As the FAO (1976) emphasized, although relevance and high scientific precision are often incompatible goals, development of indices of low relevance and precision (e.g., diversity indices) can be "misleading and worse than useless." Further, the danger implicit here is in the ascription of an inaccurate number to environmental health that may be unscrupulously regarded by some as license to pollute or develop to a particular level. Setting of directions rather than end points may therefore be a wiser management strategy.

As Cairns (1975) has elaborated, prejudicial dismissal of index approaches by ivory-tower academics is equally as dangerous. The statistical acumen needed to use and explain complicated multivariate techniques is, more often than not, unavailable to policy makers. The time lag involved in educating such individuals precludes the widespread use of multivariate approaches. Indices should not, however, be generated as a replacement to detailed statistical ordination procedures by researchers, if for no other reason than that such procedures are needed to identify representative community types for the indices (France 1990). It is important to remember that the usefulness of any index depends greatly upon the manner in which the component metrics are aggregated (CEQ 1975). Indices should be supported by mathematical models that characterize environmental interrelationships in vigorous quantitative fashion. Frequently, biologists fall into lengthy arguments about why they consider an area to be polluted or pristine based on observed community patterns (some of which, unfortunately, are analyzed by statistical techniques of dubious merit). By using indices of biotic community integrity, objectivity will replace subjective rhetoric in the assessment of shifts in environmental quality in relation to development sprawl (see chapter 5). Indeed, we will be able not only to define our watershed goals but also to measure how we progress toward them (see chapter 4). Indices are susceptible, as Thomas (1972) correctly stated, to misuse, just as all information systems are, but their use can actually promote open discussion and retard misleading environmental information that may appear when only selected raw data or complicated statistical procedures are available to a limited number from the ranks of a select scientific priesthood. Again, it is important to recognize that a biotic index is but a tool, albeit a useful one.

Part II

PROBLEM MINIMIZATION

Chapter Four

Exploring Choice

Managing the Ecological Integrity of Escaped Tigers—An Option-Strategy Protocol for Water-Sensitive Environmental Management

The view from the airplane over the patchwork quilt of the Ohio landscape was startling. Every conceivable inch appeared to have been divided up and planted, the rivers, at least from the air, offering the only nonlinearity to the scene. Try as I might, twisting my head this way and that, it was impossible to see anything that came close to resembling a forest, even along the river courses. It was one of the most depressing landscapes I had ever regarded, with not a glimpse of unmanicured naturalness to be seen anywhere. Several days later, on the ground, my first impression remained unchanged. As we followed a major river northward out of the city of Columbus, I was struck by how completely different everything was from what I was used to. Hitherto, my experience of rivers had been that the closer they were to cities, the more tortured they became, their shapes contorting as they entered the sprawl zone of the suburbs until, upon reaching the downtown core, the severe deformation obscured all resemblance of natural channel sinuosity. Here, however, the situation was reversed. The farther we followed the river away from the edge of the city and up to its headwaters, the more stressed it became in response to the massive agricultural modifications of the landscape. At one point we encountered a historic bas-relief sign on the side of the road heralding the past existence of what had once been one of the largest wetland complexes in the entire Midwest region. While at the sign, try as I might, it was impossible to glimpse even the smallest drop of water remaining anywhere on the efficiently drained landscape for as far as the eye could see. Eventually, the river, so majestic when first observed back in the city, dwindled to little more than an agricultural ditch that, had one not been informed or known otherwise, would have been impossible to guess as being the headwaters of the same river. How were these land-use decisions made that resulted in such environ-

mental abuse? And did the planners have a clear idea of what the available options were for development?

INTRODUCTION

The incorporation of ecological principles concerning landscape processes into comprehensive land-use planning is a long-established tradition (McHarg 1969; Holling and Goldberg 1970; Glekson 1971). Today, such principles commonly form the basis for textbooks (e.g., Marsh 1998) and are the foundation for planning courses (Steinitz 2002) in many landscape design curricula (Ahern et al. 2002). Conservation planning has been (Kain 1981) and continues to be (Arendt 1996) a major directive in land-use management, recently finding new importance in the field of biodiversity research (Noss, O'Connell, and Murphy 1998; Peck 1998) with its particular focus on habitat preservation (France and Rigg 1998). In particular, development of the field of alternative futures planning (Steinitz et al. 2003; see also chapter 6) often necessitates a prioritization of design options in an iterative fashion, motivated by an understanding of multiple aspirations that characterize land management decisions in complex socioeconomic-political arenas. Furthermore, landscape planning and design in the absence of any consideration of ethical responsibilities (Ahern et al. 2002) toward the "health" (Steedman 2005) of land affected by sprawl, especially in a way that is truly sustainable through time (Abbott 2005), is recognized to be of dubious and tenuous merit (Beatley 1994).

We need to explore new paradigms for recognizing, understanding, and directing development (Colby 1990). We need such "innovative diffusion" (*sensu* Richman 2005) because of the wide spectrum existing in human perceptions toward environmental health and in attitudes toward development risk (Michaels 1999). Understanding and planning ecologically sensitive and sustainable development options can be facilitated, both in concept and in execution, through careful consideration of how these various options interrelate amongst each another, as well as in relation to the wider field of environmental management. This chapter reviews two systematic analyses of options previously published over three decades ago and combines these into a new single protocol for use in environmental management. This combined option-strategy protocol is then applied to a variety of illustrative case studies concerned with broadly ranging issues of water-sensitive planning, including several dealing with minimizing problems associated with managing sprawl.

FRAMEWORK FOR SYSTEMATIC ANALYSIS OF OPTIONS

Ecological Integrity

Concepts of ecological integrity, from their origin by Jeffers and Leopold in laying the foundation for modern land ethics (France 1992a), have now been operationalized as measures for monitoring ecosystem health (Steedman 2005; see also chapter 3) as well as for guiding rehabilitative ecosystem management (Steedman and Regier 1990). In addition, for almost three decades, laws in both the United States and Canada have necessitated the maintenance of ecological integrity. To clarify the concept of integrity, the U.S. Environmental Protection Agency (EPA) convened a symposium on the integrity of water in 1975 in order to explore characteristics of ecosystems encompassed by integrity and the implications of these for effective environmental management (EPA 1975). During the symposium, it was noted that "from the many interpretations presented, it can be seen that integrity, like beauty, is in the eye of the beholder." Regier and France (1990) reviewed the document and systematically synthesized and ordered the many varied perspectives of the participants into a framework based on the degree of reform deemed necessary to achieve integrity:

1. Deep reform
   - Deep, comprehensive societal change with a broadly specified end point, firmly rooted in ecocentric principles.
   - Protection of water as a moral obligation for its inherent worth rather than as just a utilitarian resource.
   - Return of polluted systems to a pristine, unadulterated condition.
   - Indictment of conventional technological development and government regulatory regimes as inconsistent with natural/social integrity.
2. Partial reform
   - Pragmatic, sectoral, stepwise societal change within a specified general direction.
   - Admission that restoration to pristine conditions is usually impossible, but pristine conditions are a useful ideal even if unattainable.
   - Support for a mosaic approach with upgraded conventional technocentric management and science programs for ecosystems heavily utilized by humans, and alternative ecocentric management science for near-pristine areas to be conserved.
3. Incremental advances
   - Cost-effective technical improvements are applied within a society that is evolving gradually, progressively, and appropriately.

- Recognition that integrity is a multidimensional concept that is not value-free, and therefore certain trade-offs may be required and economics may sometimes dictate ecologics.
- Solutions are often viewed as engineering problems, and the ideal solution is an elegant "techno-fix" that involves only a minor "socio-fix."
- Implicit resourcism with an ultimate goal to return and maintain ecosystems to a state of beneficial use.

4. Holding the line
   - No further degradation is permitted except where society decides otherwise.
   - Simplified and explicit utilitarian objectives in water conservation, with present conditions as the primary reference point.
   - Broad application of concepts such as assimilative capacity, carrying capacity, maximum sustainable yield, and acceptable levels of risk.

5. Slowing the rate of retreat
   - Resistance to emergence of new forms of degradation and commitment to reduction in the rate of intensification and/or spread of current forms of degradation.
   - Undertaking inexpensive but visible initiatives to protect an image of concern and action with a hope that the major perceived problems will be found to be overblown or will be resolved spontaneously.

Escaped Tigers

In the late 1960s, William Haddon, working for the U.S. Insurance Institute for Highway Safety, became interested in the various management possibilities for reducing human and economic losses due to accidents, both natural and anthropogenic. In particular, a major class of ecological phenomena was considered to exist involving the way in which energy was transferred and the amount of losses occurring through escaped energy during such transfers. Drawing the analogy between detrimental energy losses and escaped tigers, Haddon (1970) developed a descriptive framework from which to characterize the possible strategies available for reducing these losses. Examples included harmful interactions to people and property of such agents as hurricanes, earthquakes, projectiles, automobiles, ionizing radiation, lightning, conflagrations, and "the cuts and bruises of daily life." Using Haddon's original ten-step framework, Steinitz (1998) translated and expanded the escaped tiger analogy, reformulating the concepts toward environmental problem management in general:

1. Prevent the marshaling of the energy
   - Target area becomes safe through removal of all tigers to a distant refuge far from presence of delectable humans; that is, recognition that problem solution is most effectively mitigated at source through complete elimination of energy in the first place.
2. Reduce the amount of marshaled energy
   - Only baby tigers or those that have been declawed are allowed to remain in target region in close association with human children; that is, if complete removal of the problem is impossible, the next best option may be to limit the potential threat by changing the dimensions of the problem.
3. Prevent the release of energy marshaled
   - Tigers, though they may be able to get out of their cages or across the moat, are securely tethered and thus cannot roam far; that is, if removal or reduction of the problem is logistically unfeasible, an alternate is to contain the problem on-site.
4. Modify the rate or spatial distribution of the release of energy
   - Only a single tiger at a time is allowed out to roam, thereby limiting contact with human prey, or if several tigers must be released at the same time, they are set free in widely separated regions in an attempt to limit pride hunting; that is, with resignation that problems will be released, the rapidity with which and where that release takes place will go far toward regulating damage.
5. Separate in space or time the energy being released
   - Tigers are allowed to roam only in restricted subregions of the overall target area (e.g., no school playgrounds), and then only during times when little children/morsels are safely inside at their desks; that is, when and where problem releases take place may play a major role in alleviating their ensuing threat of damage.
6. Separation by interposition of a material barrier
   - Tigers, though free of their original containment, are limited in their area of expanded "freedom" due to presence of backup fences; that is, widespread risks are reduced by physically restricting the zone of influence of problems.
7. Modify appropriately the contact surface
   - Nighttime curfews are instigated when escaped tigers are most likely to be hunting, and massive deforestation is instigated to prevent tigers from sneaking up on hapless humans; that is, given that some problems can never be completely avoided, exposure can be softened and damage lessened through implementation of both structural and nonstructural procedures.

8. Strengthen the structure otherwise damaged by energy release
   - Owners of tigers are held legally responsible if their pets consume humans, and a team of tough and burly tiger catchers is hired to control the problem; that is, shoring up implements, both living and nonliving, is accomplished to limit damage from problems after their release so as to restrict the overall impact.
9. Detection and evaluation of damage by generating a signal that a response is required
   - Frequency of emergency calls is surveyed, patterns of tiger sightings are monitored, and fate of disappearing children is investigated; that is, if damage cannot be prevented by the previous strategies, a move to rapidly assess past and present damage is needed to counter its continuation and extension.
10. Return to preevent conditions or stabilization of altered state
    - Remaining tigers are shot in retribution, and families have more children in compensation; that is, encompasses all measures implemented during the emergency period following damaging problem release to final stabilization after appropriate reparation and rehabilitation.

Combined Option-Strategy Protocol

The two approaches for categorizing environmental management were combined into a single option-strategy protocol by Mueller (1998):

1. Prevent energy marshaling (deep reform)
2. Reduce amount of energy marshaled (deep reform)
3. Prevent energy release (deep reform)
4. Modify spatial/rate of energy release (partial reform)
5. Time/space separation of energy release (partial reform)
6. Separation by barrier interposition (incremental advance)
7. Modify contact surface (incremental advance)
8. Strengthen structure (holding the line)
9. Generation of signal in response to damage (slowing the rate of retreat)
10. Return to preevent retreat stabilization of altered state (slowing the rate of retreat)

CASE STUDIES

By way of illustration, the management option-strategy protocol for achieving ecosystem integrity and controlling escaped tigers was applied to nine topics concerned with varied aspects of water-sensitive planning: housing development (Steinitz 1998); aquifer protection and maintenance from regional pollution and for site-specific stormwater recharge (Mueller, France, and Steinitz 2002); wetland loss-replacement mitigation (France 2003c); environmental auditing and green business sustainability (Abbott 1999, 2005); lake acidification and biodiversity protection (France 1992b); watershed agricultural development (Freemark 1999; see also chapter 7), agricultural drainage and rural stream protection (Zucker 1999; Zucker et al. 2002); and collaborative watershed management (Michaels 1999). For all cases, a succinct listing of how various management and planning choices might fit within the combined option-strategy protocol is presented as developed by each researcher. Many of the specific remedial actions suggested are covered elsewhere in this book.

Combined Option-Strategy Protocol for Lakeside Housing Development (Steinitz 1998)

1. Prevent energy marshaling (deep reform)
   - Watershed or lakeside carrying capacity limits to growth are set and cannot be exceeded, thereby preventing new homes from being built.
2. Reduce amount of energy marshaled (deep reform)
   - Only single-family homes are permitted.
   - Remove new homes.
3. Prevent energy release (deep reform)
   - New homes must be situated on the leeward side of elevation crests away from direct communication with waterbodies.
   - New homes all have state-of-the-art septic systems.
4. Modify spatial/rate of energy release (partial reform)
   - Houses are built incrementally over an extended period of years.
   - Cluster housing zoning is required, thereby preserving open greenspace.
5. Time/space separation of energy release (partial reform)
   - Phased construction process is implemented.
6. Separation by barrier interposition (incremental advance)
   - Stormwater detention basins are built to catch runoff.
7. Modify contact surface (incremental advance)
   - Friction between source and receiver is increased through vegetated buffer/filter strips.
   - Homes are not permitted in designated sensitive areas such as inflows, wetlands, etc.

8. Strengthen structure (holding the line)
   - Limnological management (e.g., biomanipulation) to reduce effects of eutrophication.
9. Generation of signal in response to damage (slowing the rate of retreat)
   - Comprehensive water monitoring program.
10. Return to preevent retreat stabilization of altered state (slowing the rate of retreat)
    - Lake restoration (e.g., fish restocking).
    - Remove new homes.

Combined Option-Strategy Protocol for Regional Aquifer Protection from Pollution (Mueller, France, and Steinitz 2002)

1. Prevent energy marshaling (deep reform)
   - Remove polluting activities from aquifer recharge areas.
2. Reduce amount of energy marshaled (deep reform)
   - Reduce the number of polluting activities.
   - Treat all pollution.
3. Prevent energy release (deep reform)
   - Contain pollution activities.
4. Modify spatial/rate of energy release (partial reform)
   - Restrict building to nonaquifer recharge areas.
   - Build in dispersed pattern.
5. Time/space separation of energy release (partial reform)
   - Phase construction along with mitigation measures.
   - Alternate development and grazing areas.
6. Separation by barrier interposition (incremental advance)
   - Fence off aquifer recharge areas.
7. Modify contact surface (incremental advance)
   - Eliminate grazing areas.
   - Eliminate roads.
   - Develop pollution-neutralizing surfaces and other best management practices (BMPs).
8. Strengthen structure (holding the line)
   - Wastewater and stormwater treatment.
9. Generation of signal in response to damage (slowing the rate of retreat)
   - Monitor streams and wells.
10. Return to preevent and stabilization of altered state (slowing the rate of retreat)
    - Develop alternative water source and abandon aquifer.
    - Desalinization and water reclamation.

Combined Option-Strategy Protocol for Site Stormwater Management for Aquifer Recharge (Mueller, France, and Steinitz 2002)

1. Prevent energy marshaling (deep reform)
   - On-site small-scale active recharge techniques.
   - Injection wells.
   - Minimize impervious surfaces.
2. Reduce amount of energy marshaled (deep reform)
   - On-site retention and recharge.
   - Collect surface runoff from site.
3. Prevent energy release (deep reform)
   - On-site retention and recharge.
   - Surround site with drains and swales to redirect runoff back to recharge area.
4. Modify spatial/rate of energy release (partial reform)
   - Single-family housing on large lots.
   - Retain runoff on site and discharge slowly.
5. Time/space separation of energy release (partial reform)
   - Small lot footprint; that is, high-rise housing.
   - Build on only impervious bedrock.
6. Separation by barrier interposition (incremental advance)
   - Cover development site with canopy and divert water to recharge area.
7. Modify contact surface (incremental advance)
   - Build underground dwellings.
   - Cover building roofs with sod.
8. Strengthen structure (holding the line)
   - Send rain into injection wells and other vehicles of recharge.
9. Generation of signal in response to damage (slowing the rate of retreat)
   - Monitor drains, swales, and water table height.
10. Return to preevent and stabilization of altered state (slowing the rate of retreat)
    - Repair/retrofit storm drains, swales, and recharge areas.
    - Abandon settlements if threshold development is reached.

Combined Option-Strategy Protocol for Wetland Loss-Replacement Mitigation (France 2003c)

1. Prevent energy marshaling (deep reform)
   - No-loss policy is in effect so that development never impinges upon wetlands.

2. Reduce amount of energy marshaled (deep reform)
   • Precise limits are set for the extent of wetland degradation permissible on a site-specific basis.
3. Prevent energy release (deep reform)
   • Development is allowed only with presence of numerous BMPs to protect nearby wetlands.
4. Modify spatial/rate of energy release (partial reform)
   • Adoption of a watershed prioritization scheme to identify and preserve those wetlands that offer the greatest functional benefits.
5. Time/space separation of energy release (partial reform)
   • Wetlands located upstream of floodplains are preserved for their role as stormwater modifiers.
   • Wetlands located downstream of developed areas or agricultural lands are preserved for their role as contaminant sinks.
   • Wetlands located in large contiguous complexes are preserved for their role as wildlife oases.
6. Separation by barrier interposition (incremental advance)
   • Unavoidable wetland degradation, that which exceeds the capacity of BMP protection, occurs only in restricted areas of larger wetland complexes.
7. Modify contact surface (incremental advance)
   • Wetlands permissible to be degraded or lost are only those that are hydrologically isolated in the watershed.
8. Strengthen structure (holding the line)
   • Compensation for wetlands lost through unavoidable development is required either on-site or through use of wetland banks.
9. Generation of signal in response to damage (slowing the rate of retreat)
   • A regimented program of monitoring and assessment of threatened or already degraded wetlands is enforced.
   • Plan is initiated to identify those degraded wetlands that would reestablish the greatest functional capacity to the watershed if they were restored.
10. Return to preevent and stabilization of altered state (slowing the rate of retreat)
    • Comprehensive wetland restoration within a watershed perspective begins in earnest.

Combined Option-Strategy Protocol for Business Enviro-Sustainability (Abbott 1999, 2005)

1. Prevent energy marshaling (deep reform)

- Business transformation with radical resource productivity and closed-loop production.
- All business solutions based on protection of natural capital.
2. Reduce amount of energy marshaled (deep reform)
   - Programs to systematically reduce negative environmental and social impacts through audits.
   - Overall resource efficiency improved, and economic measures broadened.
3. Prevent energy release (deep reform)
   - Environmental management broadens to embrace sustainability.
   - Protect natural capital and invest in social capital.
4. Modify spatial/rate of energy release (partial reform)
   - Programs to reduce environmental footprint of business.
   - Some consideration given to social capital.
5. Time/space separation of energy release (partial reform)
   - Pollution prevention programs and closed-loop environmental management systems.
6. Separation by barrier interposition (incremental advance)
   - Environmental management systems developed to international standards.
   - Begin to question where and how environmental activity can support business objectives.
7. Modify contact surface (incremental advance)
   - Develop environmental management system.
   - Awareness of business ecological "footprint."
8. Strengthen structure (holding the line)
   - Develop rudimentary audit programs.
   - Start thinking in a systems approach.
9. Generation of signal in response to damage (slowing the rate of retreat)
   - Ad hoc programs for key, easily perceived environmental risks.
   - Monitoring and measuring taking place but not linked to business planning.
10. Return to preevent and stabilization of altered state (slowing the rate of retreat)
    - Comply with existing laws (or at least try to).

Combined Option-Strategy Protocol for Biodiversity Protection from Lake Acidification (France 1992b)

1. Prevent energy marshaling (deep reform)
   - Coal banned as a viable fossil fuel.

2. Reduce amount of energy marshaled (deep reform)
   - Only low sulfur content coal is permitted.
   - Use of alternate energy sources is permitted.
3. Prevent energy release (deep reform)
   - Outdated power plants are closed.
   - Remaining power plants have scrubbers installed.
4. Modify spatial/rate of energy release (partial reform)
   - Limitations set for sulfur dioxide emissions.
5. Time/space separation of energy release (partial reform)
   - Dirty coal-burning power plants can only operate in regions having adequate natural buffering capacity.
   - Sulfur dioxide emission banking and trading between sensitive and insensitive regions is permitted.
6. Separation by barrier interposition (incremental advance)
   - Tall emission stacks with high dispersal capabilities are not permitted.
7. Modify contact surface (incremental advance)
   - Regional application of lime via aircraft deposition.
8. Strengthen structure (holding the line)
   - Routine and moderate site-specific liming of recreational lakes.
9. Generation of signal in response to damage (slowing the rate of retreat)
   - Monitoring of chemistry and ecological integrity of acidifying lakes.
10. Return to preevent and stabilization of altered state (slowing the rate of retreat)
    - Return to circumneutral pH in stressed lakes through massive liming.
    - Restocking of lost species.

Combined Option-Strategy Protocol for Agricultural Development (Freemark 1999; see also chapter 7)

1. Prevent energy marshaling (deep reform)
   - Conception of farming as part of the larger ecological mosaic in both space and time with environmentally sensitive crop management.
   - Organic methods used, and no genetically modified organisms permitted.
2. Reduce amount of energy marshaled (deep reform)
   - Pastured animals excluded from sensitive areas.
   - No net loss of natural areas, and road development curtailed.
3. Prevent energy release (deep reform)
   - Wide-scale adoption of integrated pest management regimes and soil conservation practices at source.
4. Modify spatial/rate of energy release (partial reform)

- Adoption of BMPs to conserve soil and prevent off-site movement of agrochemicals.
5. Time/space separation of energy release (partial reform)
   - Restrict intensive cropping to only locations of prime topography and soils.
6. Separation by barrier interposition (incremental advance)
   - Employ buffer strips around noncrop habitats.
7. Modify contact surface (incremental advance)
   - Retire marginal farmland.
8. Strengthen structure (holding the line)
   - Provide incentives to farmers for producing ecological benefits.
   - Enforce penalties for ecological damage such as soil or biodiversity loss.
9. Generation of signal in response to damage (slowing the rate of retreat)
   - Implement routine chemical monitoring for nontarget aquatic organisms and human health.
   - Populations of endangered, threatened, and rare species protected and monitored.
10. Return to preevent and stabilization of altered state (slowing the rate of retreat)
    - Abandon unsuitable and degraded fields and convert them to other land uses.

Combined Option-Strategy Protocol for Agricultural Drainage and Rural Stream Protection (Zucker 1999; Zucker et al. 2002)

1. Prevent energy marshaling (deep reform)
   - Food and fiber production of native species is adapted to premodification hydrologic regimes and excluded from stream corridors.
   - Channel and floodplain elevations and stream corridor widths determined by geologic processes.
2. Reduce amount of energy marshaled (deep reform)
   - Food and fiber extraction (not cultivation) is allowed within stream corridors.
   - Rotation of extraction areas and other site management strategies to limit regional degradation.
3. Prevent energy release (deep reform)
   - Manipulation of water table is permissible for food and fiber production of native species on upland flats and slopes.
   - Maintenance of stream corridor widths to accommodate changes in flow regime and channel morphology.

4. Modify spatial/rate of energy release (partial reform)
   - Stream hydrologic regime and morphology are allowed to be altered in relation to regional plans to maintain overall ecological integrity by facilitating agricultural production of nonnative species.
   - Livestock grazing on the floodplain and in streams is limited to non-sensitive areas.
5. Time/space separation of energy release (partial reform)
   - Floodplain vegetation is managed to maximize the filtering out of agro-chemicals.
   - Local water quantity and quality are carefully managed.
6. Separation by barrier interposition (incremental advance)
   - Vegetative filter strips, detention ponds, and natural wetlands are used to reduce agrochemical movement into streams.
7. Modify contact surface (incremental advance)
   - Fencing is used to restrict livestock grazing in streams.
   - Levees are used to regulate water flow in the floodplain.
8. Strengthen structure (holding the line)
   - Areas of wet soils currently in production are improved by drainage to decrease conversion of remaining wetlands into agriculture.
   - Streams are allowed to be channelized in accordance to a regional policy of maintaining water quality.
9. Generation of signal in response to damage (slowing the rate of retreat)
   - In-stream biological, chemical, and physical monitoring are used to gauge changes in environmental integrity.
10. Return to preevent and stabilization of altered state (slowing the rate of retreat)
    - Streambanks are hardened with riprap to prevent erosion and channels deepened and straightened to accommodate increased runoff and prevent flooding.

Combined Option-Strategy Protocol for Collaborative Watershed Management (Michaels 1999)

1. Prevent energy marshaling (deep reform)
   - People and industry choose to locate in a particular watershed out of a commitment to place.
2. Reduce amount of energy marshaled (deep reform)
   - In moving to a particular watershed, people and industry accept that they must abide by building design codes and BMPs.
3. Prevent energy release (deep reform)
   - Regulation and enforcement dictate human occupancy and activity.

4. Modify spatial/rate of energy release (partial reform)
   - A quota system is imposed to determine who can undertake activities (such as water discharges into local streams), when, and in what quantities.
5. Time/space separation of energy release (partial reform)
   - Wetlands and other environmentally sensitive areas are excluded from development.
6. Separation by barrier interposition (incremental advance)
   - People are excluded from riverbanks due to placement of fences to restrict erosion damage.
7. Modify contact surface (incremental advance)
   - Stream tributaries are encased in underground conduits to minimize pollution from nonpoint sources.
8. Strengthen structure (holding the line)
   - Property owners are held legally responsible for polluted runoff flowing from their land into public waterways.
9. Generation of signal in response to damage (slowing the rate of retreat)
   - Water quality and quantity are monitored, and potential causes of poor conditions are investigated.
10. Return to preevent and stabilization of altered state (slowing the rate of retreat)
    - Stakeholders work together to develop and implement watershed restoration.

CONCLUSION

Watershed protection, management, and restoration often operate most effectively if approached incrementally. The combined option-strategy framework for environmental action outlined in this chapter serves to clearly display the balance between quixotic aspirations and realistic expectations. By providing such a context, progress toward wished-for goals can be measured. In the absence of such a framework, progress often remains unrecognized, and the danger is that goals may possibly be dismissed as being unachievable. This occurs because, without context, the work of environmentally sensitive landscape planners and watershed managers may begin to resemble nothing more than the frustrating and disillusioning labors of Sisyphus. To avoid becoming jaded, it is important to have a clear framework upon which to easily identify the goal(s) being aspired to as well as to locate in proximal reference future objectives that might eventually be desired (see chapter 3).

Recognizing that public education is one of the most pressing requirements for effective watershed management (France 2005; see also chapter 2), the integrity–escaped tigers framework for option-strategy selection may have its greatest utility in facilitating communication among concerned parties by providing a common lexicon or familiar argot (as is also the case with the biomonitoring indices described in chapter 3). Dialogue in order to achieve better watershed management and planning evaluation is fostered because the focus is shifted from being based on ends to being based on means. By examining the option-strategy protocol outlined here, it is possible to recognize where it is we are presently situated in the broad spectrum of management/planning options while also being able to see where it is we may wish to be heading for. As the economist Oliver Wendell Holmes stated, "The great thing in this world is not so much where we stand, but in which direction we are moving" (Abbott 1999). Importantly, through adopting this option-strategy methodology, we have a clear presentation of the means for achieving each of those "deeper" (in terms of reform) or more progressive objectives. By focusing on means, therefore, it is possible that the ends may take care of themselves along the way. This protocol for watershed development options and strategies can thus help us to understand the behavioral barriers to environmental improvement by offering a practical tool for improving environmental planning and decision making toward an end of achieving sustainable futures (Abbott 1999, 2005; see also chapter 7).

Chapter Five

Establishing "Enough"

Empirically Determining the Limits to Growth in Watershed Development Planning

The last few miles of the drive to Waquoit Bay on southern Cape Cod reveal an astonishing degree of development. Hundreds of homes of a postwar vintage squat beside one another on their postage-stamp lawns, all seemingly jockeying for advantageous position in relation to views south across the beautiful Long Island Sound. A little farther inland and away from the estuarine bay, several new housing developments are under construction. I leave the car and walk around a half-finished construction site that has been recently carved out of the scrub pitch pine forest and squeezed in between small, vernal wetland pools. Along one new access road I photograph a sign indicating a turtle crossing and then scramble down the bank to see the wildlife underpass purposely created for this purpose. Hopefully, I smile ruefully, the turtles will also be able to recognize that this is the one place designated for them to safely cross the soon-to-be busy road during their spring migration from wetland pool to pool. My attention shifts to the piles of sand excavated from a nearby hole destined for a housing foundation. Reaching into my backpack I remove a water bottle and pour its contents upon the ground, noticing the speed at which the liquid disappears into the permeable surface. Later I examine a recently installed septic system of the newest technology and wonder about the aged systems glimpsed earlier in the mounded backyards in the older postwar neighborhood. Returning to the car, I drive the kilometer down to the edge of the estuary, completing in minutes the journey that will take the effluent from the septic systems a half decade or more to travel through the groundwater. The surface water of the bay looks superficially beautiful, but I know that it deceptively hides serious problems underneath. Walking out across a conveniently located pier, I stare down into the water and search in vain for any beds of the ecologically important eelgrass that I know once existed there in abundance. Instead, all I see are large clumps of invasive and biologically sterile filamentous algae drifting about like tumbleweeds in the nearshore desert of the bay. Turning back to scan the houses along the shoreline, both the old ones and those newly constructed, which I know to be responsible for the desertification of the estuary, I wonder about the lack of planning restrictions that has allowed all this development to happen, and I ask the pointed question, "When is enough, enough?"

A PROBLEM

Landscape designers and land-use planners are often preoccupied with the particulars of place. A good designer or planner, like a good engineer, embraces the detailed characteristics and localized idiosyncrasies of her or his development site. The danger is that sometimes in the desire to tease out the nuances about place there is a tendency to forget about how that place is situated in the wider space. Perspectives of landscape processes are frequently ignored. Such a limited place-particular view is insufficient in ensuring the protection of ecosystem integrity as now mandated by both Canadian and U.S. law (France and Weiskel 1997; see also chapters 3 and 4).

There is a need to explore varied and innovative approaches for incorporating ecological concepts into landscape design and planning curricula (Rodiek and Steiner 1998; Johnson and Hill 2002). Despite the assumption often implicit in many studios and courses and in professional practice, designed landscapes can only rarely be completely uncoupled from their surrounding ecosystems. Just as the old adage states that the most interesting things are those that frequently occur at the borders between maps, so it is that the most significant ramifications of design projects frequently occur off-site. Landscape planners need to be educated about the broader, or lateral, cumulative impacts of their projects on larger spatial scales (e.g., O'Neill, Williams, and Shuler 1997; Golodetz and Foster 1997). For projects that may influence waters or water resources, the obvious scale of impact delineation is that of the watershed (Heathcote 1998; France 2005). Simple watershed-level "understanding," though a marked improvement over the frequent isolated fashion with which many students and practitioners approach their projects, is in itself not enough. There is a need to instill a way of viewing the world by examining the implications of project design and development at the earliest possible stage, through adoption of empirical predictions arising from cross-(eco)system analysis.

A SOLUTION

Landscape planners and managers should be able to predict and evaluate the effects of land-use alterations rather than to react only to observed damage. Extrapolative methods are therefore required. The need to develop predictive capabilities to move management sciences from a reactive mode to a *proactive* mode, with measurable benefits to human and natural systems, has been heralded as being the most essential requirement for aquatic resource management (Naiman et al. 1995) and is a requirement for effective watershed planning (Schueler and Holland 2000). During the 1990s, the Limnology Group at McGill University, under the guidance of the late Robert Peters (Kalff 1996; Pace and del Giorgio 1996), developed an approach to environmental problem solving in which predictive capacities are used to generalize from experience through use of simple regression models, thereby replacing studies of each different landscape location and each new potential stress as if they were always unique (e.g., Peters 1986, 1991; Rigler and Peters 1995; Hakanson and Peters 1995). This chapter very briefly outlines five examples of such ecological empiricism that can provide tools for watershed development planning.

CASE STUDY EXAMPLES

Urbanization and Stream Water Quality

The Index of Biotic Integrity (IBI) was developed as an agglomorative and integrative measure to assess fish community health based on the metrics of species richness, local indicator species, trophic composition, and fish abundance and condition (Karr 1981; see also chapter 3). It provides an invaluable tool for environmental management based on assessing ecosystem health (Steedman 2005). Steedman (1988) adapted this approach to form models to predict the effects of urbanization on water quality of Toronto streams. The IBI was found to be positively related to both the proportion of the watershed covered by forest and the proportion of the river channel bordered by riparian forest and was found to be negatively related to the proportion of the watershed in urban land use (i.e., impervious surfaces of pavement and buildings). And as might be expected, land use immediately upstream of sample stations was determined to be most strongly associated with stream quality as measured by the IBI. Interestingly, Steedman developed a multiple regression model that led to formation of a simple contour plot in which to predict the impacts of sprawl.

For landscape planners and urban designers, this empirical study, assembled by comparing the IBI values from a set of streams in subwatersheds of ranging urbanization, offers the following useful information to aid in watershed development planning: if the shift in rank from "good" to "fair" stream quality is taken as the societal "threshold" of degradation that is deemed acceptable, then that level of degradation is reached if 75 percent of the riparian forest is removed under conditions of 0 percent urbanization at one extreme, to 0 percent further removal of riparian forest under conditions of 55 percent urbanization at the other. Within this zone of degradation, many opportunities exist for varying the extent of forest removal and of urbanization in order to ensure that the threshold to unacceptable stream health is not exceeded. The opportunity exists, of course, to work backwards from a desired result of no declines in stream health to what corresponding level of urbanization would be permissible to ensure such resource protection.

Shoreline Cottage Development and Fishery Yield

Because phosphorus is the limiting nutrient for algal growth in many lakes, empirical relationships can be constructed between watershed phosphorus export and the size of nuisance and potentially detrimental algal blooms. Both lake phosphorus concentration and algal abundance increase in relation to agriculture and urbanization (Meeuwig and Peters 1996) as well as to shoreline cottage development (Hutchinson, Neary, and Dillon 1991; Hutchinson 2002). Dillon et al. (1986) conducted detailed mass balance studies of phosphorus dynamics for watersheds in central Ontario and generated a series of serially related regression models to predict the carrying capacity of lakes to shoreline development. Lakewide, average cottage use was found to be positively related to lake phosphorus concentration, which itself was positively related to the abundance of algae. Algal abundance was then negatively related to the amount of deepwater oxygen remaining from decomposition, which in turn was positively related to the catch of deepwater sport fish. In short, more nutrients mean more algae, which means less oxygen due to the breakdown of those algae, which in turn means less fish yield due to hypoxia and consequent constrictions in deepwater habitat.

For landscape planners and aquatic resource managers, this empirical study, assembled by comparing limnological data from a group of lakes of ranging shoreline development, offers the following useful information to aid in watershed development planning: if a 50 percent increase in annual cottage user days is the build-out level deemed socially acceptable, the model predicts that this could result in a 12 percent increase in algal abundance, which in turn would bring about a corresponding 8 percent decrease in sport-fish yield. The opportunity exists, of course, to work backwards from a desired result of no declines in sport-fish yield to what corresponding level of shoreline cottage would be permissible to ensure such resource protection.

Riparian Clear-cutting and Lake Metabolism

In many situations, the amount of externally produced (allochthonous) carbon transported to lakes greatly exceeds that produced within lakes (autochthonous). In such lakes, bacterio-plankton communities are found to consume more carbon than the phytoplankton (algae) can themselves produce (i.e., based on respiration or consumption rates being in excess of photosynthesis or primary production rates). These lakes are therefore reliant upon external energy supplies such as riparian litterfall (France, Culbert, and Peters 1996) to sustain their metabolism (Del Giorgio and Peters 1993). France and Peters (1995) compiled literature data on the input of terrestrial litter to many lakes in order to predict the potential consequences of riparian clear-cutting on the balance between algal production and bacterial respiration, this measure being important as it influences the transfer of food and contaminants through food webs. The proportional contribution of carbon from airborne litterfall to the total lake carbon budget was found to be negatively related to existing algal production, and the proportional contribution of phosphorus from airborne litterfall to the total phosphorus input was found to be positively related to the ratio of lake surface to watershed area. By combining these relationships with one linking the actual amount of litterfall input to the percentage forested shoreline, France and Peters generated contour plots predicting the effects of clear-cutting on the metabolism of boreal lakes in northwestern Ontario.

For landscape planners and forest managers, this empirical study, assembled by comparing metabolism and litterfall input data from lakes of ranging shoreline deforestation, offers the following useful information to aid in watershed development planning: for oligotrophic (low nutrient) lakes with small drainage basins, half to complete removal of shoreline trees can produce decreases of 4–9 percent in algal production and of 8–17 percent in bacterial respiration. The opportunity exists, of course, to work backwards from a desired result of no alterations in lake metabolism to what corresponding level of shoreline deforestation would be permissible to ensure such resource protection.

Coastal Eutrophication and Eelgrass Abundance

Estuaries are often closely coupled to coastlines through groundwater-borne nutrient transport (Valiela, Cummins, and Shearer 1992), which in the case of additional inputs from residential septic systems can contribute up to half of the total nitrogen load. Short et al. (1996) and Short and Burdick (1996) developed a series of empirical models that enabled linking coastal housing in

New England to the decline in areal coverage of eelgrass beds, a habitat that is critically important for supporting fisheries, stabilizing sediments, and purifying estuarine waters. In the preliminary model, the increasing number of houses in a watershed over time was found to be negatively related to the decreasing areal extent of eelgrass beds. The subsequent model was spatially based on various subbasins in another estuary. Here, the number of houses within each subwatershed was found to be positively related to the amount of nitrogen being released into that respective portion of the estuary. Since nitrogen loading for different subwatersheds was found to be negatively related to the size of eelgrass beds, this allowed a predictive model to be constructed between the number of houses in the watershed and eelgrass area.

For landscape planners and coastal housing regulators, this empirical study, assembled by comparing eelgrass data from systems of ranging housing extent, offers the following useful information to aid in watershed development planning: doubling the number of individual septic systems causes a doubling in the amount of nitrogen exported to estuaries, which in turn can decrease the areal coverage of eelgrass beds anywhere from 5 percent to 50 percent depending on the starting density of houses. The opportunity exists, of course, to work backwards from a desired result of no declines in eelgrass abundance to what corresponding level of housing density would be permissible to ensure such resource protection.

Rural Development and Wetland Biodiversity

Wetlands, though recognized as providing centers for threatened or endangered species biodiversity, are nevertheless still disappearing at an alarming rate in rural North America (France 2003c). Findlay and Houlahan (1997) examined empirical relationships between the species richness of various taxa in southeastern Ontario wetlands and the extent of land-use modification in terms of road construction and forest removal or conversion to farmland. Species richness was found to be positively related to both wetland area and the proportion of forest cover, and it was negatively related to the density of paved roads. Multiple regression analysis was then employed to examine the proportional residual variation or strength of model fit in relation to distance from the wetland edge where the land-use modification occurred. Surprisingly, the authors found that both the removal of forest cover or the increase in density of paved roads exerted the same negative impact upon species richness as would a shrinkage in size of the wetland itself and that these former effects were significant at distances of up to 1–2 km from the wetland edge. The implications of these results for land-use planning are profound, given that existing laws only regulate development within narrow 120 m buffer strips beside the water.

For landscape planners and regional resource managers, this empirical study, assembled by comparing biodiversity data from wetlands in landscapes of ranging road density and extent of forest cover, offers the following useful information to aid in watershed development planning: a 15 percent decrease in wetland species richness can result from a decline in forest cover of 20 percent or an increase of 2 m/ha in density of hard surface roads within 1–2 km of a wetland. The opportunity exists, of course, to work backwards from a desired result of no declines in wetland biodiversity to what corresponding level of road density or forest clearance would be permissible to ensure such resource protection.

IMPLICATIONS AND IMPLEMENTATIONS

In the absence of data particular to the region of study, it is possible to develop empirical models using literature data as was accomplished in the clear-cutting example of France and Peters (1995) reviewed here as well as other examples such as the lake eutrophication model of Meeuwig and Peters (1996). What may be lost in such cases in terms of regional specificity can be compensated for by gaining a wider applicability of models being generated.

The empirical approach reviewed in this chapter is based on the concept of selecting as simple a suite of predictor variables as possible that can enable a priori judgments to be made concerning watershed development planning through the use of straightforward regression analysis. Such simple metrics as outlined in the examples in this chapter include percentage riparian or watershed forest coverage, road density, or number of houses or cottages, all of which are easily obtained through GIS analysis or air photo interpretation. Another well-studied example includes the use of percentage-impervious surface coverage as a surrogate measure for the extent and effects of urbanization (e.g., in terms of increased runoff, stream temperatures, stream erosion, and woody habitat removal) and expressed with respect to its deleterious influences on aquatic biota (e.g., Schueler and Holland 2000).

In some situations, it may be possible to develop empirical models useful for watershed development planning through even further simplification. Here, the assumption is that the driving variable truly responsible for environmental damage is ultimately the number of people residing in the watershed. In other words, it may be possible to formulate models relating watershed population density to aquatic resource quality, as, for example, with respect to lake and estuary eutrophication (Goldman 1993; Meeuwig and Peters 1996), nitrogen export (Cole et al. 1993), or aquatic biodiversity (Jones and Clark 1987). Such a procedure is certainly in line with the working mandate of the journal *Environmen-*

tal Planning B: Planning and Design: "the notion that complex systems must be met by powerful simplifications that extract the essence of things" (Batty 1998). Such population-based methods begin to embrace the social dimension of landscape planning necessary to ensure long-term and long-range ecological sustainability (Linehan and Gross 1998).

How then do we go about integrating such concepts into watershed development planning? First, from an educational perspective, the cardinal tenet of viewing all development projects from a holistic watershed framework must be presented and reiterated again and again until it becomes the status quo. Given general acceptance of the importance and benefits of examining multiple ecosystems exposed to varying degrees of sprawl, individual site-specific designs can be conceptually reconnected to the larger landscape through use of empirical predictive planning, as demonstrated in the examples above.

What is particularly important to advance when fostering the technique of empirical ecology in watershed development planning is that it represents a prognostic means for the setting of upper threshold limits or "carrying capacity" (*sensu* Doenges et al. 1990; Lazar, Peterson, and Calvo 2000) based on estimating the repercussions of future sprawl. As such, it is a logical *first* step in minimizing the problems of development undertaken before the screening process for judging individual site-development suitability, as described in chapter 6. The strength in applying this approach is that it removes much of the subjective rhetoric, arm waving, and "what if" guesswork involved when trying to assess site suitability in the type of scenario planning forecasting described in chapter 7. It is conceivable that a tiered approach might be applicable. First, examine or develop a model of watershed population-carrying capacity to predict if the proposed increase in human population density (or its surrogate, number of houses) accompanying the development of a particular project will likely generate serious environmental repercussions. Next, examine or develop empirical models based on easily measurable environmental metrics such as the percentage of forest land in the watershed, the density of roads, the extent of impervious coverage, or the like that might explain some of the residual variability about the upper-tier model.

Of interest here is that watershed development planners and managers can use such methods for both ecosystem restoration and the creation of environmentally benign project designs in futures forecasting. For example, given such-and-such an existing population or housing density currently in the watershed, and given such-and-such a proposed increase in this through development of the intended new project, how can we then reduce the repercussions of this exacerbated environmental stress through techniques of reforestation, reduction in road density, etc.? In other words, not only can development planners proactively design watershed landscapes to minimize detrimental environmental repercussions, they can also estimate the improvements to existing conditions likely to happen through restorative tree planting, road consolidation, or pavement removal. What such empirical predictive models will not do, however, is offer guidance as to precisely where to actually go about planting those forests or placing those roads or houses, in short, assessing just where development should or should not occur (see chapter 6). Again, it is important to recognize that these empirical models operate only in establishing threshold criteria early in the overall comprehensive planning process. In this respect, such models are identical with visual quality objectives developed with respect to limiting the maximum amount of logging (Berris 1995) in that both techniques more closely resemble what might be called "watershed development prescriptions" rather than detailed evaluations of the opportunities and constraints characteristic of itemized and rigorous watershed plans.

Subjectivity enters into the procedure in determining the acceptability threshold criteria that are posited to limit repercussions from development. The particular degree of environmental disturbance that the client or society can live with or that legislation may dictate is set at the beginning. For example, if a level of 10 percent reduction in eelgrass habitat or fish IBI is deemed acceptable, then the empirical models predict that we can build so many houses, remove so many trees in the watershed, etc. The important underlying strength in using this approach for watershed development planning is that it goes far toward reducing the likelihood of future surprises. The advantage of this in watershed management is crucial. In short, utilization of prognostic empirical models offers planners and developers a means to expect the unexpected, a key strategy in applying environmental adaptive management (Holling 1978).

Chapter Six

Examining Sites

Assessing Site-Development Potential in Terms of Water Vulnerability and Other Environmental Impacts

Although informed about what would be seen, I was still surprised by my first encounter with the antiquated remains of previous inhabitants that I stumbled across deep within the woods of the Harvard Forest in central Massachusetts. There were old building and cellar foundations, stream diversion sluice gates, abandoned farm ponds, and, of course, beautiful stone walls, all found amidst what to the casual eye would appear to be a virgin forest. What, I wondered at the time, had determined where these early settlers had located their home-steads? A year later I returned to the area and visited a new housing develop-ment that was in the process of being constructed on a large property hewn from the dense woods that had grown up in the century or two since the time of the first European pioneers. Overall, the site seemed to have several things going for it, but there were also several attributes that seemed to make it less attrac-tive: it was nearby both a major road and an area of protected natural land; it was on an elevated rise yet was surrounded by wetlands and small streams; and there were some old stone rows present although views were limited due to the dense surrounding forest. What had convinced the developer that this particular parcel of land was a good site for situating the dozen or so homes that were now being constructed? Several years later, and working with a group of planning students, we visited a handful of sites in the area and ranked them as to their suitability for potential or present development. Our assessment criteria were a series of simple variables dealing with water vulnerability, environmental impacts, site amenities, and estimated development costs. And the specific sites we examined for potential development ranged in their overall suitability from "poor" to "good." Interestingly, but perhaps not surprisingly, over the years of revisitations and many evaluations by different groups of students, sites that had been originally selected by the pioneers consistently rated higher than did those established in the early to mid-twentieth century, which in turn seemed to be better situated than the more recently developed sites. Was this simply a situation of the best sites being developed first? And if so, at what point is a decision made in terms of the law of diminishing return when it comes to development, when the remaining sites are evaluated as being simply unsuitable for consideration?

INTRODUCTION

Development Frameworks for Ecological Planning and Conservation Design

> Every new development should be based upon a fairly thorough (but not necessarily costly) analysis of the site's special features, both those offering opportunities and those involving constraints.
>
> R. Arendt, *Conservation Design for Subdivisions, 1996*

Steinitz (2002) developed a robust and useful framework in which to integrate ecology into design school curricula through the generation of a series of models targeted toward six different questions concerning land-use planning.

1. How should the landscape be described?
   Addressed by representation models
2. How does the landscape operate?
   Addressed by process models
3. Is the current landscape working well?
   Addressed by evaluation models
4. How might the landscape be altered?
   Addressed by change models
5. What predictable differences might the changes cause?
   Addressed by impact models
6. And how much should the landscape to changed?
   Addressed by decision models

There is an obvious parallel between this framework of inquisition and investigation and the questions used to introduce chapters in the present book. Steinitz (2002) argues that to be effective and efficient, land-use planning should progress through these questions by applying the appropriate models of representation, process, evaluation, change, impact, and decision in an iterative feedback. Adoption of such a procedure offers promise in being able to assess the vulnerability (the risk of potential harm from the impacts of land-use change) of the area under investigation.

Arendt (1996) outlined a process for organizing development around a central tenet of conservation planning of protected lands arranged into an interconnected network. The first phase of development planning is the objective collection and analysis of background information, which involves four distinct steps:

1. Understanding the locational context
2. Mapping natural, cultural, and historic features
3. Integrating the information layers
4. Prioritizing objectives

Once the background phase is completed and the data collated, Arendt (1996) believes that often the overall pattern of open space and development appropriate for each site becomes rather obvious. In this case, it is possible to progress to the design phase, which involves an additional four steps:

1. Identify all potential conservation areas
2. Locate the house sites
3. Design street alignments and trails
4. Draw in the lot lines

The overall goal is to maintain livability on the somewhat smaller lots needed in conservation subdivisions. The next challenge is to find ways to link individual conservation subdivisions to create a regional interconnected open-space network. Once this is accomplished, the community is well on its way to actualizing Aldo Leopold's concepts of building a new land ethic (Arendt 1996).

Large-scale Computer Analysis Evaluations

Sprawl development grows like a spreading cancer, rapidly covering the landscape in ill-advised and poorly situated construction projects. The magnitude of the problem, involving millions of square kilometers each year in North America, suggests that one way to get hold of the horns of the crazed beast in an attempt to manage or contain its rampage is to examine the ramifications of development on the large landscape scale.

Geographic information systems (GIS) have emerged as an extremely powerful tool in water-sensitive planning. The ability to map watershed attributes as varied as soil moisture (Felkner and Binford 2002), riparian buffers (France et al. 2002), land-lake linkages (Cantwell 2002), or surface permeability and aquifer recharge potential (Mueller, France, and Steinitz 2002) is an important step in identifying resources for protection from future development. This is the bottom-up approach promoted by Schloss (2002). Unfortunately, like any powerful tool, GIS has been used as an excuse to identify areas that are imagined to be capable of absorbing more development—what Schloss criticizes as the "top-down" approach.

Resource or bottom-up GIS analysis leads to preemptive planning and protection, which in turn helps toward fostering watershed stewardship. Stewardship comes about through education (France 2005), and it is here where GIS serves its most important role in water-sensitive planning (see chapter 2). Through providing convenient visualizations of complex and occult attributes, GIS allows stakeholders to become informed about not just the current status of their watershed but also the status of past conditions as well as the predicted status of future conditions given different development scenarios (see chapters 2 and 7).

There is a logical framework for undertaking watershed planning through GIS analysis: critical lands analysis $\rightarrow$ land capability analysis $\rightarrow$ prioritization of areas of special concern $\rightarrow$ determination of areas most likely to become developed $\rightarrow$ combination of all elements into a final planning summary (France 2002b).

It is important to also recognize a pertinent, cautionary lesson for water-sensitive planners, for it is the very elements that makes GIS so effective as a communication and education tool that also seduce many into using the techniques in a superficial and cavalier fashion. There is a need to move beyond the common use of GIS analysis to produce snazzy, computer-based presentations and instead to push the tool toward new and carefully thought-out directions in watershed management. In the end, it is important to remember that GIS is a means toward an end, never the end itself (France 2002a).

Some of the multiple objectives, directions, and advantages in watershed management that can be achieved through improving the use of GIS analysis (Schloss et al. 2002) include:

- Recognition and circumvention of gaps in knowledge through use of GIS modeling.
- Education of communities to think in an entire watershed context through enabling visual comprehension of everyone's place in the landscape.
- Establishment of voluntary controls to development and acknowledgment of the importance of land conservation.
- Movement toward use of GIS in a bottom-up management approach; that is, identification of resources to be protected from any future development

including wetlands, groundwater recharge areas, habitat for threatened species, fisheries, etc.

• Fusion of the two GIS approaches through iterative feedback to provide the different interest groups with a logical strategy for spatial analysis. That is, first, where are the critical areas that need to be protected; second, where can new development easily occur due to available infrastructure; and third, where are the intersection points?

• Increased communication facilitation and community building by taking the message directly to the town council.

• Understanding of the importance of proactive planning; that is, the need to act now to preserve special features of the watershed.

• Embracing the guiding principles of low-impact development.

• Further transparency and access to information for the public to foster local empowerment in decision making.

• Small decisions on the local scale have to be informed from a watershed perspective that must link immediate site-specific knowledge to long-term watershed inventories and future projections.

• Increased ecological sophistication of the public fostered through computer technologies.

• Movement toward technical standardization and national referencing of appropriate GIS approaches.

• Development of clear visions of the future through alternative futures land-use planning.

• Strengthen governmental management and enforcement.

• Need to jar people into thinking and planning on larger scales rather than being lost in the idiosyncrasies of individual sites.

One of the most useful (and simple) GIS-based models for predicting the aquatic effects of site development is that of Purdum (1997). Here, aquatic vulnerability is interpreted from the interaction of land-use induced change with the sensitivity of the systems to change. The sources of land-use induced change are spatially assessed through information predicted from database overlays on nutrient loading, erosion and sedimentation, stormwater runoff, adjacent wetlands loss, and alteration of stream morphology. The sum of these land-use induced changes are obtained from a simple weighting analysis and categorized as high, medium, low, or none. This information is then combined with a similarly weighted assessment of the drainage intensity and thus potential energy in the landscape to create a model of the intensity of the landscape for change. And finally, these data are combined with weighted estimates of the sensitivity of the drainage basin to produce a final appraisal of the vulnerability of the landscape to change.

The important point here is Purdum's (1997) belief that the GIS-based analysis is by no means the end product. Instead, he cautions that such vulnerability mapping must be interpreted cautiously as being relative to the particular study area. The benefit of undertaking such analyses is in their being able to "direct more site-specific investigation to areas which are spatially located and prioritized as contributing to high, medium or low vulnerability of steams and rivers. Site-specific investigation of signs of eutrophication, erosion, pollution, wetland loss and stream channelization are made more efficient by reducing the problem to a relatively small number of locations where they are most likely to be found."

Small-scale Site Visitation Evaluations

There is a need to ground-truth computer models with site visitations. Site-specific idiosyncrasies can often outweigh or obscure characterizations formulated on computers when locations are represented simply as GIS data. There is an important need to experience landscapes physically just as much as mentally in order to be able to generate the most useful appraisals of their suitability for development in relation to the potential vulnerability of their surrounding resources. Environmental inventories that provide a catalogue and description of the features and resources of the area being investigated are an essential first stage in land-use planning (Marsh 1998). These data, in combination with an examination of opportunities and constraints, allow for sites to be assessed in terms of their potential to accommodate development. Site visits are often essential to allow for generation of a series of rules of thumb to prevent problems with siting and design (Steinitz 2002).

There is general concordance in the various lists that have been produced of the variables deemed important for site inventory and development assessment. Arendt's (1996) list includes soils, wetlands, floodplains, slopes, significant wildlife habitats, woodlands, farmland, historic/cultural and archeological features, views into and out from the site, and aquifers and their recharge areas. Marsh's (1998) list includes topography, soils and wastewater disposal, groundwater and aquifer protection, stormwater discharge and management, watersheds and drainage networks, streamflow and floodplains, runoff and water quality, soil erosion and stream sedimentation, riparian landscapes, solar aspect and heating potential, microclimate considerations, ground frost, vegetation, landscape ecology and wildlife habitat, and wetlands. And Steinitz's (2002) list includes wetlands, erosion, and water.

SITE EVALUATION RANKINGS

The accelerated rate at which watersheds are being developed requires procedures for rapidly identifying sites that will exert as few impacts as possible on receiving waters. Additionally, development also has the potential to influence wildlife diversity as well as human and resource utility and habitability. The following discussion of site evaluation impact criteria was adapted from the detailed GIS analyses used in the core planning studio for a township in the Central Uplands region of Massachusetts (Steinitz 2002). The area is now covered by the secondary regrowth of a transition hardwood-hemlock-white pine forest following agricultural abandonment in the late nineteenth century (Fuller et al. 1998; Foster, Motzkin, and Slater 1998).

The following framework for site evaluations is based on conducting careful walkthroughs of the area under investigation, a simple soil percolation test, and use of both local and regional topographic maps. Each site analysis took a team of four to six students about an hour to complete. Importantly, assessment results for the same location by different groups of students were found to be in accordance much more frequently than those by the same group of students when adjudicating different sites; that is, the approach truly estimates intersite suitability, not merely interassessor appraisal variability. Interestingly, these site visitations provided rankings of locations that were often found to generally, but not always, agree with the large-scale, computer-based GIS assessments of the area for the same purposes.

Water-Sensitive Planning

The earth's hydrological cycle has been altered severely through centuries of environmentally deleterious human activity. Due to its corporeal form, water is an important integrator of environmental disturbance across spatial scales ranging from small subdivisions to regional drainage basins. As a result, local site-specific actions have cumulative effects on larger landscapes (France 2002a).

Vulnerability of Wetlands

Wetlands are often the most vitally important landscape feature sensitive to sprawl development. The following four principles of wetland functionality are summarized from France (2003c):

1. Wetlands function as giant sponges in that they slow down and absorb runoff, then gradually release it over a prolonged period, thereby reducing the risk of flooding.

2. By slowing down the rate of movement of water across the landscape and thereby promoting sediment deposition, wetlands operate like giant kidneys by entrapping and treating a vast array of contaminants.
3. In some watersheds, the most important role of wetlands may be their ability to structure and maintain biological integrity (for example, wetlands are the most biologically productive habitats on earth and thus function as wildlife diversity centers).
4. Wetlands, long regarded pejoratively as "wastelands," are now recognized as being providers of a great number of benefits to humans such as aesthetic beauty, recreational open space, important archives of history, and locations for environmental education.

Unfortunately, no landscapes have borne the brunt of environmentally insensitive development more than have wetlands. In the United States alone, for example, eighty million square hectares or almost half of the original wetlands have been lost due to agricultural and urban development.

A strange imbalance exists between the scale at which wetland losses are felt by society and the scale at which wetlands are preserved (France 2003b). Often the most important role that wetlands play is related not to any specific single wetland but rather to the cumulative effect of many wetlands on larger-scale landscape processes. In short, wetlands are not isolated entities but are linked to their surrounding landscape in terms of sensitivity to terrestrial disturbance, and the impacts of development sprawl need to be considered from a watershed-scale perspective in terms of the following principles:

• The magnitude of the effects of development on any single wetland are a reflection of the extent and proximity of the impacted wetland to other wetlands in watershed. Because there is a functional interdependency of wetlands such that they operate together as complexes, the environmental impacts of removing isolated wetlands may be more severe due to a lack of functional redundancy.
• Not all wetlands are created equal in terms of either their ecological role in watersheds or their estimated likelihood of successful replication through loss-mitigation creation. Specifically, vernal pools are the most sensitive and the hardest to create anew, followed by forested swamps, then wet meadows, and lastly open-water wetlands with macrophytes.
• The watershed position of wetlands relative to potential development is important to consider in respect to their ecological role and the estimated severity of environmental damage should they be removed. Wetlands higher in the watershed are important for flood control, those lower in the water-

shed are important for chemical absorption, and those situated in riverine riparian zones are important for sustaining wildlife.

• The extent of previous wetland loss in the watershed influences the severity of additional wetland damage from continued development. In other words, if there are many surrounding wetlands still present, the detrimental effects of altering a single wetland will be less severe.

Riparian Forest Buffers

The region where land meets water—the riparian ecotone—is known to demand special attention in environmental management (e.g., USDA 1998). Riparian buffers function protectively as the first line of defense for water bodies from land development, such as, for example, with respect to soil erosion (France 2002c) or reciprocally for protecting human occupants of floodplains in terms of water management (Zucker et al. 2002). Because riparian buffers provide not only these functions but also serve as human amenities in green recreational corridors (Flink 2002; see also chapter 10), much attention has been devoted to measuring their size and extent on a landscape scale (Schloss 2002; France et al. 2002). What is most important is the need for bridging, conceptually as well as physically, across spatial scales.

Mitchell (2002) repeatedly makes the point that to be truly effective, riparian buffers must be coupled to the larger landscape of whole watersheds and continuous habitat areas. The importance of this simple precept for the profession of water-sensitive site development cannot be overstated. This is particularly the case for concerns about wildlife biodiversity. For example, although a buffer strip of only a hundred feet or so may be sufficient to filter out sediments and entrap contaminants (e.g., France 2002c), such widths are often woefully inadequate for protecting riparian wildlife (Forman 1997).

Concepts of landscape ecology such as fragmentation, connectivity, edge effects, patches, nodes, etc. (Dramstad, Olson, and Forman 1996; Peck 1998) should be part of shoreline planning. One of the greatest challenges in establishing networks of shoreline buffers is in avoiding or minimizing gaps, which can later be filled in through localized restoration efforts (see chapter 10). Watershed planners must therefore learn how to situate their regions of interest and study back into the larger landscape in order to effectively mitigate harmful land-use changes. For example, roads may have a negative influence upon riparian wildlife (e.g., directly through roadkills or indirectly through interfering with seasonal migrations) even though they may be located many kilometers away from the water (chapter 5).

Mitchell's (2002) thesis becomes even more significant in his encompassing of the sociology implicit, yet frequently ignored, in riparian forest protection. The role of education in fostering initial interest and then in sustaining surveillance is of critical importance (France 2005; see also chapter 2). Public surveys often demonstrate the support professed by landowners for both human and environmental (wildlife) benefits accruing from shoreline protection. Watershed planners desperately need this type of information at an early date in order to justify to the skeptics (who may hold the purse strings) that their intents are obviously in the best interests of both the wildlife *and* the human populations.

Riparian forest buffers thus offer many environmental benefits that need to be kept in mind during the first round of assessing site-development potential. The following list, adapted from the Massachusetts Riverways Program (Cohen 1998)—one of the most effective such state agencies in the country— summarizes the functions of riparian forest buffers and justifies their preservation during site development.

1. Flood control and mitigation of stormwater damage
    - Floodplain area stores water
    - Vegetative barrier to slow down flows and therefore to decrease storm peaks
    - Roots open up soil and increase percolation
    - Transpiration takes up water
2. Wildlife habitat
    - Ecotones are transition zones with consequent high biodiversity
    - The dynamic equilibrium of rivers produces diverse patterns of vegetation
    - Critical corridors for wildlife movement
    - Importance of dead snags, windthrow, and woody debris as forest habitat
3. Fisheries protection
    - Large woody debris creates pool habitat and entraps downstream movement of organic matter
    - Shading is important for temperature regulation and consequently serves to increase the water oxygen levels
    - Food source supply of leaves and insects
4. Groundwater protection and water
    - Many wells are located in riparian zones and thus hydrologically connected to rivers
    - Vegetation slows down water movement and therefore increases purification
    - Vegetation increases soil percolation and maintains continual baseflow to streams during dry periods

- Maintains a healthy hyporheic (interstitial spring-fed) zone important for stream insects
5. Pollution prevention
   - Vegetation slows down water movement, leading to deposition of nutrient-laden, oxygen-using sediment and organic matter
   - Phytoremediation of trace contaminants (both urban and agricultural) through vegetation providing a substrate for pathogen breakdown

The important multifaceted roles played by riparian forests in sustaining ecological functions make them only slightly less important on a watershed perspective in this regard than wetlands. As such, protecting riparian areas to buffer aquatic systems from land disturbance is of paramount importance for environmentally sensitive development and figures strongly in site evaluations.

- The ground-surface slope from the proposed development site through the riparian buffer strip and to the water body is of major significance in terms of influencing the erosion potential. The steeper the surface slope, the greater the movement of sediment on the landscape (France 1997b) and the less attractive the site is for development.
- The average width for the riparian forest is critical for the ability of the buffer to entrap sediment. The greater the width of the buffer, the more likely it will prevent the incursion of soil into the water from site development.
- The unbroken longitudinal extent of the riparian forest is critical for enabling wildlife movement (Forman 1997). The more fragmented the riparian forest buffer, the less likely it is presently functioning as a wildlife corridor and, as such, the less critical it is to prevent any further tree removal from development compared to a well-forested and utilized corridor.
- The position in the watershed of the potential development project will influence the severity of its impact on rivers due to removal of riparian trees. Food webs in streams shift from being predominantly fueled by terrestrial leaf litter in the headwaters to being progressively fueled more and more by algae farther down the watershed. As a result, the higher up in the watershed the development is, the more sensitive the streams will be to removal of any riparian vegetation.

Water Quality

The greatest threat to water quality comes not from the direct input of effluent from manufacturing plants but rather through nonpoint-source contamination carried in the runoff from a wide range of sources. Because many contaminants are physically bound to soil, understanding the threats posed by nonpoint-source pollution necessitates being able to predict the dynamics of soil movement upon the landscape (Purdum 1997).

- The nature of the potential source material will of course affect the likelihood of its movement. Soils vary in their inherent susceptibility to being mobilized by rainfall and the resulting potential for interrill erosion (France 1997b). Obviously, the greater the degree of surface compaction, the less erodible is the material and the less likely is the threat of nonpoint-source pollution.
- Soil mobility is of course influenced by the aspect slope of the ground (France 1997b). The steeper the slope of the ground, the greater the erosion energy potential and the more likely the threat of nonpoint-source pollution.
- The overall ground surface topography (Purdum 1997) and presence or absence of transport impediments (France 2002c) will influence soil movement. The more convex the topography, the more erosion energy will be reduced through dissipating surface-water movement. In contrast, if the topography is concave, water will be concentrated and soil can be moved greater distances with a consequent increased likelihood of nonpoint-source pollution of downslope water bodies. The greater the extent of ground-surface coverage by live vegetation (trees, grass, etc.) and large obstructions (boulders, windthrow, etc.), the shorter the distance soil will be transported and therefore the less likely the threat from nonpoint-source pollution.
- Protecting the quality of drinking water from reservoirs requires particular diligence (Blau 2002; Benjamin 2002). Therefore, a simple measure of the riverine linear distance and connectivity from nearby water bodies to any drinking water reservoir will affect the overall suitability of the site for potential development.

Septic System Suitability

Degradation of groundwater occurs when contaminants are introduced into the aquifer from diffuse sources such as agricultural and urban runoff as well as from leaking septic systems. Although groundwater is less frequently polluted, once this happens it is much slower to recover from pollution episodes that would be considered relatively mild for surface waters (e.g., Mueller, France, and Steinitz 2002). And although the duration, type, and intensity of contamination will determine the risk to groundwater quality, the susceptibility of surface waters to nutrient enrichment from septic systems is influenced by landscape features.

- The physical nature of the surface and subsurface material (i.e., soil type, bedrock depth, etc.) is important for influencing wastewater treatment. Soil profiles of high permeability and filtration are ideal for establishing septic system leach fields. Situations characterized by presence of impervious clays will mean that sewage effluent will not have the same opportunity to be cleansed before it is transported to streams and lakes. Such sites will, as a result, be less suitable for development.
- The aspect slope and water table depth also influence wastewater treatment by septic fields as well as the likelihood for groundwater contamination. Slopes of less than 5 percent are good for septic trenches, as they allow for slow percolation and better water treatment than if the slopes were steeper. Shallow water table depths obviously pose a greater danger from septic system contamination than those of greater depth where the effluent has a longer treatment path before it communicates with the groundwater.
- Sites with abundant vegetation are more suitable for potential development than barren sites because plants can uptake nutrients (and other contaminants) through phytoremediation.
- Once again, the distance from the proposed septic field to nearby water bodies (and especially to any drinking water reservoirs) will affect the overall suitability of the site for potential development.

Wildlife-Sensitive Planning

There is often an inherent and deeply based conflict between the inhabitation of landscapes by humans and by wildlife. In fact, habitat destruction and degradation is the major cause of endangerment of species in the United States (Noss, O'Connell, and Murphy 1997). Thus, habitat-based conservation is critical; that is, the key to preserving species is in preserving important ecosystems. Because the magnitude of threats to biodiversity from rampant development is such a serious global problem, approaches to selecting potential sites for human inhabitation must be made based on an imperative to intermesh into the landscape with as little intrusion as possible upon biological integrity.

There is a need to provide and adapt principles of conservation biology to conservation planning. Noss, O'Connell, and Murphy (1997) provide a useful list of the principles, both philosophical and practical, for habitat-based conservation planning. Among those are the following, some of which are explored in more detail in the site appraisals below:

- Ecosystems are not only more complex than we think but more complex than we can think.
- Nature is full of surprises.

- The fewer data or more uncertainty, the more conservative a conservation plan should be.
- The less the predicted impact of a project on species or ecosystems, the less scientific scrutiny is needed.
- Biodiversity conservation must be concerned with many different spatial and temporal scales.
- Species well distributed across their native range are less susceptible to extinction than species confined to small portions of their range.
- Large blocks of habitat, containing large populations, are better than small blocks with small populations.
- Blocks of habitat close together are better than blocks far apart.
- Habitat in congruous blocks is better than fragmented habitat.
- Interconnected blocks of habitat are better than isolated blocks.

Endangered Species

The most serious ramification that might arise from sprawl development is to bring about the local extirpation of endangered species. Sensitivity of endemic animals and plants to human interventions in the landscape, though variable, is often a barometer for the overall state of health of the environment (chapter 3). Often by the time species loss is recognized at regional scales, the local site-specific impacts that cumulatively caused the loss have gone unrecognized for years. Serious, a priori attention must therefore be paid to wildlife-sensitive planning at smaller spatial scales where the impacts of development can be more quickly recognized and remedied.

- Although wetlands contribute to only about 5 percent of the total land coverage area in North America, more than a third of all rare and endangered species are found in these habitats (France 2003c). Consequently, the presence of wetlands on or near a potential development site can limit its suitability for that purpose.
- In New England, forests have undergone a remarkable recovery in areal extent over the last century. As a result, it is not forest species that are particularly rare but rather those species that are characteristic of old agricultural fields that need special protection. Therefore, in this type of landscape, it is those sites with an absence of uniform forest cover that are more likely to harbor rarer species and thus be less attractive for potential development. In other words, locations characterized by dense forest cover will actually be more suitable for development than those of an open forest and field mosaic.
- Given the extent of regional sprawl, the presence of lands placed under protection as reserves or land trusts are likely to harbor a high proportion of

endangered species through their role as wildlife oases in a developed and depauperate desert. As such, the suitability of such locations for potential development can be seriously compromised relative to those in which there are no nearby bioreserves.

- Endangered wildlife are often found in locations where people are not. Therefore, sites with an absence of anthropogenic influences (which can be loosely gauged based on the distance from the nearest town) have a higher likelihood of being associated with wildlife species in need of protection from development than in locations adjacent to towns. Sprawl development is therefore much more likely to detrimentally impact endangered species than infill development.

Biodiversity

The distribution of biological species across the landscape is neither uniform nor random but rather is extremely patchy such that hot spots of biodiversity occur, as do areas that can be nearly devoid of life (Forman 1997). Recognizing those particular locations expected to harbor a rich diversity of species would obviously aid in the comparative appraisal of sites for potential development.

- Ecotones are transition zones between different types of landscapes. As such, their complex habitat structure allows for an overlap of the home ranges of many different species. One of the most notable ecotones that harbor an incredibly diverse group of associated species is land-water riparian regions. Therefore, it is important to protect these habitats from nearby development. As a result, the suitability of sites for development decrease in relation to their proximity to riparian wildlife corridors.
- The next most obvious hot spot for biodiversity that can easily be discerned is the presence of ecotones between open fields and closed forests. Such a mosaic of variable habitat patches will attract a richer array of species than uniform habitats of either one type or the other. In consequence, the greater the frequency of such mosaic patches on the landscape, the less suitable the site is for potential development.
- Even in nonecotonal landscapes, wildlife diversity is extremely patchy in its distribution. There are often strong positive relationships between habitat complexity as measured by the variability in the structure and type of vegetation and the number of wildlife species residing in the many different niches located there. Therefore, such sites become less attractive for development compared to those characterized by monospecific, uniformly aged stands of trees.

- Once again, the influence of anthropogenic disturbances have negative effects on wildlife diversity such that the farther a potential site is from nearby towns, the less attractive it is for development compared to a site situated adjacent to the town.

Fragmentation

One of the basic tenets of undertaking wildlife-sensitive development through the lens of landscape ecology is recognition that most animals are mobile, not sessile, creatures. Indeed, for many species, movement is their very key to survival, an organism's "home range" being the essential area necessary for searching for habitat and food, avoiding predators, and finding and attracting a mate. Though occasionally development can have a direct effect on species survival (as, for example, erosion entering rivers and destroying trout spawning beds), more often its effects are insidious, reducing a region's biological integrity by fragmenting the landscape and thus interfering with the movement of wildlife.

- Roads can exact a considerable negative effect upon regional wildlife through their role in carving up the landscape and impeding animal movement (Forman et al. 2003; see also chapters 2 and 5). As a consequence, the presence of roads already bisecting an area suggests that inclusion of another subdivision development there will be less serious than if the development occurred in a completely virgin, forested landscape. This results because the former proposed development would be inserted into the existing framework of established roads, whereas to provide access to the latter proposed development, new roads would have to be constructed.
- Another concern is how the new proposed development will dissect the landscape into isolated "island" patches surrounded by an inhospitable "sea" of open space. The greater the likelihood that the proposed development will isolate such a patch of habitat, the less suitable that site will be for development.
- Given that in many areas it is the presence of forests that sustains regional biodiversity, obviously sites that could be built on land that has already been developed (e.g., underused agriculture fields, abandoned postindustrial properties, etc.) are preferable compared to those that would entail forest clearance. The greater the opportunity to recycle previously used land, the less serious will be the effects of new development there in terms of fragmenting the landscape for animals.
- Most wild animals shy away from humans and their pets and buildings. Because of this, the density of existing buildings on the landscape will influ-

ence wildlife movement: if too dense to be able to squeeze in between, the structures will function as a wall; if spread out with adequate greenspace in between, the structures will not interfere with movement. The question for assessing new development becomes how will the added structures affect the overall porosity of the landscape for wildlife movement?

Connectivity

The corollary of landscape fragmentation is habitat connectivity. Animals actively search out and exploit travel linkages between habitat patches (Dramstad, Olson, and Forman 1996; Peck 1998). Development must therefore be inserted into the landscape with as little intrusion as possible upon these animal thoroughfares.

- Often the most widely used wildlife movement corridors are those occurring within streamside riparian zones. Potential sites that would risk the severance of these important migration corridors are thus unsuitable for development.
- Presence of large forested tracts of land function as both seed areas for and major attracters of wildlife and, as a result, are essential for sustaining regional biodiversity. Consequently, corridors leading to and from such areas are bound to be popular with animals. Because of this, the more proximal a site is to such large bioreserves, the increased vigilance that is needed to not sever those wildlife arteries.
- Wildlife have the ability to leapfrog across open expanses between isolated "island" habitat patches. Therefore, both the number and the size of the patches of undeveloped land will affect regional biodiversity. An important question for assessing the potential of sites for development is, how will the new buildings hinder the ability of animals to move from patch to patch? In this perspective, an optimal location for development would be one distant from such gaps between patches.
- The suitability of linear strips of land in functioning as movement corridors for wildlife depends on the size (width and length) of these connectors. The best connectors are those that are short and fat; the worst are reciprocally those that are long and skinny. The better a site is for development, the better its ability to leave a landscape in which corridors have the highest probability to maintain their connectivity status.

Besides the previous eight water and wildlife evaluation criteria, an additional three criteria based on site amenities and another three criteria based on site construction and maintenance are useful for assessing the overall development suitability. These will be covered below in much less detail than those described previously, with the admitted recognition that in certain situations the specific importance of this latter group of six criteria could be at least as important for determining the overall suitability of a site for development as those environmental ones that are the central focus of this chapter.

Site Amenities

Agricultural Potential

- The chemistry and organic matter content of the soil will of course influence suitability for crop production.
- The agricultural history of the site is important for its present-day potential for crop production. Land currently in production is more favorable than former agricultural land that may be depleted in nutrients or appropriate soil.
- Whether or not the site needs forest clearance before crop planting will also influence its suitability for agriculture.
- Unless nonpesticide organic farming will be adopted, the distance from water bodies is an important variable to consider.

Visual Quality

- The presence of forest copses are always looked upon favorably from a perspective of site aesthetics as well as for providing screening to hide the new development from neighbors or vice versa.
- The presence of water substantially increases the attractiveness of the site and allows developers to charge higher purchase or rental prices (known as the "water premium" in real estate development).
- The elevation and the aspect of the view significantly influence the attractiveness of any site for development. Also, the ability to build on the mid-slope rather than on the top of a hill (the latter of which would detrimentally affect the view of neighbors) will raise the desirability of the site for development.
- The extent of proximal development in terms of roads and other buildings can play a major role in the aesthetics of a site.

Historic/Cultural Resources

- The presence or reuse of historic buildings on the property to be developed can increase its overall attraction to both investors and potential inhabitants.
- Likewise, the presence of old stone rows and farm foundations adds a his-

torical thickness to the landscape that, if preserved and even emphasized in the final development plan, can add substantially to the amenities the site possesses.

- In the same vein, remnants of certain types of previous land use such as abandoned farm fields can increase the aesthetics of the potential development site.
- And finally, if the site either contains or is situated nearby old country carriage lanes, its attractiveness for development can increase.

Site Construction and Maintenance

Energy and Microclimate

- The orientation of the site will be important in terms of the exposure of its buildings to sunlight and therefore the potential for passive heating. In northern locations, south-facing development sites are more favorable than those whose aspect is oriented toward the north.
- The exposure of the site to wind will affect its development suitability in terms of avoiding winter arctic blasts or capturing cooling gusts, depending on the geographic location being examined and the corresponding harshness of winter cold or summer heat.
- The elevation of the potential development site will also influence its temperature. In many situations, the ideal site location will be on the midslope, thus avoiding damp air in the valleys or the cold winds on the summit.
- Proximity to large bodies of water can increase the suitability of a site in terms of providing thermal modulation.

Projected Construction Costs

- The nature of existing land use will influence a site's suitability for development. For example, if there are existing buildings present, can they be reused or do they have to be torn down?
- The construction of a site necessitates having adequate access. In this regard, the presence of, and proximity to, existing roads will be important in reducing development costs.
- The slope and surficial geology will greatly influence site construction. The steeper the slope, the more expensive the construction of buildings. And the shallower the bedrock, the more work often involved to create building footprints.
- Because one consequence of site construction is soil movement, the proximity to water bodies will influence the consequent need for rigorously

enforced best management practices (BMPs) to prevent erosion damage to aquatic resources.

Wastewater Treatment

- Decentralized, on-site treatment of wastewater necessitates appropriate space to be allocated for construction of such systems. Therefore, if the development footprint is too small to insert such a technology, the cost of examining alternative treatments rises.
- Decentralized wastewater management works best in situations of low slope to increase the exposure time of sewage to biological treatment.
- As was the case for site construction, the presence of, and proximity to, existing roads is important for enabling servicing of the wastewater management systems.
- And as for all aspects of site development where there is a likelihood that contaminants (in this case nutrients) can be transported by overland or subsurface water, the distance from lakes and streams will influence the suitability of the site.

CONCLUSION

Ranking of Potential Development Sites

The overall suitability of a site for development can be quantified by ascribing the simple weighting of 1 for "poor," 2 for "fair," and 3 for "good," for each one of the evaluation criteria (table 6.1). An ideal site for development would therefore have the maximum total score of 168; that is, the 14 evaluation categories multiplied by the 4 criteria per category multiplied by the evaluation grade of 3 for "good" for each assessment. And an incredibly bad site for development would have the minimum total score of 56; that is, the 14 evaluation categories multiplied by the 4 criteria per category multiplied by the evaluation grade of 1 for "poor" for each assessment.

Table 6.1. Scorecard of abbreviated evaluation criteria for assessing site suitability for potential development

Evaluation Criteria	Poor (1)	Fair (2)	Good (3)
Vulnerability of Wetlands			
• Wetland proximity	___	___	___
• Wetland type	___	___	___
• Watershed position	___	___	___
• Wetland loss	___	___	___
Riparian Forest Buffers			
• Ground slope	___	___	___
• Width	___	___	___
• Longitudinal extent	___	___	___
• Watershed position	___	___	___
Water Quality			
• Source material	___	___	___
• Slope	___	___	___
• Topography and transport impediments	___	___	___
• Distance to water	___	___	___
Septic System Suitability			
• Permeability and filtration	___	___	___
• Slope and water table depth	___	___	___
• Phytoremediation potential	___	___	___
• Distance to water	___	___	___
Endangered Species			
• Wetlands	___	___	___
• Old fields	___	___	___
• Protected lands	___	___	___
• Anthropogenic influences	___	___	___
Biodiversity			
• Riparian ecotones	___	___	___
• Mosaic patches	___	___	___
• Vegetation variability	___	___	___
• Anthropogenic influences	___	___	___
Fragmentation			
• Roads	___	___	___
• Habitat patches	___	___	___
• Developed land	___	___	___
• Building density	___	___	___
Connectivity			
• Riparian corridors	___	___	___
• Distance to large reserve	___	___	___
• Patch number and size	___	___	___
• Connectors' size	___	___	___
Agricultural Potential			
• Soil suitability	___	___	___
• Past site history	___	___	___
• Forest clearance needed	___	___	___
• Distance to water	___	___	___

continued

Table 6.1.   Scorecard of abbreviated evaluation criteria for assessing site suitability for potential development   (*continued*)

Evaluation Criteria	Poor (1)	Fair (2)	Good (3)
Visual Quality			
• Forest	___	___	___
• Water	___	___	___
• Elevation	___	___	___
• Anthropogenic constructions	___	___	___
Historic/Cultural Resources			
• Historic buildings	___	___	___
• Old stone rows and farm foundations	___	___	___
• Abandoned farm fields	___	___	___
• Old country carriage lanes	___	___	___
Energy and Microclimate			
• Sunlight slope	___	___	___
• Wind exposure	___	___	___
• Elevation	___	___	___
• Water	___	___	___
Projected Construction Costs			
• Existing land use	___	___	___
• Distance to roads	___	___	___
• Slope and geology	___	___	___
• Distance to water	___	___	___
Wastewater Treatment			
• Construction space	___	___	___
• Slope	___	___	___
• Distance to roads	___	___	___
• Distance to water	___	___	___

Maximum rank = 14 _ 4 _ 3 (all "good") = 168
Minimum rank = 14 _ 4 _ 1 (all "poor") = 56

Chapter Seven

Engaging Time

Frameworks for Modeling Scenarios of Alternative Development Futures

The speed of development was almost beyond belief, so much so in fact that I had to sit down by the shore to take it all in and try to comprehend what it was my eyes were telling me. It was my second visit to Hangzhou, China, and the changes in the cityscape were glaringly obvious even though the two visits had been separated by a mere six months. On the other hand, maybe I shouldn't have been so surprised considering that I knew at the time that nearby Shanghai actually had one-quarter of all the sky cranes in the entire world there for new construction projects! Perhaps this was all part of some sort of frightening competition whereby each Chinese city was attempting to grow at the fastest rate, seemingly at the expense of all other considerations. Gazing out across the incredibly picturesque and richly historic West Lake and past the few remaining relics preserved from when the city had been the capital in the time of Marco Polo, I noted that the skyline was marred by wave after wave of high-rise buildings spreading out in the distance toward the mountains and the famous tea plantations and monasteries located there. Soon, unless checked and redirected, all would be engulfed in one enormous sprawling city, and the future of West Lake would be as dire as that of the few surviving streams that struggled their beleaguered way through the metropolis toward the historic lake. How was it possible for the city to achieve its desired UN World Heritage Site status in the face of such massive economic pressures from the rapidly expanding Chinese economy? This was the question that had brought me and a group of professors and students to Hangzhou. Viewing the jewel of the lake against the encircling city reinforced, however, that it would obviously be a daunting task to attempt to answer that question. Again noticing buildings where none had existed less than half a year ago, it seemed impossible to grasp the rapidity of the change. Perhaps if one had a way to forecast what the future could look like, might this provide a sobering shock and bring reality therapy to those officials in charge of supervising development. What can be done, then, to predict what the effects of development might be on the ecological conditions of a watershed? And is there a way to describe and compare what the various choices might offer in terms of how to proceed with that development?

INTRODUCTION

Gaps often exist in the production of scientific information and the delivery of those insights in a useful form for people to act upon (Hulse, Branscomb, and Payne 2004; see also chapter 3). Furthermore, there is need to develop place-based relationships between environmental policy and implementation (Freemark 2000), particularly in relation to trade-offs that can often exist among ecological, social, and economic aspirations, and in a form that not only supports but actually encourages objective discussion abut what the future might look like on the ground.

As Neils Bohr humorously, but aptly, quipped, "prediction is difficult, especially when it is about the future" (Steinitz 2000). There are six questions that are important for understanding how watersheds will respond to development, adapted from Steinitz (2000):

1. How should the landscape be described?
2. How does the landscape operate?
3. Is the landscape working well?
4. How might the landscape be altered?
5. What differences might the changes cause?
6. Should the landscape be changed? If so, how and by whom?

The truly critical question in assessing the implications of increased population pressure and watershed development is the fourth one. And the easy answer is that there are thousands of ways that the landscape can be altered through time. So the challenge becomes how to get all the options down to an attractive number so that stakeholders can start to think about, discuss, argue about, and act on the projected changes in their living spaces (Steinitz 2000).

One approach that is beginning to receive widespread interest among land-use planners, particularly those dealing with large-scale, highly contentious water-driven issues, is alternative futures scenario modeling. This technique enables predicting impacts of land-use alterations on ecological processes, integrating human dimensions into effective planning, and developing an understanding of the uncertainty of impacts and associated risks of various development scenarios (Hulse et al. 2000; Steinitz et al. 2001; Santelmann, Hulse, and White 2001; Hulse and Gregory 2001; Dole and Nieme 2004; Van Sickle et al. 2004). And most importantly, the alternative futures approach provides a framework to effectively incorporate science into the community-based decision-making process. Major components (Baker and Landers 2004; Hulse, Branscomb, and Payne 2004) include:

- Characterization of the trajectory of landscape change and formulating these as a series of defined alternative future scenario assumptions.
- Development of spatially explicit alternative future landscapes through models that reflect varying assumptions about land and water use and the range of stakeholder viewpoints.
- Modeling and evaluating the likely effects of the landscape trajectory and alternative futures on key and valued ecological and socioeconomic end points.
- Characterizing and synthesizing the differences between the alternatives.

The alternative futures approach has its roots in build-out analyses that have been used for decades by land-use planners as a tool to predict future development patterns and their effects. The build-out methodology is directed toward promoting sound land-management decisions by providing growth projections, assessing the impacts of existing growth, and encouraging actions to reduce the impacts of growth (CBP 1998). The regulatory options available for managing sprawl that are often included as elements of build-out analyses include:

- Forest conservation
- Stream buffer protection
- Rural clustering
- Increased development potential in growth areas
- Transfer of development rights to growth areas
- Extending sewer service to designated growth areas
- Protective agricultural zoning
- Purchase of development rights
- Management needs strategies

CASE STUDIES

Hydrological Frameworks for Riverine Development (Steinitz 2000)

Carl Steinitz likes to quote Herbert Simon's definition of design as being an active verb in that "Everyone designs who devises courses of action aimed at changing existing conditions into preferred ones" (Steinitz 1990). The common element shared among the following cases (Steinitz 2000) is that hydrologists are acting as the designers due to their models driving the systems that underlie the land-development scenarios being examined. In the first study dealing with the Santa Margerita River in Camp Pendleton in California, the central focus is on water availability. In the second study concerning the Jordan River in Israel, the Palestinian Territories, and Jordan, the central issue concerns the economic use of water. And in the third study based on the San Pedro River in Arizona and Senora, groundwater is the central issue. Also, all three studies deal with large-scale regions and decision choices that are based on highly contentious water-driven issues.

Steinitz always makes clear that the role that he, his students, and his research collaborators assume is not to provide the answer to any particular problem but rather to provide a range of possibilities from which the answer can be derived. In a sense, this takes full advantage of the researchers' physical and emotional distance from these projects that, due to their contested nature, are seen by locals as zero-sum games rather than win-win situations. And the underlying strategy is to construct a time framework that looks twenty to forty years ahead. This framework recognizes that adapting to the worsening pressures of change cannot be immediately enforceable but rather acknowledges that it will take them some time to be able to thwart development with effective protection measures. Another advantage in alternative futures modeling is its ability to detect and then measure hitherto occult agents of change. In this regard, whereas indirect effects can remain unnoticed by casual observers when examined independently, their cumulative modification by land use may become overt when investigated interactively (Steinitz et al. 1996).

Camp Pendleton

Five river basins flow through Camp Pendleton, and the largest of these, the Santa Margerita, is the last large unchannelized river in southern California (Steinitz 2000). Unlike most places in southern California, Camp Pendleton has no direct connection to water imported from distant locations. Today, the area is regarded as one of the few places with very little development and considerable open space. In reality, 100 percent of Camp Pendleton is used by the military, and bombs are dropped there frequently, whereas the abutting areas are subject to randomly located subdivisions spreading over the landscape. Briefly (further details can be found in Steinitz et al. 1996), demographic predictions suggest that over the next forty to sixty years, up to a million people will move into the area. These growth forecasts were used to predict alterations in land use.

The development alternatives model (Steinitz 2000) addressed two foreseeable problems. First, the region has the highest biodiversity in the western United States. And second, because the air base is built on the valley floor downstream from off-base suburban development, it has been subjected to being buried under a meter of silt during twenty-year storm events. The immediate, short-term answer to solving the flooding problem would be to build a levee surrounding the base to protect it from future flash floods. The long-term solution involved some hard decisions about landscape management.

The representation stage of investigation used GIS-based data on land cover and terrain mapping. The landscape operation stage used soil models that influenced hydrology, which influenced fire, which influenced vegetation, which in turn influenced biodiversity. One question was how the projected increases in urbanization would affect regional biodiversity; the other question dealt with the worsening flooding problem. The challenge is that currently 100 percent of the private land outside the military reserve is zoned for development with nothing set aside for public open space or conservation. Therefore, given the plans to pave over most of the upstream area, what can be expected in terms of the resulting biodiversity and flooding?

The constructed flood assessment model (Steinitz et al. 1996) tracks land-use changes through soil changes through vegetative cover changes to runoff and infiltration changes. In short, the model links alterations in land-use from development to changes in runoff. The modeling exercise involved taking a twenty-five-year flood and running it through several scenarios of differing development. The models revealed that under predicted build-out conditions, the peak of the flood would double and that the damage from a ten-year flood would essentially become as severe as that presently characterizing a twenty-year flood (see chapter 2 for discussion of a similar problem).

For the investigation stage of land alteration, students generated six alternatives:

1. A group of regional urban centers (this is the plan favored by the developers).
2. A group of high-density subdivisions scattered over the land.
3. Present trends are followed, but then a widespread wakeup occurs midway through with consequent damage-minimizing adaptive management concerning what nature remains.
4. Privatized conservation by millionaires with land trusts.
5. Small villages are built that are linked by bus.
6. Everyone is concentrated into one place .

The impact stage of investigation was based on constructing a decision matrix of development alternatives versus environmental variables (Steinitz et al. 1996). One result showed that the sprawl and scattered development option would generate the most detrimental effects on regional biodiversity. An important result was that none of the various alternatives were found to solve the problem of flooding on Camp Pendleton, and all left major gaps in landscape connectivity important for biodiversity conservation (see Chapter 6). Other, site-specific investigations (Steinitz et al. 1996) looked at various restorative designs for constructing percolation basins for flood attenuation and wildlife habitat, as well as the siting of proposed developments distant from wildlife corridors (see chapter 6).

A more detailed follow-up study addressed the locations of potential conflicts (Steinitz 2000). For example, the places where both the developers and the conservationists desired the land tended to be next to the riparian corridors, a location the first model had warned would be of greatest risk from development. As a result, a second group of students focused on preserving riparian areas and offered suggestions based on environmentally sensitive development guidelines (such as in chapter 6).

Most results generated from this seventh alternative proved to be better in terms of both reducing flood risk as well as preserving biodiversity (Steinitz 2000). In particular, the development futures model estimated that it would cost $270 million to acquire the land rights to achieve the desirable conservation pattern needed to reduce flooding. When compared to the estimated costs of $3 billion to relocate the air base, or the $250 million required to channelize the rivers as per the initial plan, the land management scheme raised by the scenario modeling proved economically sensible. Given that placing riparian areas in protective land trusts would also bring about obvious wildlife protection (as opposed to the opposite occurring if rivers were channelized to increase their floodwater storage capacity), the land acquisition option seemed the obvious one. Unfortunately, however, the big problem is that federal law does not presently allow for Department of Defense funds to be spent off base. So, in order to implement the suggestions raised in this study, a change of law would be required—something that is currently being examined.

Jordan River Valley

The Jordan River valley contains one of the world's most culturally important rivers even though at the present time it is but a remnant of its former state. The river is the northern portion of the Great Rift Valley through which prehistoric hominids made their way from Africa into Europe. As part of a studio project, Steinitz and his students undertook a study of how the concepts of political coexistence, cooperation, and partnership in designing alternative futures might be brought about for the region of the Israeli town of Beit She'an, the Palestinian Territories city of Jenin, and northern Jordan (Steinitz et al. 1999).

In its heyday, Beit She'an had been a very important city due to its strategic location astride the west-east main road from Mediterranean to Baghdad and the north-south road from Damascus to Cairo. Today, the region is considered a social and economic backwater from all three jurisdictions. Israeli land is situated in the lowest portion, and much of the region in the Occupied Territories lies atop rolling hills. The primary land use in the area is agriculture, with, however, an important difference being that it is accomplished through widespread irrigation in Israel.

Early into their period of background research, the students decided that the real alternatives to development were not physical but rather political options (Steinitz 2000). As a result, the study investigated the development consequences of what might happen under conditions of:

- Coexistence—three independent nations acting in their own self-interests and within their boundaries and having very little to do with one another.
- Cooperation—three independent nations that on some topics might make bilateral or trilateral decisions for the benefit of all.
- Partnership—three interdependent regions of their nations that undertake many joint ventures and integrated land-use planning.

All the jurisdictions forecast a doubling of their respective populations within the next half century in a place that has already experienced a substantial water deficit (Steinitz et al. 1999). Water and its use is the volatile element for the entire region. For example, there is a marked disparity in water consumption rate between Palestinians and Israelis (actually a ten-to-one variance). A pressing question thus becomes, what would happen to the landscape and its inhabitants in consequence of changes in water policy? Already there is a progression to transform open agricultural fields into high-tech indoor greenhouses as well as a major increase in water recycling on the Israeli side. On the Jordanian side, a major canal shunts water to the capital city of Amman, which is growing so rapidly that it has daily water restrictions in place. The studio project (Steinitz et al. 1999) was based on examining the existing conditions and then conceptually transforming the landscape through a doubling of the overall population size along with corresponding changes in infrastructure and agriculture. Additionally, various changes in conservation efforts were looked at that would require different investment policies among the governments.

The Middle East Water Project—a joint Harvard and MIT independent research venture—was used to assess the implications of the three alternatives (Steinitz 2000). The Water Project model is a very detailed economic hydrology model, and its input is a set of socioeconomic objectives. The output from the model is a menu of varying land uses that include different types of agriculture directed toward a goal of optimizing economic returns and minimizing water shortages. The model was run based on assumption sets provided by the land-use planning students in order to determine the results of the different development scenarios.

One aspect of the research examined the comparative land use and ensuing site hydrology based on construction of each of a Palestinian village, a Jordanian village, and a kibbutz. Another area of investigation looked at the role of desalination of both groundwater and Mediterranean water to supply the area. Also, the concept of a partnership with joint venturing in water policy to create a free market to trade water among the stakeholders was studied. A major conclusion of the studio (Steinitz et al. 1999) was a recommendation to move toward a controlled hydrological system in order to capture, treat, and reuse agricultural water and wastewater.

The students also applied a conservation plan that would maintain existing protected areas as no-build zones, protect sensitive wetland areas such as the Jordan River in addition to other rivers and wadis, and join existing open spaces and vegetated areas with green corridors to increase ecosystem connectivity and ecological fitness. Such a move toward greenspace conservation was thought to provide opportunities for multinational tourism development, given that the area is on the major flyway between Africa and Europe and is already popular among bird watchers due to migrating storks stopping at the fishponds located there. The long-range strategy (Steinitz 2000) is to expand the studio project by making informed suggestions for the creation of a Jordan River World Heritage Park as well as a Peace Park straddling the river at the point where all three countries meet.

San Pedro River Basin

The San Pedro River in southern Arizona and northern Mexico, the last free-flowing river in the Southwest, is one of the most contentious rivers in the United States (Steinitz 2000). The riparian corridor, an important stopover on the Canada to Central America flyway, harbors the highest bird diversity in the United States and is thus protected under NAFTA. The Nature Conservancy has placed the corridor on its list of the "Last Great Places in the Western Hemisphere," and maintenance of riparian vegetation is a joint obligation of both Mexico and the United States.

Problems exist, however, due to the transborder movement of contaminated water and out-of-basin recharge. The biggest problem, however, is due to the effects of urbanization and agriculture on groundwater resources. Groundwater extraction lowers the water table, which in turn affects vegetation and threatens critical habitat for wildlife. Because of this, many tributaries are already dry for most of their length and for most of the time. The situation is only expected to get worse due to the rapid growth of the greater Tucson region. Already houses are starting to fill up the river valley and draw even more water from the ground. Land-management difficulties ensue because of differences in land owner-ship—private in the United States and public in Mexico—as well as the polar-ization in outlooks of Americans in the area; that is, both very right-wing and also very environmentally minded individuals are present.

The major driving system for the region is the rapid population growth and consequent rate of development. This will change the land cover, which will change the fire regime, which will change the vegetation patterns, which will then change the groundwater recharge, stream flow, and local precipitation (Steinitz 2000). The crucial question in all this is whether the affected stream-flows will remain sufficient to be able to maintain the riparian vegetation (essen-tially willows and cottonwood) necessary for biodiversity. Thus, the goal for the study, described in detail in Steinitz et al. (2003), was to model processes of the predicted change. Specifically, these goals were to aid decision making by:

- Identifying and evaluating regional water management options and their implications for biodiversity.
- Assessing the impacts of future land-use and development options on water and wildlife concerns.
- Demonstrating a flexible and practical approach to planning in order to fos-ter cooperation among stakeholders having vested interests in the region's future.

The study developed a model of development probability that was based on a five-layer groundwater model. The outputs produced included 3-D render-ings of water table depths depending on land-use changes and corresponding groundwater well locations and withdrawal rates (Steinitz 2000).

Scenarios were not based on design as in the Camp Pendleton study or on politics as in the Jordan River study. Instead, the alternatives were based on twenty-six active policy debates taking place in this area in terms of population, growth and planning issues, water management issues, and land-management and conservation issues. About one hundred interviews were conducted to assess the political issues upon which to create scenarios. Topics that figured into the survey (Steinitz et al. 2003) included:

- Demographics
  Quality of life
  Population forecasts
  Distribution of new residents

Rural residential zoning
Status of key cultural and natural locations
Visual preferences

- Water management
  Domestic water use
  Irrigated agriculture
  Vegetation management for stream flow
  Stormwater management

- Land management
  Ranching
  Leasing of land for conservation
  Fire management
  Landscape ecological pattern
  Protection of species habitat
  Species diversity
  Urban growth

This information was used to create ten scenarios for change distributed under three broad categories based on predicted development alternatives. Futures modeling was undertaken to base land-use and hydrological changes on these scenarios.

In each case, a scenario had a set of constraints based on these categories, and the computer program allocated four different types of housing subject to those constraints. Real-time computer simulations were developed that showed the interaction between development and groundwater wells. Shown clearly were the drops in water table depths due to the development and what the consequences of this would be for vegetation patterns and consequent wildlife habitat. Those options that restricted irrigated agriculture and concentrated the development were found to have less serious implications on groundwater reserves. The prognosis is that unless development is curtailed or tightly regulated, serious environmental problems will ensue. The lesson is that proactive action in terms of water-sensitive planning is required immediately rather than time spent later in courtrooms debating consequences as the river life continues to disappear (Steinitz 2000).

Management Frameworks for Agricultural Development (Freemark 2000)

The environmental consequences of modern agricultural production have occurred at a rate exceeding the adoption of ecologically sustainable conservation practices (Santelmann, Hulse, and White 2001). Serious concerns exist over soil erosion, degradation of water quality, biodiversity, and human quality of life (Freemark 1995; Berger and Bolte 2004). In particular, the major cause of nonpoint-source pollution in North America is due to agricultural land use. For example, nutrient transport associated with sediment movement from agricultural land poses problems for the eutrophication of the Mississippi and Missouri rivers and eventually the Gulf of Mexico ecosystem. This study was interested in how differences in land-use policies and practices could be implemented in a group of small (five thousand to eight thousand hectare) watersheds and second-order streams, and was motivated by a desire to point the way to achieving agricultural policy goals (Nassauer, Corry, and Cruse 2002; see chapter 4).

Agricultural development is regulated by federal and state policy. A large, interdiciplinary team of biologists, physical scientists, and sociologists was brought together to investigate the implications of projected development on midwestern agricultural watersheds in the corn belt region of Iowa (Freemark 2000). Almost all the land in the study area is in private ownership, and the predominant land-use is agriculture (mostly corn and soybeans). Pasture land is also abundant, and some forests are present along the stream courses.

The idea of the study was, like all alternative futures modeling exercises, to use a detailed characterization of the present as a platform upon which to make predictions about the future. Scenarios were based on projected futures for the year 2025 and designed through a year-long iterative process in consultation with disciplinary experts in agriculture (described in detail in Santelmann, Hulse, and White 2001). The research group decided to look at a projection of current trends and provocative but plausible future directions for federal agricultural policy under an assumption of no climate change effects. For comparative purposes, a presettlement (ca. 1800) condition was recreated based on vegetation reconstruction using the soils data base and knowledge of the relationship of different soils to plant communities. All future scenarios that were developed assumed that the landscape would embody profitable agricultural production, would embody public concerns about biodiversity and water quality, and would be affected by market forces and agricultural policies from all levels of government; the scenario also assumed that both agricultural and environmental policies would reflect societal perceptions, values, and concerns (Freemark 2000). In all cases, landscape ecology principles were used to design the predicted future landscapes under auspices of each development scenario. In particular, the following attributes were examined (Nassauer, Corry, and Cruse 2002): field patterns and livestock enterprises; conservation practices; and farmsteads, towns, and cultural practices, along with the expected effects of their change on landscape network and grain, water quality and quantity, agricultural production, and public acceptance.

The first investigated scenario was based on the current trends of industrialization of agricultural production under existing regulatory frameworks. This was found to result in many more row crops, use of BMPs, more precision in the agricultural use of nutrients and chemicals, less woodland/grassland area as soybean production rose, buffer and filter strips three to six meters wide, a doubling of farm size with a consequent halving of the number of farms, and the proliferation of confined feedlots.

The second scenario focused on issues of water quality in terms of nutrients and suspended solids. Under this aspect, BMPs to reduce erosion and nutrient transport would increase, riparian buffers would increase in size, wetlands would be created to detain nutrients from runoff, and these off-channel storage areas would be used to absorb stormwater. A shift to more livestock grazing and forage crops was also part of this scenario.

The third scenario that dealt with biodiversity and conservation restoration was the most provocative (Freemark 2000). Bioreserves would be created, prairie pothole wetlands would be restored, riparian buffers would be expanded to function as corridors for animal movement, more fencerows would be established, perennial strip intercropping would be applied, organic farming and agroforestry would dominate with a consequent reduction in nutrient use, nonfarmers would move into the area due to the watershed becoming more attractive through use of native plantings, and all feeding operations would be confined and strictly managed for manure.

The different scenarios were evaluated based on a spatially distributed water quality model of the EPA, a spatially explicit model of biodivesity based on habitat associations and population dynamics, and a spatially grounded model of economics and human dimensions based on interviews and analysis of perceptions of the willingness of farmers to adopt innovative practices (Freemark 2000). A series of graphs was generated in which to compare across all future scenarios along with historic scenarios in terms of the change relative to the present (Santelmann, Hulse, and White 2001). In other words, how are these alternative watershed futures scenarios performing relative to how the present landscape is operating? For example, in terms of water quality, how much water, sediment, and nutrients are coming off the land?

Such an approach allowed for the comparative assessment of implementing the various potential landscape treatments in terms of providing a measure of risk (Freemark 2000) and addressed the following questions:

- How much change will happen to which particular species under which specific development scenario?
- How will the economic return from the land be influenced through application of the various scenarios?

• What are the economic penalties if there is a move toward more environmentally beneficial landscape development?
• And if there are trade-offs in terms of return from the land, what sort of economic incentives must be looked at to compensate farmers for land held in bioreserves?

A critical step to gauging the implications of watershed development alternatives is to obtain an understanding of the human dimensions in relation to the predicted land-use changes (Santelmann, Hulse, and White 2001; see also chapter 2). The study produced visual simulations of the landscapes under the different scenarios in order to illicit favorability responses from a group of farmers selected from the wider bioregion, but specifically not from the particular watersheds under investigation (Freemark 2000). Because the researchers were interested in examining the broadest range of options for agriculture, they felt that had they used members from the watersheds under investigation, it would have constrained the possible options generated and discussed. This would occur because most residents would defensively stick to their beliefs that what they were doing right now was correct, and they could obviously not get past the hypothetical issues of the future scenarios with respect to whose particular piece of land was going to be taken away to make a bioreserve. Due to the imagined difficulties in engaging in such an open dialogue, it was therefore deemed more useful to work with people who dealt regularly and professionally with farmers rather than the farmers themselves.

A major part of the study equally important to human perceptions was to integrate economic decision making with ecological assessments to examine economic barriers to implementing each proposed scenario (Coiner, Wu, and Polasky 2001). Such economic concerns have the potential to become obstacles to the application of ecological guidelines in land-use planning. By evaluating the economic returns from the various agricultural production scenarios, the accruing ecological benefits can be related to their cost to the producer, thereby helping policy makers in decisions about subsidies or incentives that might be necessary to landowners (Santelmann, Hulse, and White 2001). In this respect, alternative scenario modeling can help in exploring the limitations in the current state of understanding about the sustainable development of the watershed.

CONCLUSION

The use of future scenarios is therefore a tool for engaging in discussion about alternative choices for land-use management and development, and particularly what the implications of those choices might be for the kinds of aspirations we have about ecology, sociology, and economy in our watersheds (Steinitz et al. 2001). Spatially explicit comparisons of present land use with past land uses as well as with various alternative futures will help provide a spatial and temporal perspective for decision makers (Freemark 2000). In so doing, these methods can have the capability to catalyze change in cultural attitudes and even inspire action in terms of how and where land development occurs and what may be possible as corrective measures. Such an approach is used to inform community-based decisions regarding land and water use through facilitating consensus building (Baker et al. 2004) by:

- Helping to clarify differences of opinion by forcing stakeholders to be very explicit about their individual goals and the priorities used to create the specific future scenarios under consideration.
- Enlarging these goals and priorities to a systemwide format of different landscape futures.
- Identifying the changes to be expected and linking these to specific locations in the watershed.
- Evaluating how these development alterations will affect land and water resources and other socioeconomic characteristics.

Alternative future scenarios of landscape change are most important for helping decision makers visualize and evaluate alternative choices through the generation of GIS-based computer simulations. Such a futures approach therefore takes abstract goals such as enhancing water quality or restoring biological diversity and translates these into specific land-use practices (Santelmann, Hulse, and White 2001). One very important part of the alternative futures model-building is the generation of the actual change scenarios through use of a citizen- or expert-driven approach or some combination of the two, each having its own set of benefits and detriments (Hulse, Branscomb, and Payne 2004). These scenarios are the means to achieving various alternative futures. However, unlike histories based on facts, scenarios rely on assumptions of the future and must be understood to be predictive judgments of what might be likely to happen (Schearer 2005). Though it is certainly true that the scenarios help to facilitate discussion of planning options across stakeholder groups, professional disciplines, and levels of management, the critical challenge is to formulate realistic visions of what is pragmatically possible, reasonable, and feasible at the same time as avoiding hubris by giving a false impression of high precision. Scenarios are thus required that offer more than prescriptions of doom and gloom or Arcadian richness; that is, they need to help feed into a program of concrete action to help move all from a pessimistic to an optimistic state.

Part III

PROBLEM MITIGATION

Chapter Eight

Framing Sites

Jonathan Swift's Bane—Communicating and Implementing Strategies for Protecting Water Quality from Stormwater Runoff

It is always informative to visit land-development projects during the process of their construction. Here, before the architectural and landscaping veneer is applied, one can see the ground floor of creation, as it were, recognizing both the strengths and weaknesses of the design. The new development project near the river in Minneapolis was a wonderful example of the new paradigm of stormwater management. It was easy for our group to follow the course of water through the site, the series of open channels and small detention basins wrapping their way around the foundations of the future buildings. Already, even before occupation, the stormwater management system was playing an important role in entrapping sediment from the construction site before it could be transported to the river. And what was particularly interesting was that every basin had a set of parallel tracks leading into it to enable a small vehicle to drive down the ramp for periodic excavation and removal of accumulating sediment. Also, as I looked around the site, I was struck by the overt engineering aspect of the project, with little attempt being made to hide the infrastructure behind a veil of naturalness. It was obvious what the project's intended role was, and that it was created through human artifice. Although there were groupings of aquatic plants in several plunge pools that seemed to be already on their way to growing into small pocket wetlands, these were connected by highly engineered structures through which the stormwater runoff would move. And linking all was a system of trails along which future residents could stroll. What could this particular site teach us? Was it possible that all the attention paid elsewhere to the design of completely natural-looking stormwater management projects, several of which actually excluded people, was somewhat misplaced? Was it just as important in the end that these projects also provide opportunities for people to experience water as well as to attract wildlife? Later, as I flew out of the city and stared down at the vast sea of concrete parking lots surrounding many of the suburban malls, my good mood produced by the aforementioned site visit was dimmed. Certainly, I thought, does this not show how amending existing land-development regulations to reduce the amount of parking stalls required per square footage of commercial space may ultimately have an even greater role in mitigating the effects of sprawl than dozens of site-specific designs, no matter how inspiring the latter may be or how well they operate? Clearly, the best solution is adopting both water-sensitive planning and design in concert.

INTRODUCTION

By all accounts, eighteenth-century London—one of largest cities in the world at that time—was an incredibly dirty and unhealthy place. Food slops and chamber pots were thrown out of windows to be mixed with horse droppings and animal remains into a grand slurry of contamination whenever it rained. "Filth of all hues and odour doth seem to tell, what street they sail'd from, by their sight and smell," recounted a dismayed Jonathan Swift during one visit to the capital. Today, stormwater runoff still represents the largest source of nonpoint-source pollution in cities, a veritable cocktail of organic and inorganic contaminants often referred to as "urban slobber." Input of untreated runoff into receiving streams and other water bodies can severely impact resident fauna (see chapter 5). As a result, many techniques have successfully been implemented for protecting urban water quality (see reviews by Horner et al. 1994; Schueler and Holland 2000). This chapter outlines two such approaches, one operating from a planning perspective, the other involving site design.

GEORGIA'S WATER QUALITY LAND DEVELOPMENT PROVISIONS (FERGUSON, NICHOLS, AND WEINBERG 2000)

Atlanta, Georgia, has the dubious "honor" of leading other major U.S. cities in terms of the imbalance between increases in physical size relative to increases in population size. This growth has produced a major construction boom in terms of new subdivisions, schools, office parks, and shopping centers that have exacted harmful consequences for Georgia's aquatic systems (Nichols, Ferguson, and Weinberg 1997). And although it would be easy to blame developers for all of the ensuing environmental problems, the reality is that they are just following ordinances in use by local municipalities. There is a need, therefore, to reexamine and modify the existing land-development regulations.

The report "Land Development Provisions to Protect Georgia Water Quality" prepared by the School of Environmental Design at the University of Georgia for the Georgia Department of Natural Resources Environmental Protection Division (Nichols, Ferguson, and Weinberg 1997) has been a major landmark in helping to understand and manage watershed development. The report was distributed to more than ten thousand Georgian residents in its first two years of publication and won a national award (Ferguson, pers. comm., 1999). Although intended to produce many of the same results as that of the manual developed for the San Francisco region (Richman et al. 1999), the Georgia report does this "at the planning level via relevant provisions in municipal development ordinances, rather than individual designers working under those provisions" (Ferguson, pers. comm., 1999).

Ferguson, Nichols, and Weinberg (2000) describe provisions that could be modified or added to local development regulations for the purpose of protecting water quality. The outlined provisions were developed from reported experiences and studies around the country and refined in dialogue with a task force of Georgia citizens, developers, and planners.

Municipal ordinances where these provisions could be used include zoning and subdivision ordinances, erosion and sediment control laws, drainage ordinances, and design standards documents. These types of documents control the construction and use of impervious surfaces by defining and segregating land uses, defining options for transportation, and specifying the dimensions and materials of streets, parking areas, and residential lots (Ferguson, Nichols, and Weinberg 2000).

The report can be regarded as a partial "menu" from which each municipality can select specific appropriate provisions and adapt them to local conditions. The report explains the provisions' roles in water-quality protection by addressing the quality of stormwater runoff and its effects on safety and cost (Nichols, Ferguson, and Weinberg 1997). In this chapter, the provisions are grouped into four general categories, the intended purpose for each originating from Ferguson, Nichols, and Weinberg (2000) and the highlighting of other selected issues abstracted from Nichols, Ferguson, and Weinberg (1997).

Overall Measures of Development

Density Zoning

Purpose. Development intensity can be regulated by the quantity of development on a site as a whole, not by minimum lot size. Density zoning gives flexibility to adapt to site-specific topography and drainage, locating streets, homes, and lots in ways that are at once economical, environmentally protective, and appropriate to local markets (Ferguson, Nichols, and Weinberg 2000).

Issues

- Density zoning may enable house clustering and dedicated open space in some developments.
- The layout flexibility requires site analysis (as described in chapter 6) to identify floodplains, stream buffers, steep slopes, valuable trees, etc.
- Economic savings can result in construction and maintenance of roads, utilities, and drainage infrastructure.
- Density zoning enables the preservation of sensitive environmental areas regardless of whether or not they are protected by ordinances.

Stream Buffers

Purpose.   Reservations of undeveloped land adjoining stream channels operate as stream buffers. Undisturbed buffer vegetation filters in-flowing runoff, prevents channel erosion, and creates habitats for functioning ecosystems (chapters 1 and 6). Siting construction away from drainage courses avoids the costs of flood damage and poor drainage.

Issues

- Residential property values increase due to presence of naturally vegetated stream buffers.
- Directing development away from riparian areas requires density zoning.
- Protecting broad, undeveloped floodplains allows rivers to achieve a cycle of balanced hydrologic function.
- Streamside buffers are appropriate places for public recreation greenways (chapter 10).
- Buffers on private lots can achieve many ecological goals (chapter 10).

Limited Impervious Cover

Purpose.   The proportion of a site covered in impervious roofs and pavements without treating the runoff can be controlled. Limiting unmitigated impervious cover controls the generation of runoff and pollution at the source while allowing development of any type and intensity.

Issues

- Impervious caps (as in chapter 5) of about 10 percent have been found to protect aquatic resources.
- Developers can trade an amount of stormwater mitigation—e.g., various low-impact development (LID) techniques such as bioretention swales, porous pavers, green ecoroofs, etc.—for an amount of impervious cover.
- Unless this provision is integrated with that of density zoning, which will allow increased development in some areas provided compensations are made in terms of applying mitigated techniques, sprawl can be encouraged by requiring all developments to be of low intensity.

Land-use Combination

Purpose. Blending different, but mutually supportive, land-use types in the same zoning districts can be an important land-development provision. Certain types of commercial and office uses can be combined with residential uses, reducing dependence on automobiles and the pavements they require as well as the consequent auto emissions and runoff.

Issues
- Compact land-use strategies combining work and shopping close to homes will create more walkable and thus healthier cities.

Paths for Biking and Walking

Purpose. This provision creates public facilities that allow individuals the choice of nonautomotive transportation. Biking and walking reduce automobile use and the pavements autos require as well as the consequent emissions and runoff.

Issues

- Because the cost to individuals of nonautomobile transportation are low, this provision benefits low-income communities.
- In order to create a citywide system of safe trails, it will be necessary to work with developers, who must dedicate the easements and can contribute to the city path construction fund (chapter 10).
- Off-street foot and bike paths are compatible with stream buffers (chapter 10).

Infill Zoning

Purpose. Relatively high-density, mixed-used development or redevelopment is allowed where it would be compatible with an existing neighborhood. The local concentrations of runoff and pollutants are of course high. But infill development limits impervious cover and auto usage in the region as a whole. It accommodates some growth without destroying pristine areas and without requiring this part of the population to demand large quantities of pavement to support routine automobile use.

Issues

- Often the most suitable location for infill zoning is in the midst of old neighborhoods where the pattern is already established.
- Redeveloping previous sites can often improve runoff quality through application of new technologies and approaches (Nichols, Ferguson, and Weinberg 1997).

Streets and Pavements

Limited Street Width and Curbing

Purpose. This provision (Ferguson, Nichols, and Weinberg 2000) limits street development to only that needed for each street's specific function, thereby limiting both runoff and construction cost. Narrow pavements encourage cautious driving and eliminate the "speedway" feel of wide streets. They do not hinder emergency access where they are correctly applied only to streets with little traffic and little on-street parking.

Issues

- Because curbs are often pollutant traps that prevent runoff from infiltrating the soil, their limitation will improve water quality.
- On streets with low traffic volume, sidewalks are not needed.

Limited Pavement in Turnarounds

Purpose. Pavement areas at the ends of cul-de-sacs are unnecessary and should be eliminated. In the centers of turnarounds, pavement is unusable for vehicles. Replacing it with vegetated soil reduces runoff and provides infiltration and treatment. This reduces construction cost but requires provision for maintenance.

Issues

- The vegetated central spaces in the "doughnut" turnarounds can become visual amenities to neighborhoods.

Limited Amount of Parking

Purpose. Unused portions of parking areas will be eliminated in this provision. In commercial and office areas, parking areas have been oversupplied. Limiting parking reduces paved areas and runoff. It also reduces construction cost and land consumption.

Issues

- Parking areas are the largest component of impervious cover in commercial and industrial zones.
- Excess parking adds no value to a commercial development, and though unused by commuters it can be used profitably by rainfall or by runoff.
- Large, free parking lots encourage the use of automobiles by solo drivers and thus contribute to traffic congestion throughout the community.
- The effects of limited parking are reinforced by infill zoning, land-use combination, and alternative transportation.

Porous Pavement Materials

Purpose. The purpose of this provision is to replace impervious pavements so the underlying soil can absorb rainfall and treat pollutants. Porous pavement materials can economically provide safer driving surfaces than the impermeable materials they replace; however, they should be avoided on steep slopes.

Issues

- Porous materials include porous aggregate, porous turf, plastic geocells, open-jointed paving blocks, open-celled paving grids, porous concrete, porous asphalt, and soft porous surfacing (see Ferguson 2005).
- Because they are better drained, porous asphalt and concrete pavements produce better traction in wet weather as well as less glare and noise.

- Use of porous concrete and asphalt adds about 10 percent to the cost of pavement.
- Parking lots are ideal surfaces for use of crushed aggregates or open-celled pavers (Nichols, Ferguson, and Weinberg 1997).

Drainage

Drainage in Vegetated Swales

Purpose.   Vegetated swales carry, store, treat, and infiltrate runoff in contact with permeable soil. Where vegetated swales replace curbs or drainage pipes, they reduce construction cost (Ferguson, Nichols, and Weinberg 2000).

Issues

- Swales can replace the functions of curbs and gutters in street drainage while at the same time adding ecological benefits.
- Swales also reduce maintenance costs by allowing organic matter to decompose and become part of the soil rather than having to remove it through street-cleaning operations.
- By slowing down runoff movement, vegetated swales help to reduce flood peaks.
- Because of the need to limit erosion, swales work best along streets with slopes of less than 8 percent.
- Careful attention needs to be paid to swale location, design, and construction to promote infiltration and limit impounding of runoff.

Swale Biofiltration Velocity Control

Purpose.   Velocity control in swales assures effective runoff treatment and infiltration by prolonging contact with soil and vegetation. Although the quantity of treatment is small in a few large storms, the cumulative long-term effect of many small storms is vital.

Issues

- Techniques such as check dams and elevated culverts contribute to slowing down water movement in swales.
- Ponding ideally should be limited to twenty-four hours, which will maintain healthy flora and complete decomposition of organic matter into humus.

Treatment of "Hot Spots"

Purpose. It is important to assure runoff treatment specifically at a few small, highly concentrated runoff and pollutant sources such as dumpster pads and gasoline stations. This provision secures "point" treatment, even where treatment of runoff from other impervious surfaces cannot receive the same degree of careful attention.

Issues

• "Hot spots" generate concentrated pollutants far in access of what might be expected due to their limited size and thus need to be addressed early in managing land development.
• Treatment of these areas is highly feasible particularly because it is focused in area.

Inlet Labeling

Purpose. Identifying swales and drainage inlets to the public increases knowledge about the vital purpose of these structures. This inhibits dumping of pollutants and educates the public about the environmental systems around them.

Issues

• The use of stencils in both older, established areas and new developments is a proven educational tool adopted by many municipalities.

Construction Process

Limited Clearing, Grading, and Disturbance

Purpose. It is important to try to confine construction work to those areas where it is actually required. This provision preserves existing trees and pervious soils that attenuate, treat, and infiltrate rainfall and runoff.

Issues

• Use of clearly delineated zones of no activity, carefully thought-out plans for phased construction, and adequate installation of erosion-control measures will limit site disturbance (Nichols, Ferguson, and Weinberg 1997).

There is a misconception that the best way to go about limiting the harmful effects of sprawl upon watershed functionality is to focus on constructing technical solutions to mitigate the problem. Although these can be effective on the scale of individual sites (as shown, for example, by Wenk 2000 in the next section) or occasionally even on a scale of neighborhoods and cities (e.g., Poole 2005), there is no denying that this form of restorative care is based on treating the symptoms rather than on addressing the problems of watershed dysfunction. In some ways, then, the attempt to retool zoning bylaws as described by Ferguson, Nichols, and Weinberg (2000) has the possibility to contribute very significantly to improving the health of entire watersheds. Such nonstructural approaches to mitigating the problems of sprawl, for example, by changing parking codes or through allowing for mixed-use infill development, will produce widespread benefits.

CONTINUITIES IN WATERSHED PLANNING AND DESIGN (WENK 2000)

Problems with Civic Infrastructure and the Cult of Naturalness

Ecologically sensitive cultured landscapes, those that have a certain human quality to them, are civic and typically urban. It is important to deal with these landscapes at a continuum of the three realms of policy, system, and site, otherwise opportunities will be missed in terms of dealing in a deep and meaningful way with some of the major ecological problems of our cities (Wenk 2000). These issues are thus as much a social as an ecological aspect of a city's health, and it is important to seek out and work at the interface of these connections in terms of developing what might be called a "civic infrastructure" (*sensu* Poole 2005).

Currently, most development projects deal with sites, whereas policies deal with watersheds. There are some disconnects between policy and practices, between the physical and the ideal, that need to be bridged, because practices are often constrained by policies and frequently don't integrate very well (Wenk 2000). These issues become important to address in several ways.

There are a number of barriers to implementing what water-sensitive designers are trying to accomplish as a profession. One of the most serious is that society collectively has a very narrow view about what the "natural" is all about. Typically, stormwater management designs are characterized by very natural-looking ponds filled with ducks and cattails. Unfortunately, this is an ideal of nature that has very little to do with the realities of an urban ecology. And in focusing on only naturalistic schemes, a huge potential is missed to make these truly cultured landscapes as much a part of the city and the civic landscape as they are of the natural world.

Wenk's projects, in contrast, are typically more about public works then they are about ecology. Urban streams and drainage-ways are controlled by public works departments that have a set of engineering standards and details and a way of going about doing things that are very pervasive and very difficult to change but are essential for the water-sensitive designer to work through. Therefore, in order to deal with waterways in a city in a responsible manner, it becomes necessary to deal with the public works departments. And by engaging in this dialogue, the way in which one thinks about urban water becomes completely transformed (Wenk 2000).

Within such a civic infrastructure mind-set, another problem soon realized is that policies are often ahead of realities. The realities of maintenance, for example, especially public works maintenance, drive stormwater management designs unless the projects are very specialized cases, such as demonstration projects that are going to be maintained differently. Although maintenance is often ignored, it is critical when planning urban stormwater projects to think about maintenance and to work with the agencies that are controlling, owning, and maintaining those waterways in order to be effective environmental managers.

And finally, the main barrier to undertaking effective protection of water quality is the deep resistance to change (Richman 2005) in terms of the conceptual shift that is necessary to move designs from being regarded as innovative to their final acceptance. Wenk (2000) believes that many public works departments are still trapped in an old paradigm of thinking and operating, for example, in regard to their frequent downright denial about the significance of nonpoint-source pollution that arises from stormwater runoff.

Review of Built Projects: Barriers and Suggestions

The Woodlands development in Texas, designed in the 1970s by the seminal landscape architect Ian McHarg, is a wonderful and influential project (one of the first) that integrates stormwater management into the design of a new community; Village Homes in California is another such project (Francis 2003). But according to Wenk (2000), the reality is that there are a number of different aspects of the Woodlands project that don't work all that well. In Woodlands, the oft-heralded stormwater designs lack a civic or human quality that is crucial to a successful urban project. For example, some of the drop structures holding back water are simply dangerous, some ponds come across as unsafe and unfriendly, and some of the open drainage-ways, although they may work from a hydrologic point of view, are also very uninviting in terms of open space for citizens. Wenk (2000) believes that there is a need to take stormwater projects to the next level in terms of dealing with the humanness of the space.

Many of Wenk's projects are in Colorado, which is a setting shaped by water coming off the mountains into a cultural landscape (Woodward 2000). At present, Colorado streams have baseflows due to runoff from massive development sites where previously the streams barely existed prior to the development. In this regard, water and how it is influenced by development are very visible and obvious on the High Plains. For this reason, it is of vital importance to make people part of the scene by producing designs with a human quality, which brings added value to a project beyond simply reestablishing natural functions.

A shortcoming of many stream restoration projects is that often, preoccupied as designers and engineers are with a goal of "restoring" hydrologic naturalness, they frequently do not truly recognize and engage the extreme hydraulic forces characteristic of urban streams. Wenk's urban projects, in contrast, do not look completely natural but have a built-in buffer to absorb the forces of water runoff generated from development. It is essential to be aware of and design for these strong forces if a goal is to have people coming down to encounter water (as, for example, via gatlike steps in one of his projects) for direct physical contact when safe opportunities permit. It is also possible to select beautiful plants that are tough enough to sustain extreme flows to stabilize banks. Wenk's (2000) message is to be eclectic and open to a myriad of ideas and not be held to a rigidity of naturalness in an ecologically sensitive project.

For example, in another of Wenk's stream restoration projects in a former mined valley, he placed the new stream overtop a rubber liner. The new stream is certainly contrived to look like what a natural stream would be, with pools and meanders as well as the use of soils and plants collected from nearby construction sites to restore the natural communities along the river. So is it natural? Perhaps given the artifice in such projects, Wenk (2000) believes that the term "re-creation" is more apt than "restoration" when referring to urban waterways.

The aspiration in constructing such projects is to find the balance between form and function. But in some ways a project can also not work because its plantings may be ahead of the maintenance capabilities of the civic works department in a particular urban drainage district. So in order to be successful, it becomes important to think past the design to the concerns of ongoing maintenance. Most cities are terrified about what they will have to do from a maintenance perspective when dealing with nonpoint-source pollutants and complying with their federally issued permits. In this regard, a common concern is how many times it will be necessary for the civic works department to have to remove the accumulated sediment. This issue is critically important for every stormwater project and if not addressed could kill great design concepts because they failed to deal with the sediment maintenance question. One of the challenges with urban water management is to take the concentrated water and spread it back out on the landscape, and one of the ways to do this is by using dams. For example, two old U.S. Army Corps of Engineers stormwater ponds are now some of the richest wetland habitats in the greater Denver area and have cleaned up the water substantially. It is important, therefore, to be open-minded about some of those engineering projects that seem at first to be anathema to good ecological practice. Wenk (2000) believes that dams can be beautiful objects in a landscape. By reusing such old infrastructures, people are allowed to ascend to the top of the dam, making the structures civic and humanly scaled. Water systems and pedestrian paths can thus be integrated to create a series of deliberate and functional landforms that contribute to the overall acceptance of the project.

Looking at a development site in terms of its water budget forces a new perspective in how to think about the location (Wenk 2000). Such an approach involves dividing the site into sections and then calculating the amount of stormwater storage needed to sustain proposed wetlands or turf areas. What this does is to promote the planning of functional landscapes based on water budgets, thereby enabling the detailed design of specific features that can be sustained by the stored water. In other words, such a strategy is significant in its approach of regarding stormwater runoff as a resource rather than as a waste product.

In Minneapolis, the redevelopment of old public housing built over a creek that had since settled and caused the buildings to fail became a very complicated project. The neighborhood sued the city and the federal government over multiple social and physical problems. Wenk's (2000) plan was to reconnect the neighborhood with the surrounding city through a series of parks with a linear parkway at its core. The entire site was divided into subcatchments, and water budgets were calculated. This enabled the creation of landscapes based on the desired removal of phosphorus using a treatment train that is fairly typical in function (Apfelbaum 2005) but whose form is purposely given a civic quality at the same time by constructing a series of components resembling the sort of details seen in public works engineering manuals. Each created landscape in this project functions in a very specific and deliberate way to clean stormwater. Designs were based on the very humble and mundane storm drains producing fluvial patterns that give shape to the landscape in a number of different contexts. Both functional and civic qualities were combined, for example, in the use of level spreaders to infiltrate water before a daylighted creek, and landforms were designed to integrate the "city beautiful" tradition of the Minneapolis park system into a stormwater infrastructure system.

Wenk (2000) argues that landscape designers of stormwater management systems need to deal better with barriers or practicalities of narrow views of what is ecological responsibility. The only way to establish truly functional stormwater management systems is to work closely with public works departments and especially to deal better with integrating policies and practice. In terms of the latter, for example, practice and policy can be confounded in the western United States where water rights are owned. So, if you design a new management system to capture and make use of stormwater on your site, you take away its downstream transport and what a legally entitled antecedent user may have planned for it. It is critical in such a case to deal with water rights issues even if a beneficial use is planned for the stormwater. The very complicated legal system necessitates water rights being allocated and moved between different sources when dealing with large projects.

Chapter Nine

Functioning Art

Ripple Effects—Creating Treatment Wetland Parks

Fishtrap Creek, in the town of Abbotsford, located inland from Vancouver, was the first multipurpose, created wetland that I had visited, and the scene was both instantly inspirational and now, through a filter of time and memory, nothing short of transformative. As I strolled through the site along the many trails and past the picnic shelter, the gaming tables, the seating benches, the pedestrian bridges, the scenic overlooks on hills or suspended over the water, pausing here and there to read an interpretive sign about wildlife or site history, I kept having to tell myself that all these wonderful park attributes were actually extras, ancillary to the wetland's main intended purpose of stormwater detention and treatment. The integration of beautiful landscape architecture with utilitarian environmental engineering was a marvel. Just before leaving, I watched from the elevated overlook as lunch-hour joggers from nearby offices weaved their way about children in strollers and painters with easels, eventually ascending the steps to where I was watching and, in an established local ritual, tagged the historic railway tie beside an interpretive sign before heading down again. Such "functional art"—the seamless fusion of form and function, or what might be called "sustainable aesthetics"—is certainly not new. Recently, for example, I had a water heater self-destruct on a wintry Thursday morning and was forced to have to wait until Monday night for the repair service. During that interval, I boiled water on all four stove burners and filled the bathtub to a depth of several inches with the water. Sitting mostly high and dry above the water, I soon realized that the bathing/cleaning experience was not going to work. Then, in a moment of inspiration, I bounded out of the bathtub and into the living room. Opening the glass display cabinet filled with the accumulated bric-a-brac of travel mementos, I removed a beautiful metal-worked, nineteenth-century hamman bowl from Damascus, which, upon returning to the bathroom, was soon put to its intended use as a bathing ladle. Was this not the key to the success of the previously visited stormwater wetland, the fusion of form and function in the creation of a beautiful and functional object, that in the case of the wetland was a landscape that both ameliorated the detrimental effects of sprawl at the same time as operating as a park that engaged the public?

INTRODUCTION

Can a few conspicuous solar homes, constructed wetlands, bike paths, recycling industries, wildlife habitat corridors, organic agricultural plots, and wind farms really be the key to saving the world? Isn't a much greater transformation needed in global economic, political, and social institutions?

R. Thayer, *Gray World, Green Heart*

We live in what Aldo Leopold has referred to as a "world of wounds" (France 2006), one in which there is irrefutable evidence that we (or at least the next few generations after us) are balancing precariously on an apocalyptic cusp. "Human beings and the natural world are on a collision course. Human activities inflict harsh and often irreversible damage on the environment and on critical resources. If not checked, many of our current practices put at serious risk the future we wish for human society." This 1992 statement from a document called "World Scientists' Warning to Humanity" is illuminative because it does not originate from some fringe collection of tree-hugging "green-nicks" but rather was signed by more than half of all living Nobel Prize winners.

The image of the Earth as the ship *Titanic* moving blissfully and blindly forward on its collision course with destiny, the band playing away and people engaging in revelries of excess, all in ignorance of their imminent fate, is a compelling and often-used environmental metaphor. It is also one germane to the question of realities, illusions, and efficacies of nature-sustaining design (France 2003d). Though champions of sustainable design may herald its critical role in keeping us on track away from the looming threat of icebergs bearing such scary labels as "global climate change" or "global biodiversity loss," a skeptic or cynic might take a different message from the metaphor. In short, the key question is whether the roles of designers in shaping our built environments offer anything more helpful than, for example, architects configuring better deck chairs (more comfortable perhaps or those that can double as life rafts) or landscape architects providing a more favorable arrangement of the chairs (so as to enable a better view of us all going down perhaps).

THE PROMISE OF SUSTAINABLE SITE DESIGN

The special issue of *Time* magazine published on August 26, 2002, in conjunction with the Johannesburg World Environment Conference, was entitled "How to Save the Earth." Here for the fist time, mixed in between the usual doom-and-gloom articles and arresting images of people begging for food, roads clogged with automobiles, wetlands shrinking due to drought, and elephants marching off toward extinction, was a collection of pieces dealing with the promising role of sustainable design in moving us back from the cusp of natural apocalypse. The message is one of profound importance, representing as it does a high visibility coming of age for a movement that ironically, while enjoying increasing popularity amongst the lay public, still remains largely marginalized within the design professions themselves. For example, Hagan (2003) comments that for architects, environmentalism is embarrassing because "it has no edge, no buzz, no style. It's populated by the self-righteous and the badly dressed. Its analysis is simplistic, its conviction naïve, its physics dubious, and its metaphysics absurd. It's a haven for the untalented, where ethics replace aesthetics and get away with it." But for how long can the design professions continue on their titanic course, oblivious to their role in promoting or saving us from our collective fate?

There is some reassuring evidence to suggest that the design professions might very well be on the verge of taking their first baby steps toward a paradigm shift in their relationship to nature and sustainability (France 2003d). Long-time champions (e.g., McDonnough and Braungart 2002; Murcutt, Cooper, and Beck 2002) have recently been joined by a cadre of what *Time* referred to as "some of the most prominent names in architecture [who] have turned green." The sentence quoted above continues, however, with the caveat that this greening by the architectural illuminati exists "at least for *selected* projects" (*Time* 2002 [my italics]).

Landscape architects, in turn, now seem to be scrambling to embrace both the concepts and practices of sustainable design after a decade of near silence following the publication of Lyle's (1985) *Design for Human Ecosystems* and Thayer's (1994) *Gray World, Green Heart,* as witnessed by two recent books dealing with the subject. *Sustainable Landscape Construction* (Thompson and Sorvig 2000) represents nothing short of a watershed in the evolution of educating landscape designers in how they should approach their projects. The ten guiding principles offer a set of practical alternatives to the business-as-usual manner common within the profession:

- Keep healthy sites healthy
- Heal injured sites
- Favor living, flexible materials

- Respect the waters of life
- Pave less
- Consider origin and fate of materials
- Know the costs of energy over time
- Celebrate light, respect darkness
- Quietly defend silence
- And maintain to sustain

And *Constructed Wetlands in the Sustainable Landscape* (Campbell and Ogden 1999), though much narrower in scope, presents a unique blending of science, engineering, landscape architecture, and environmental art together with regulatory planning and site development to advance nothing less than a new vision for how to manage this one important aspect of our built environment.

In 1988, the Council of Educators in Landscape Architecture (CELA) defined sustainable landscapes as those that "contribute to human well being and at the same time are in harmony with the natural environment. They do not deplete or damage other ecosystems. While human activity will have altered native patterns, a sustainable landscape will work with native conditions in its structure and functions. Valuable resources—water, nutrients, soil, et cetera—and energy will be conserved, diversity of species will be maintained or increased" (Ahern et al. 2002).

Academic programs are now being retooled to capitalize upon the interest shown among students for sustainable design. The University of Michigan, for example, was recently seeking "a designer and scholar who is knowledgeable and experienced in the application of ecological principles to the analysis and design of the landscape and built environment. . . . The new faculty member will interact with students and faculty who have diverse interdisciplinary interests related to sustainability such as energy-and-resource-efficient building design, green structure and infrastructure, landscape ecology, healthy buildings, urban ecosystem management, and life cycle assessment. . . . The new faculty member should establish a strong program of scholarship in sustainable design and demonstrate achievement in professional practice" (Ahern et al. 2002).

And at the Harvard Design School, a student award will be implemented in the near future (France 2003d). Available to students in all departments, one award will be given each semester for "the option studio project that most exemplifies principles of sustainability regardless of the topic of the studio." The strategy here is to raise awareness of these principles and call attention to the importance of embedding them in the design process rather than seeing them as "add-ons" in a special (and potentially marginalized or token) separate design competition award. Briefly, student projects will be judged based on their addressing four key principles of sustainable design:

1. Maintains, fosters, or improves upon human and environmental health
2. Considers and is adaptable to future situations
3. Is technologically and ecologically realistic
4. Can be economically viable

The truly important question is, however, how is all this being played out in the real world of practitioners, far removed from stogie and possibly unengaged academic halls, the shelved and possibly forgotten though important books, or the glamorous spotlight of reporters from international magazines?

MORE THAN GREENWASH HYPE?

The design professions are certainly no more immune to the vagaries of faddism than are any other area of study and practice (France 2003d). One can easily become cynical about the environmental realities lying underneath the verbal veneer. In many instances, scratch a touted sustainable design and what one finds underneath is sustainable rhetoric masquerading as something more than what it really is. There is perhaps no more egregious example of this than "ecorevelatory design," which has been likened to presenting an attractive bauble that is actually just making "business-as-usual look nice" (France 2000). This begs the question as to what exactly is the nature of the "business" of landscape architecture. Is adding the adjective "green" or "sustainable" before "landscape architecture" redundant, or is it establishing an improbable oxymoron?

It may come as a shock to the uninitiated to learn that being a landscape architect, just like being an ecologist, is certainly no guarantee that either will be an environmentalist. Personal motivations of the former to want to place their design fingerprint upon the landscape and of the latter to wish to understand the mysterious inner workings of nature can often be at odds with a desire to "preserve, protect and restore environmental integrity" as mandated in the 1972 U.S. Clean Water Act (see chapter 3). The reality of the situation is that much of the landscape architecture profession, though speaking lofty-sounding words with a self-congratulatory green tongue, can be characterized by having a gray heart, or certainly one that is no greener than those possessed by the environmental engineers whom the designers are so often quick to lambaste (France 2003d).

Motivated by fear that "the future of the profession is at stake," the American Society of Landscape Architects adopted a declaration on the environment and development. This action was an attempt to encourage landscape architecture to play a "key role in shaping an ecologically healthy and regenerative world in the 21st century" rather than degrading into "little more than a minor decorative art" (ASLA 1993a). Despite the oft-repeated assertion by Ian McHarg that "the study of environmental ethics, with its roots in ecology, is absolutely crucial to landscape architecture," very few design education programs have incorporated a course in such into their curricula. A 1992 survey revealed that only three of forty-three programs had ever offered a full course on environmental ethics taught by a landscape architecture faculty member (ASLA 1993b). This had been regarded as being not only extremely embarrassing but also "outright dangerous" (Ahern et al. 2002).

Landscape architecture voices high claims about collectively advancing wise stewardship of the land, yet its education base never promotes such, thereby seriously compromising the intended stewardship role. The chair of the ASLA Professional Interest Group on Water Conservation has decried the frequent failure of the profession to live up to its ethical responsibility for "the stewardship and conservation of natural, constructed, and human resources" (Patchett 1999). This "failure of contemporary landscape architects to articulate their role satisfactorily as 'stewards of the land'" is due, Scarfo (1989) argues, to a grand delusion inspired by an antiquated romantic ideal of landscape husbandry that is completely out of place and time with the technology-driven realities of the modern profession.

The debate about the motivations and environmental efficacy of landscape architecture rages again and again in the pages of the profession's premier popular magazine, *Landscape Architecture,* as do claims about the benefits ensuing to the world, human and natural, from the installation of the high-visibility projects presented therein. In a recent article about the 2002 ASLA Awards, jurors referred to "the dearth of ecologically sensitive designs" from which to pick the "flawed presence in so much of the work" that was submitted and the overall impression that "the profession is only giving lip service" to sustainable design (Anon. 2002). It appears that little has changed in the decade since Thayer (1994) harshly criticized landscape architecture as being "dominated by the creation of pleasant, illusory places which either give token service to environmental stewardship values, or ignore them altogether."

"Architecture," it has been provocatively said, is "a destructive act," with the concept of "green architecture" being as oxymoronic as "green SUVs" (France 2003d). The most serious question that can be asked about landscape architecture is thus whether it too represents, in the end after all is said and done, either an environmentally constructive or a destructive activity. In the recent John Sayles's film *Sunshine State,* in which the protagonist plays a landscape architect, the profession certainly doesn't come off very well. Overall, the impression given is that landscape architects come in after the dust has settled and the raped and murdered terrain is laid bare and that their major job is to be landscape corpse beauticians, applying a little mascara (trees) here and there before the funeral (human inhabitation).

Realistically, in the landscape design of public parks and open spaces, can one hope for (expect) more? We can quickly gauge as to how effective the profession is in generating environmental benefits in this regard by reviewing the projects covered in the pages of *Landscape Architecture* magazine. Luckily there exists a convenient way in which to make such objective appraisals.

One of the most exciting and promising developments to encourage sustainable design is the Leadership in Energy and Environmental Design (LEED) Green Building Rating System, which evaluates the environmental performance of buildings and sites. In particular, a subset of those criteria that are appropriate to water-sensitive design includes incorporating such strategies as minimizing parking spaces, reducing impervious surfaces, installing nonpoint-source stormwater treatment (e.g., bioretention swales), building green ecoroofs and rain gardens, and developing on-site water reuse systems (see chapter 8 for a discussion of some of these strategies).

A review of the past decade of projects covered in *Landscape Architecture* magazine (France 2003d) from such a water-sensitive design perspective reveals a striking absence of environmental consciousness in the bulk of the projects featured: less than a third explicitly dealt with concerns about water management and thus achieved moderate to high LEED water-rating credits, and of the remaining two-thirds fewer than 10 percent of all the potentially available LEED water credits could be awarded.

So what does this tell us about the adoptability of the conviction about "green" architecture with respect to "green" landscape architecture? First, a good number of those projects that scored low or zero in terms of water-sensitive LEED credits were a probable improvement over what had existed on the site previously and thus, it might be argued, represent less of an insult to nature than had a building (no matter how wonderful it is designed) been constructed there. But, given that landscape architects pride themselves on being much more environmentally sensitive compared to their architect brethren, it may be that such a self-righteous attitude needs to be tempered somewhat. In the end, perhaps the best that can be said about landscape architecture is that in its entirety, as represented by the reportage in the pages of its namesake magazine, it appears to be neutral in its ability to sustain nature. Carl Steinitz (2003, personal communication) provocatively concludes that a significant amount of landscape architecture might actually do more harm than good.

Should we really be surprised by such a conclusion? Those most in the know are certainly not. One of the few articles in *Landscape Architecture* on the LEED credit system concluded by questioning why there has been so little involvement by landscape architects in developing and applying the system. The answer gives credence to my contention that as a group landscape architects are, despite the green verbiage, really gray at heart: "Many landscape architects feel that they design sustainable landscapes as a matter of course in their general practice and that they don't need LEED to guide them. There is also a misguided assumption that all built landscapes are 'green'" (Calkins 2001). Of course, as even this admittedly simple examination showed, such arrogance is unwarranted, instead supporting Thayer's (1994) earlier contention that "most products of landscape architecture are simply not sustainable by any definition." In Thompson and Sorvig's (2000) book in which they review more than a hundred sustainable landscape projects, they too grapple with the troubling reality that the creation of green (here referring to color, not sustainability) growing spaces by humans can actually hurt the environment. Never, they note, should we forget that no matter how naturalistic or sustainable a created landscape appears or is touted to be, it is never a substitute for real nature free from human meddling.

"FUNCTIONAL ART" DEMONSTRATION PROJECTS: THE KEY TO SUCCESS IN SUSTAINABLE SITE DESIGN

Given that in Thayer's (1994) words, "the majority of the work done by [landscape architects] . . . could not possibly be justified under official ASLA rhetoric pertaining to environmental stewardship or sustainability" and that the best that perhaps we can ask from any site design project is that it "tends" toward sustainability, are there examples that break out of the prevalent dogma?

Although there is unequivocal evidence that land-use planning makes substantive contributions to sustaining natural resources—for example, in watershed management or low impact-development (France 2002a)—in all honesty one must remain skeptical about whether landscape architects working on the site-specific scale can affect enough positive physical alterations in the landscape to enable them to play an effective and direct role in this regard. This is not to say, however, that such efforts are insignificant in fostering environmental stewardship through the indirect means of ecological restoration and experiential education (France 2005).

The secret for corrective environmental action to sustain nature is to motivate and inspire people (France 2003a, 2005). This can be brought about not only by preserving the few relict greenspaces that still exist far removed from cities but also, at the same time, by educating and directly engaging individuals in the recognition and repair of damaged landscapes. And, it is specifically through melding the worlds of engineering and aesthetics, developing what might be called "functional art," where landscape architects can truly contribute to sustaining nature. The reason for this is that neither art and design nor science and engineering alone has much of a track record to be proud about in terms of instilling love and motivating action about saving the natural world (France 2003d); that is, it is hard to look at a sterile engineered waterway like the Los Angeles River and become inspired to go out and protect other, still-natural rivers, just as it is difficult to imagine how interacting with a piece of landscape artistic frippery such as a tree clipped to resemble a poodle will galvanize action to preserve anything.

There is possibly no better challenge anywhere to C. P. Snow's assertion of the two solitudes in the worlds of art and science than Caudwell's belief that "Art is the science of feeling. Science is the art of knowing. We must know to be able to do. But we must feel to know what to do" (Eckbo 1950). The pressing question then becomes can the "feeling" of art and "knowing" of science be married through landscape art and architecture as a means for sustaining nature (see case studies described in France 2003d; France and Fletcher 2005; Brukilacchio and Hill 2005; Harries and Heder 2005: North 2005; Damon and Mavor 2005)? The answer is, I believe, a qualified "yes," as shown most clearly in the recent development of functional and beautiful stormwater wetland parks.

NATURE BY DESIGN: CREATING TREATMENT WETLAND PARKS

Wetlands combine the beauty of aesthetic form and ecological function in a way that few other landforms can match. As such, they have been, and will certainly continue to be, important elements in site design and landscape planning (France 2003c). There is a long-established tradition in the creation of scenic wetland gardens. Indeed, it can be argued that the birth of landscape design began with the publication of *Sakuteiki* and its instructions about how to build Japanese water features (Takei and Keane 2001). And modern landscape architecture is often thought to have started with Olmsted's work on the scenic and functional Back Bay Fens wastewater treatment park system (Spirn 1995). Over the last several decades, however, wetlands have been constructed primarily by engineers and scientists to ably support the functions of flood prevention and water quality improvement. Although these latter systems have functioned well, their generally square, boxlike shapes have provided little wildlife benefits, and they have been places where people have shied away from rather than been attracted to. Today, nowhere has the union of art and science been more successfully accomplished than through the creation (often led by landscape architects) of treatment wetland parks that, in acknowledgment to the seemingly all but forgotten vision of Olmsted, combine both environmental management and ecotourism. This represents a conscious shift in focus from "constructing" wetlands to "creating" wetlands. In this regard, Salvesen's (1994) quotation of Dickens from *Pickwick Papers* is apt. "The whole difference between construction and creation is exactly this: that a thing constructed can only be loved after it is constructed; but a thing created is loved before it exists." This serves as a powerful maxim by which to redirect wetland creation as an evolving and maturing discipline (France 2003c).

The movement from single-purpose treatment wetlands toward multifunction designed wetland parks is one of the glowing success stories in nature-sustaining landscape design, capturing the civic element discussed in chapter 8. No longer are ecological benefits such as wildlife habitat or human amenities such as environmental education treated as mere ancillary benefits; instead, they are becoming acknowledged as being equally important in their own right compared to the functions of water management (France 2003c).

Requirements for this new paradigm of creating treatment wetland parks (Bays et al. 2002) include:

- Multidisciplinary team right from the start; that is, all created wetland parks that have public use applications should involve a landscape architect, a hydraulic engineer, a wetland designer, a site civil engineer, and a watershed process engineer or hydrologist, all sharing a strong belief in "osmosis learning."
- Need to explore new and varied ways of allowing people to become enriched by their wetland experiences while at the same time not disturbing wildlife.
- Opportunities for multiple uses need to be brought into planning and design discussions much earlier in the process, and both the public and public works officials need to be included (see chapter 8).
- Need for much more documentation about the challenges, successes, and lessons learned from established wetland creation projects.
- Cardinal requirement for more rigorous post-construction monitoring in order to persuade others that these projects have value.
- More attention paid to safety concerns of wetlands as part of public works projects; that is, the liability issue in the United States compared to such places as Canada and Europe may be the single greatest limitation to the design of aesthetically beautiful wetland parks that encourage unfettered visitor access.
- Avoidance of hubris; that is, we should not lose sight that what we are really designing (at least in the short term) is an interpretation or surrogate of nature and not necessarily real nature (though well-designed projects may evolve toward such over time).

- Honest acknowledgment of the ethical and practical weaknesses and limitations involved in wetland mitigation.
- Further education of clients toward moving from site-specific design issues to larger regional planning objectives; that is, water does begin or end in the wetland.
- Embrace the concepts of, and find ways to further promote, "diffusion innovation" (*sensu* Richman 2005) in terms of education.
- Always remember that no matter who is paying the bills, the ultimate client is the place—the landscape.

The following ten projects, arranged in order from naturalness to artifice, have won numerous awards and are worth briefly introducing as important examples of visionary wetland creation, ably demonstrating the effective achievement of the multiple objectives of designed function and form in sustainable landscape architecture (France 2003d). These projects are described in more detail in France (2003c) along with further corresponding references.

At Fort Devens, outside of Boston, a team of landscape architects and environmental engineers combined forces to design a wetland to treat parking lot runoff at the same time as providing wildlife habitat restoration and human amenities. Here, a small, naturalized, rocky waterfall has the double utility of aerating and improving water quality at the same time as providing a focal point for humans to sit down and view the planted field of native wildflowers surrounding the treatment system.

The Potawot Health Village in Arcata, California, uses creation of stormwater detention wetlands to establish a network of trails and meditation points as part of the therapuetic program for a Native American health facility. Here, the attractive wetlands, designed by a collaborative team of engineers, landscape architects, and tribal healers, in addition to curing environmental aliments, are used as the centerpiece to address the spiritual and cultural aspects of traditional healing.

Fishtrap Creek, outside of Vancouver, is a wonderful case study showing how the insight and dedication of a landscape architect was able to convince city officials to transform original plans for a traditionally engineered detention basin into a vibrant wetland system that serves the function of flood protection as well as providing an attractive and highly popular new city park. Inclusion of numerous stylized structures into the naturalized park environment demonstrates a perfect balance of form and function.

Longacres Business Park, in a suburb of Seattle, is a compelling fusion of stormwater contaminant treatment into a wetland park setting that establishes site identity and provides wildlife habitat. Significantly, this project is important in demonstrating that these various functions can be maintained in a landscape primarily designed for aesthetics that, unlike the three case studies cited above, in no way can be regarded as looking "natural." Here, the landscape architect used a planting scheme layout based on a rigid axial geometry to purposely contrast with the sinusoidal fluidity of the treatment wetland.

The Meadowbrook Pond and Wildlife Habitat in Seattle shows how the functions of stormwater detention and wildlife habitat creation can also double as a template upon which to showcase public art. Here, in a juxtaposition between art and science that is rare if not unique, park visitors can stand overlooking exposed engineering infrastructure, read interpretive signage about how the basin functions ecologically, and then, just a few meters away, sit in a plaza surrounded by art features including a reflecting sound mirror that collects and focuses the noise of floodwater as it rushes over a weir.

The stormwater treatment pond outside the Water Pollution Control Laboratory in Portland, Oregon, represents one of the most beautiful fusions of form and function in any sustainable landscape design. Wanting to lead by example, the agency, whose task it is to monitor urban runoff, created a demonstration project in which stormwater treatment, rather than being hidden, is dramatically made visible through use of beautiful and functional structures. The rock-lined dissipater used to slow down runoff inflow and the rock wall, which deflects water and therefore increases storage time, majestically emerging out of the stormwater basin have been featured on the cover of several magazines as well as Thompson and Sorvig's (2000) book about sustainable landscape construction. In contrast, a nearby piece of nonfunctional art, representing the token 10 percent of civic funding for the project, pales by comparison.

The Shop Creek restoration and stormwater management project in Denver is another project (by Wenk; see chapter 8) where it is the installation itself that provides both aesthetic amenities as well as ecological functions. Here, a soft mixture of soil cement was used to sculpt a series of attractive crescent-shaped terraces whose function is to create a network of wetland plunge pools for both the treatment and infiltration of runoff. Interestingly, the terraces are designed to erode, the art thus seamlessly blending into the landscape and slowly becoming more "natural" over time.

At the Indian Creek Stormwater Treatment Facility in Olympia, Washington, "art and science function to become one," as the facility's brochure extols. Using the metaphor of the basket-making tradition of Native Americans and its striking similarity in physical form to bioengineering techniques of shorebank stabilization, a series of elements are woven together into the overall park design. With the exception of the waterfall, whose purpose is similar to that at Fort Devens but whose design is clearly artificial, the other artistic structures subtly integrate with the landscape in a way that alternates between appearing to be natural and artificial. Here, in a project managed by the public arts council rather than the public works department, as much attention is devoted to the landscape creation of viewing trails as to the engineering construction of the different cleansing water bodies.

The Waterworks Garden in Renton, Washington, represents an innovative fusion of stormwater treatment and art activism. In this project, hydroengineers were the subconsultants to landscape architects, who in turn subbed to an environmental artist. Visitors to the garden, conceived of as one large public art project, make their way through a series of programatic "rooms" designed to symbolize a journey from the civilized to the wild. The route parallels the course of the water as it is cleansed, moving from obviously constructed to increasingly more natural waterforms, before eventually being released into the river system. Even the planting scheme is symbolic, with species placed at the top of the garden where the runoff is sill contaminated being identified by Native Americans as possessing bad omens.

Finally, the wetlands comprising the Northern Water Feature at the Homebush Bay site for the Sydney Olympics represents what might very well be regarded as the apogee of true functional stormwater artistry and sustainable landscape design. Not only is the site's runoff collected and treated in a series of obviously human-sculpted wetlands of beautiful curvilinear shape, but it is then harvested and recycled for use in both operations and site features. The most notable of the site amenities is the public art installation of a giant fountain that sends arches of water, some supplied from the nearby treatment wetland, out over a circulatory walkway.

All these projects function in improving the ecological integrity of their immediate surroundings. And importantly, due to the corporeal nature of water wherein both insults and remedies are additive and transferable to the larger landscape, these beneficial site effects are in turn felt downstream, contributing to sustaining nature of the entire watershed. Also, because these created wetlands are so beautiful in their designed form, they are truly inspirational, serving an educational role in motivating activism to protect natural wetlands located elsewhere (France 2003d).

Though many designers debate about the right balance between naturalness and artifice, form and function, in sustainable ecological design (see chapter 8), these projects show that function needn't occur at the expense of form. Also, in terms of form, there is a gradient in the display of the designer's imprint. Fort Devens, Potawat Healing Center, and Fishtrap Creek all look "natural" to the public eye, whereas Longacres is obviously designed by humans. Meadowbrook and the Portland Laboratory might be referred to as "art in the park," the former's installations designed to bring about clarity in the engineered structures, the latter's installations actually doubling as the engineered structures themselves. For Shop Creek, it is the purposely erodible installations that will ensure sustainability through time. For the "park as art" Indian Creek and the Waterworks Garden, the landscape itself is designed as the feature of functional art. And for the Northern Water Feature, not only is the landscape design a work of functional art, but the artistic installation actually celebrates the cleansing process in a gesture of sustainable reuse. In the end, there is no real dichotomy between form and function after all, for as Thompson and Sorvig (2000) correctly note, there are many examples in the non-human-designed world where aesthetic form follows ecological function in sustainable nature.

SUSTAINABLE AESTHETICS AND THE EXPERIENCE OF NATURE

Functional art lies at the success of ecologically sustainable designs that will inspire action beyond the bounds of the site (France 2003d). Mozingo (1997) is correct in her conclusion about the absence of aesthetics in many ecological design projects that send the viewer fleeing to the nearest Italian garden for a visual fix, no matter how ethically responsible one feels after spending time acknowledging the sustainable benefits of the former. It needn't be this way, of course. As outlined in this chapter, it is possible to fuse concepts encapsulated in the movingly poetic and hauntingly beautiful gardens of Kyoto or Suchzou with modern water treatment engineering and stormwater management. This has generated a series of remarkable projects whose widespread acceptance by scientists and artists alike has been inspirational for many to go out and play an active role in preserving the few remaining natural wetlands in their landscapes. Thayer (1994) is right on target again when he states, "Simply put, sustainable landscapes need conspicuous expression and visible interpretation, and that is where the creative and artistic skills of the landscape architect are most critically needed."

The most important role that landscape design plays in sustaining nature on a global scale may very well occur through the deliberate use of experience to inspire and instruct about the role of humans in nature (France 2005). All of the wetland projects cited above serve to anchor *participants* (i.e., not just superficial viewers) to a deeper understanding about the important role played by water in all our lives. The idea, always swirling just beneath the surface of such projects, is that "the more we learn about and experience water, the more we are moved to give ourselves over to it—to deeply and profoundly immerse ourselves in its physical essence and spiritual nature, and in so doing, reciprocate by preserving its presence in our enriched lives, untainted" (France 2003a).

Chapter Ten

Fixing Home(scapes)

Communicating the Benefits of Retrofitting Residences and Neighborhoods for Waterfront Buffer Gardens and Greenways

It had been a long day of paddling around the small Ontario lake, pulling up the minnow traps set the night before and enumerating their catch before releasing the animals back into the nearshore water. Even though most of our attention had been focused on the lake, there was no ignoring the variability we observed in the character of the shorelines that overlooked each of our sampling sites. Some locations, distant from any inhabitation, still had their natural forests. And several of the inhabited properties had retained some of their shoreline trees, the cottages glimpsed through the filter of vegetation. In many cases, however, the lots had been completely cleared of natural vegetation, there being nothing but green manicured lawns running straight down from the back doors right to the water's edge. At one site that was still under construction, the new owner was standing outside on his elevated deck, coffee cup in hand as he proudly surveyed the devastation in front of him that was his property, ignorant of the ecological damage his actions were inflicting upon the lake. My companion, bitter after a day of viewing other such egregious acts of environmental insensitivity, gestured at the sole tree remaining on the property and yelled out to the owner that he had missed one. After a moment's pause, the response from the landowner was such that we thought it wise to quickly paddle on. Was there an alternative to this grotesque transposition of urban lifestyles to rural, holiday retreats? Was there a way to inspire some sort of shoreline stewardship? Years later, this time in my neighborhood in Cambridge, I led a take-back-the-shoreline walk around a nearby pond in which the abutters had over the years encroached upon public land. Because the newly drafted master plan for the area (see chapter 12) had highlighted the encroachment problem and called for establishment of a public trail system, we felt we were armed with a solid justification for our actions. The

135

homeowners (and their purposely directed dogs) thought differently, however. Thinking back many years to the encounter in the Ontario lake, I was struck again by the strong emotions that issues of waterfront ownership and access can engender. People truly desire being near water, and for those not fortunate to be able to do so in terms of their residences, the creation of public greenways can be one important way to bring this about.

INTRODUCTION

The public perceives industry as the destroyer of our waters. But when we look at many of our recreational waters, we find no industry. The public has difficulty realizing that individual landowners can damage lakes and rivers, often unwittingly, in their bid to urbanize their residential and cottage shorelines.

Lindsay Penney, quoted in Kingsmill (1997)

Thus has nature placed and preserved at the very gates of Boston riches of scenery Chicago or Denver or many other American city would give millions to create, if it were possible. Stupid indeed will be the people of greater Boston if they fail to perceive and attend to their interests in this matter before the opportunity is lost.

Visionary landscape architect, Charles Eliot, ca. 1900

Buffer Strips

The shoreline region where the land meets the water—the riparian ecotone—is known to demand special attention in environmental management due to it being the place where life gathers at "a bridge between two worlds" (Korth 1999). Buffer strips are more than green eyelashes (France 2002d). Shoreline buffers can function protectively as the first line of defense from land development, for example, with respect to water bodies from soil erosion (France 2002c) or human occupants of floodplains from flooding (Zucker et al. 2002).

Because of their ecological importance and function as human amenities (Flink 2002), much work has been devoted to measuring the size and extent of buffers on a landscape scale (Schloss 2002; France et al. 2002). Mitchell (2002) makes the point that to be truly effective, shoreline buffers must be coupled to the larger landscape of whole watersheds and continuous habitat areas. This is especially the case for concerns about preserving wildlife biodiversity where the issues of landscape ecology such as fragmentation, connectivity, edge effects, patches, nodes, etc. (Forman 1997; see also chapter 6) should be incorporated into shoreline planning.

Many states and provinces have shoreline protection acts or sets of buffer strip guidelines in place (e.g., France et al. 2002). The situation in New Hampshire (Anon. 1999) is representative in this regard in that it establishes minimum standards for future subdivisions of the riparian forest and lists the prohibited and permitted uses and development of the shoreline. Prohibited uses include salt storage yards, auto junk yards, and solid or hazardous waste facilities. Developmental uses that are permitted include public water supply or sewage treatment facilities, hydroelectric facilities, public utility lines, and existing solid waste facilities. The minimum standards for future development include the size and configuration of all new lots, erosion control devices, septic systems, architectural structures, and various characteristics of the buffer strip left in place.

Home Buffers

When considered in aggregate, the area comprised by residential properties is vast and their cumulative effect upon the environment profound (Bowers et al. 1998; Kingsmill 1997). Americans are truly obsessed with lawns, which together represent an area of more than fifty thousand square miles (roughly the size of Pennsylvania) and whose care costs add up to $30 billion per year as well as requiring the use of a third of the total municipal water supply (Montgomery 1997). Often this obsession is transferred from the suburban to the vacation landscapes, the result being that shorelines can resemble a sea of groomed grass that harbors little life. Lakes can therefore often be likened to sterilized bathtubs (Kingsmill 1997). Problems with groomed shorelines include erosion and sedimentation, excessive growth of aquatic plants and algae, loss of wildlife habitat, attraction of nuisance animals such as geese, and loss of leisure time due to maintenance requirements (Henderson, Dindorf, and Rozumalski 2003).

Buffer zones restore ecological functions that are reduced or limited by traditional lawns, and an increasing number of educational documents exists to provide guidelines to help homeowners become better environmental stewards. These take the form of, for example, the following:

- Educating that "it's better to have a partial view of a healthy lake than a totally unobstructed view of a sick lake" (Kingsmill 1997), or that "no matter how far you live from a body of water, your property is part of a watershed" (Anon. 1998).
- Listing the benefits of shoreland buffers (Korth 1999; CBP 2001) and iden-

tifying the importance of shoreland areas for wildlife with recommended plantings and their associated wildlife values (Anon. 1997).

• Increasing understanding about the natural conditions of a property, listing certain grasses and plants to use as alternatives to short grass lawns, planting recommendations for natural pollution barriers, and tips for landscape maintenance (Anon. 1998; CBP 2001).

• Describing techniques of preserving existing growth, microclimatic site analysis, alternatives to traditional lawns, plant selection, and landscape management (Bowers et al. 1998).

• Providing ground-cover alternatives to grass lawns and offering suggestions for erosion control, soil improvement composting, and water conservation and protection (Anon. 1996; CBP 2001).

• Supplying suggestions for the architecture of buffers in terms of site preparation, plant installation and maintenance, shoreline stabilization, and good stewardship practices (Henderson, Dindorf, and Rozumalski 2003).

Several of these documents offer advice on establishing what might be called a "shoreline aesthetic." Anon. (1998) mentions that beautiful plants can equal beautiful lakes in terms of using up phosphorus before it reaches the water, and Bowers et al. (1998) encourage the development of a natural aesthetic capitalizing on the natural processes of change. Through providing schematic plantings plans and before-and-after diagrams, Anon. (1996) and especially Henderson, Dindorf, and Rozumalski (2003) advance the concepts of "greenscaping" and "lakescaping" as viable strategies for protecting wildlife and water quality. The report described in detail below (PRCWA 1999; Roolf and Lambright 2000) builds upon this tradition and advances it one step further in terms of integrating aesthetics and science into the concept of waterfront buffer gardens.

Neighborhood Greenways

There has been an increasing recognition of the importance of protecting scenic areas and viewsheds, such as those areas bordering rivers, as one attribute of comprehensive watershed management (Anon. 2000). Further, water-sensitive planning should transcend consideration of mere physical spaces. Greenways can very much be used to help define and instill a quality of life for humans at the same time as shaping a sustainable future (France 2002e). Greenways, once regarded as only recreational amenities, are now recognized to provide many more benefits to communities, functioning as sort of green "main streets," and represent models for integrating human and environmental objectives in land-use planning that come together in concepts of open-space stewardship (Flink 1993, 2002). Not only does modern greenway planning address the capability of these linear parks to ably serve their original resource purpose for humans in terms of tourism, protection of historic settlements, alternative transportation corridors, and increased nearby property values, such planning also considers these river borders with respect to their roles in flood-plain management, water-quality protection, and wildlife habitat preservation (Flink 2002). The report described in detail below (CRJ 1998; O'Brien and Driscoll 2000) is from a time period when the shift toward adopting the multi-functionality of such a holistic greenway vision was at its conception.

Education

Public surveys demonstrate that a strong base of support exists among water-front landowners for both human and environmental benefits that accrue from shoreline protection (Mitchell 2002). Unfortunately, people often remain both physically and conceptually uncoupled from the shoreline areas in their watershed (France 2003d; Brukilacchio and Hill 2005; Bullard 2005; see also chapter 2). There is a strong need, therefore, to develop effective means of communicating the benefits of environmental protection for water-shed residents (France 2005; see also chapters 2 and 3). For this reason, information from the two reports reviewed in this chapter are abstracted below through the extensive use of quotations. In the case of the guide for waterfront buffer gardens (Roolf and Lambright 2000), this is not so much to present new information (most of this was already covered in chapter 6) but rather in order to illustrate a very good example of the language style and level of technical detail useful for communicating these important concepts to homeowners. In the case of abstracting elements from the master plan for the Upper Charles River Reservation (O'Brien and Driscoll 2000), this is because the document offers a particularly good example of highlighting the landscape architecture elements that need to be addressed in a successfully implemented greenway plan.

HELPING HOMEOWNERS TO PLANT BUFFERS: WATERFRONT GARDENS (ROOLF AND LAMBRIGHT 2000)

Many suburban watersheds include riverfronts and lakeshores that were long ago divided up into home sites. Developed before environmental laws were enacted to protect shorelines, these homes commonly have manicured lawns that go right to the edge of the river. The Parker River Clean Water Association of Massachusetts, working with a local professional landscaper, assisted three homeowners and one commercial property in planting waterfront gardens that used habitat-enhancing native plants in a designed and landscaped arrangement (PRCWA 1999). The intention was to provide convenient models for homeowners to adopt at the scale of a house lot that looked attractive and fit within an individual's budget (Roolf and Lambright 2000).

The gardens were planted in the spring and fall with the assistance of the homeowners and volunteers. Diverse sites were sought in the application process: one was on the sunny bank of a large tidal river, another in a shaded area where freshwater and tidewater meet, and the third on the marshy banks of a small freshwater stream. The last site was a local business in which a buffer was planted around a storm drainage ditch leading into a tributary of the river.

Obstacles to the project included concern from the homeowners over obtaining necessary environmental permits, aesthetics, and the regulatory aspect of planting a new buffer area that they might not legally be able to remove if they changed their minds (Roolf and Lambright 2000). Several of the home properties also had septic system issues that needed to be considered in the final design.

A guide to planting waterfront gardens for homeowners was published that included recommendations for specific native plants, samples of designed buffers, and resources for further information (PRCWA 1999). The mandate of the guide was to educate homeowners in how to:

- Enhance bird and wildlife habitat
- Attractively frame their view of the water
- Control erosion from their properties
- Eliminate onerous and time-consuming lawn care
- Improve water quality

Information from this guide (Roolf and Lambright 2000) is abstracted below.

A Guide to Planting a Landscaped Buffer to Protect Your River, Stream, Wetland, or Pond

At the Water's Edge

The guide begins by informing homeowners that not only are waterfront locations "special places" for humans but they also play an important ecological role in both conservation biology (i.e., as wildlife corridors) and water-quality protection (i.e., as filter strips). Next, the guide heralds the merits of both natural and landscaped vegetated buffers:

You may like the way a natural buffer looks—a wild and carefree collection of native plants. If that's what you have, and you like it, your best bet is to let nature alone.

However, if you have an existing lawn down to the river, stream or neighboring wetland, you may want to plant a buffer using native plants in a landscaped arrangement. Some native plants are particularly attractive—with showy flowers and autumn color. A buffer does not have to be a tangle of "weeds." (Roolf and Lambright 2000)

Landscape Design and Ecology

The guide goes on to illuminate the environmental utility of waterside vegetation in terms of modifying water temperature, providing berries as food and hides for habitat for wildlife, roots that will take up nutrients and prevent erosion, grasses to form physical filters, and seasonally blooming native perennials to attract butterflies.

A Bounty of Buffer Benefits

The guide itemizes the following benefits accruing from landscaping with native plants (Roolf and Lambright 2000):

- Beautify your yard.
- Frame your view of the water.
- Reduce the need for herbicides and pesticides (natives are adapted to local conditions, so they need less "life support").
- Reduce your lawn-watering bill.
- Filter out pollutants and metabolize toxic chemicals.

Next, the guide lists the following results that homeowners will notice about their properties:

- Increased habitat for birds, butterflies, and wildlife
- Less erosion
- More shade to keep the water cool for fish
- Less muddy water running into the river when it rains

Designs

The guide presents two detailed buffer designs, each including a recommended planting list, a schematic plan, and an estimated budget (see PRCWA 1999). The first design is for a "Bungalow on the Pond," with the following textural information:

This buffer design is for a shady area with moist soil full of organic material. Existing trees are incorporated into the design, which adds native grasses and flowering perennials. This theme emphasizes reds, pinks, and purples with several shrubs providing year-round foliage color in addition to the seasonal blooms of the perennials. White flowers add delicate contrast. Plants are grouped in odd-numbered clusters, and plants are repeated across the waterfront for cohesion. (PRCWA 1999)

The second design is for a "Home on a Tidal River," with the following textural information:

This design must withstand the elements—located on a tidal river, it is beaten by the sun, lashed by the wind, and occasionally inundated by high storm tides. We used low-growing seaside shrubs that enhance habitat and prevent erosion, while keeping the spectacular views. Periodic pruning will keep the view clear, other than this, however, the site is low maintenance. The seaside shrubs bloom in shades of pinks and whites. Beach plums and bayberries can be harvested for jelly and wax, respectively, and the birds love both. Fragrant summersweet, located near the living room window, will provide a natural incense when in bloom. (PRCWA 1999)

Why Use Native Plants?

The guide provides a small primer on the use of native plants, how to find them at nurseries, a list of sources for additional information, and a listing of selected plants ideally targeted to solve the specific problems of mitigating bank erosion, discouraging nuisance geese, removing nutrients and sediment, and supplying shading for fishes. Following this, the guide provides a list of native plants (trees, shrubs, perennials, and grasses) well suited to riparian areas based on soil typology.

Subsequent subsections of the guide outline the benefits of no-mow options for backyards and the issues of municipal weed laws in relation to growing wildflower meadows.

Beyond Waterfront Property

The guide makes the useful point that even if one does not own waterfront property, the landscaping choices one adopts can affect distant water bodies. In this respect, the guide informs the homeowner that every site has a watershed address and that plants perform the following eological functions to help protect watersheds (Roolf and Lambright 2000):

- Roots allow rainwater to soak into the ground and replenish groundwater.
- Tree roots allow for more water to soak in than do grasses.
- Lawns increase runoff rates by up to 50 percent compared to forests.
- Pavement causes nearly all of the rainwater to run directly into the river, carrying with it pollution with no filtering or groundwater recharge.
- Across the watershed, increased pavement and lawns can result in flooding during heavy rains and dry riverbeds during times of low rainfall.

This section ends with the simple precept that addresses all the aforementioned problems, "The solution: plant plants!"

Buffers in Your Watershed

This section of the guide provides a few words about how buffers are a last line of defense in stopping pollutants from entering water bodies. In addition to waterfront areas, the important point is made that there are other places where application of buffers will exact watershed benefits:

- Surrounding storm drains
- Between houses and streets (where storm drains or drainage ditches carry the water to the river)
- Along even a tiny drainage ditch that functions ecologically as a tiny stream
- Along a parking lot or driveway

Lawn Care to Protect Rivers

The guide proceeds to instruct about how traditional lawns can impact water resources due to their requirement for intensive amounts of chemical additives to stay green and healthy. This section then proceeds to describe the management techniques available to achieve the environmentally greenest lawn possible (Roolf and Lambright 2000):

- Eliminate the lawn by planting a forest.
- Ignore the lawn; over many years it will convert to a shrubby meadow itself.
- No lawn maintenance (just mow it).
- Plant drought-resistant grasses.
- Use organic fertilizers and pest control.
- Use integrated pest management.

The guide concludes with the brief sections "Riverfront Regulations," "Invasive Species," and "Index of Attractive Native Plants."

Charles River Greenway (O'Brien and Driscoll 2000)

The Metropolitan District Commission's (MDC) Upper Charles River Reservation in Boston has come full circle over the last hundred years. An initial period (early 1900s) of resource protection, park development, and heavy public use was followed by decades of neglect, abuse, and lost public interest (O'Brien and Driscoll 2000). Today, the public's historic attraction for the Upper Reservation has been reawakened by water-quality improvements (see chapter 2) and reclamation of the river's banks.

In particular, the cleaner water and the recent development of extensive greenway corridors along the river have strengthened the river's value as an ecological and recreational resource. Since 1990, the MDC has reclaimed more than fifty illegal encroachments on public park land. All of these neglected areas have been restored as a public greenway featuring a multiuse pathway, overlook decks, restored wetland areas, general habitat improvements, and extensive plantings. Implementation of this vision is providing Boston with an exemplary model of an urban river greenway corridor that encourages extensive public use while protecting and enhancing the native ecosystem (O'Brien and Driscoll 2000).

The following objectives—first laid out more than a decade ago—are now being met (O'Brien and Driscoll 2000):

- Development of a continuous pedestrian pathway system that links the Upper Charles River Reservation and its surrounding communities with the Boston Basin pathway system.
- Restoration of river banks, edges, and channels to promote both increased recreational use and the river's ecological health.
- Decrease in nonpoint-source pollutants that have been entering the river.
- Protection and enhancement of wildlife habitat.
- Provision of interpretive displays and brochures that promote the natural and cultural elements of the river corridor.
- Broadening and strengthening of constituency groups, with particular focus on joint ventures with businesses abutting the river.

The MDC master plan for the Upper Charles River Reservation (CRJ 1998) provides a clear vision about how these goals were established and, over time, achieved. As such, because the document is a particularly good example of the landscape architecture elements needed in a successfully implemented master plan, it is useful to highlight these in the form of an extended abstract below.

The Upper Charles River Reservation Master Plan

Introduction

After a general introduction to and spatial definition of the study area, the MDC master plan progresses to describe an experiential visit to the reservation in the section titled "Discovering the Upper Charles Reservation." The reader follows a hypothetical visitor as s/he strolls along the river and "discovers the beauty and uniqueness" of the landscape. The master plan next introduces the reader (or the visitor) to the seven noticeable habitat types (open water, shallow marsh, shrub swamp/wetland meadow, forested floodplain wetland, oak/pine forested uplands, and developed and nonforested upland area) by providing a description of the ecological attributes of each.

New Expectations

This brief section provides an introduction to the overall vision of the project and is worth quoting as both the challenges and aspirations are germane to many such studies:

> It is significant that over 1,000,000 people live and work within walking distance of this fascinating landscape and its rich habitats. However, much of the Reservation goes unnoticed and may be hard to find if one is not a nearby resident or a very curious explorer. Presently, there are few clues that the public is invited into this natural preserve. Once the Reservation is found, passage is difficult or impossible due to a variety of obstacles, including steep slopes, fences, thickets, discontinuous trials, and dumped or discarded materials.
>
> The master plan for the Upper Charles recommends improvements to the Reservation that focus upon restoring, enhancing, and expanding its ecological assets. This will be coupled with improved accessibility along the river corridor, thereby making its riches and excitement more easily available to all people of the region. For years to come, people will be able to enjoy the river as a unique natural and recreational resource, while learning about the river's ecosystem and the importance of our enduring relationship with it. (CRJ 1998)

Master Plan Goals

This section (CRJ 1998) represents one of the clearest outlines laying out the working goals and related objectives needed to achieve recreational and, to a lesser degree, environmental benefits in urban greenway master planning and is thus worthy of extensive quotation.

1. Improve access to the river and/or greenway for walkers, hikers, boats, canoes, bicycles, anglers, and the physically challenged

- Create multiple access points or gateways to the Reservation, and make entries more formal and visible where appropriate
- Improve pedestrian access from neighborhood streets and open-space
- Improve, expand, and create parking areas where possible
- Create or improve informational/directional signage to make the Reservation and its entries more widely known

2. Improve circulation and open-space connections along the river corridor
   - Provide a continuous public pathway on one or, where feasible, on both sides of the river corridor
   - Use low-impact boardwalks and bridges in steep and wet areas in order to achieve continuous pathways
   - Remove physical barriers blocking passage along the river's edge
   - Create safe pedestrian crosswalks and add traffic lights where necessary at bridge crossings

3. Eliminate gaps in public ownership
   - Acquire private property and/or develop public access easements
   - Work with semi-public property owners to encourage public areas

4. Reclaim all MDC property on which abutters have encroached
   - Clearly demarcate the MDC property line with fencing, guardrail, planting or boundary markers
   - In conjunction with the MDC and property owners, implement a means of removing stored and dumped materials from MDC property

5. Protect and enhance the character of open-space and the shoreline along the river
   - Enhance/upgrade areas where there are no notable views, topography, scenic structures, etc.
   - Enhance/upgrade current park land which abuts the Reservation
   - Remove trash and clean up abandoned dumping areas
   - Revegetate encroachment areas using indigenous plantings
   - Preserve as much existing riparian vegetation as possible

6. Protect and improve visual/scenic quality
   - Improve access to prime viewing spots, and create new viewing areas where appropriate
   - Selectively prune vegetation to open new views to the river
   - Promote bridges/dams as major viewing points
   - Screen poor views with new vegetation
   - Cover obtrusive structures with plant materials
   - Clean up areas along the river edge and within the corridor that impair visual quality
   - Enforce scenic easements and propose others where appropriate

7. Promote sustainable environmental quality
   - Protect sensitive ecology, such as wildlife habitat and wetland resources
   - Limit interaction between wildlife species and Reservation users
   - Improve water quality and wildlife habitat

- Improve potential for anadromous fish migration
- Promote species diversity, eliminate exotic and invasive plant species, and revegetate eroded slopes and damaged or reconfigured river banks
- Promote low maintenance by avoiding large areas of mown grass and other planting requiring extensive care
- Use native/natural recycled materials for site elements whenever possible
8. Maximize educational/interpretive opportunities
   - Explore the interpretive potential of historic buildings and sites, cultural evolution, unique natural areas, and wildlife habitat
   - Explore educational potential of natural resources, and cultural evolution of the river corridor
   - Explore partnerships for educational and interactive activities with institutional abutters
   - Limit potential conflicts between Reservation activities
   - Where possible, separate path uses (e.g., walking versus cycling versus birdwatching) through design, location, materials, and signage
9. Maximize safety of Reservation users and privacy of abutters
   - Use planting and fencing to separate public and private property
   - Emphasize good visibility from adjacent properties
   - Post safety and use regulations
   - Employ park rangers to patrol the path system on bike
   - Encourage arrangements with local police for surveillance (CRJ 1998)

Master Plan

There is no doubt that the above listing of objectives will go far toward the goal of "linking communities and bringing people together to share a common natural resource." It must be admitted, however, that this is very much a traditional landscape architecture perspective that focuses primarily on people with environmental issues interpreted in mostly a utilitarian fashion (see chapter 12 for a contrasting perspective). Indeed, the authors of the master plan do recognize this by following the lengthy list of goals above with a somewhat apologetic statement about the importance of maintaining adequate baseflow in the river (see chapter 2) that, however, were "not within the purview of the Master Plan to deal with" (CRJ 1998).

Because of this, the bulk of the master plan is taken up with describing traditional (but important) landscape architecture recommendations pertaining to:

- Entries to the reservation
- Width and material of pathways
- Location and grading of pathways
- Open-space linkages

- Bridges and crossings
- Separation from private property
- Property acquisition and easement needs
- Safety and security
- Encroachment on public land
- Interpretive features and signage
- Water use and access

The section "Habitat Reclamation and Enhancement" subsumes only one and a half of the sixteen pages of recommendations and focuses on four strategies for improving wildlife habitat within the new reservation.

Develop a Continuous Wildlife Corridor along the River. The master plan (CRJ 1988) discusses how presence of a vegetated buffer zone adjacent to the river and wetlands will provide essential habitat for feeding, roosting, breeding, and rearing of young as well as helping to mitigate sedimentation and nutrient flow into the river (see chapter 5 for a further discussion of the ecological benefits of riparian buffers). The plan then provides some hints about how to go about replanting derelict and deforested parcels of land.

Improve Habitat Structure. The master plan next briefly mentions the various techniques that can be employed to revegetate the shorelines. Interestingly, some attention is given to the importance of leaving behind fallen tree trunks and limbs and other pieces of large woody debris along the river's edge (as in chapter 1).

Reduce Plants Not Contributing to Habitat Value. The master plan does a reasonable job in explaining concerns with nonnative exotic and opportunistic invasive species. Removal techniques for both terrestrial and aquatic invasives are also outlined.

Improve Soil Quality. The master plan explains the importance of soil to the success of any of the aforementioned plantings. A brief mention is made following this of the poor conditions of the Upper Charles riverbanks due to filling, compaction, pollution, and general low fertility. Finally, the probable need to import additional loam to establish plantings beds is discussed.

The master plan then goes on to describe all the planned interventions on a segment-by-segment basis (six such for the 5.8-mile length of the greenway study area) followed by a section that guides the reader through a variety of proposed walking loops.

Implementation. The master plan (CRJ 1998) ends with an important examination of four key elements that are essential to the long-term success of any such planning effort:

- Phasing
- Project costs
- Permitting needs
- Maintenance and management guidelines

CONCLUSIONS

The word "ecology" has its origin in the Greek word *oikos,* meaning home. Ecology, then, can be regarded as the science of the home. There is a great utility in the strategy put forth by Roolf and Lambright (2000) of mobilizing homeowners to become better watershed citizens through encouraging their planting and maintenance of waterfront buffer gardens. Gardening is the number one recreational activity in the United States (Pollan 1991), and the development of hands-on, design-build activities involving direct public participation (e.g., Winterbottom 2005) is often heralded as a major factor in ensuring the long-term success of ecological restoration projects (France 2006) through fostering feelings of connection to, and stewardship of, the natural environment (France 2005).

Neighborhoods provide a sense of place and feeling of rootedness in an era of gypsy lifestyles. And greenways provide a convenient means for reconnecting people to the mostly unheeded rivers that run through and around our towns (Bullard 2005), their historic roles in forming the very communities in which we live being all but forgotten (Meyer 2005). And although it may be easy to form criticisms that the landscape architecture of such riverside corridors, in the absence of any associated attempts to improve the ecological health or integrity of those areas, is a misdirection of efforts and resources, it is not necessarily wise to do so. One of the most important functions of greenways can be through their role in increasing the visibility of rivers, as O'Brien and Driscoll (2000) emphasize. Visibility is an important first step along the way to watershed management in that one will not protect what one does not love, and one will not love what one does not first recognize (France 2003a). In this respect, greenways provide recreational opportunities that in turn may lead, with encouragement and guidance, to restoration opportunities.

Part IV

PROBLEM MANAGEMENT

Chapter Eleven

Annotation

Executive Summary of the Watershed Development Perspectives

It turned out to be one of the most frustrating professional meetings that I had ever attended. I had been invited as part of a group of civil engineers and hydrologists to provide advice on the design of a housing development that was planned for an old gravel quarry in southern Massachusetts. I had been attracted to the idea of the project when first contacted by the landscape architecture firm, since on the first pass the project seemed to offer promise of being environmentally progressive in terms of its adaptive reuse of a post-industrial site. However, it took only a few minutes into the meeting to realize that the developer was not the least bit interested in either environmental concerns or innovative design beyond what was absolutely going to be necessary in order to get the controversial project passed through the local zoning board as quickly and effortlessly as possible. "Controversial," in the eyes of local opponents, because the intended development was in a region that was already suffering from dropping groundwater levels due to decreased infiltration and increased withdrawl rates. Despite my first questions about how the new development might fit into the watershed in which it was situated, the developer stubbornly refused to focus on anything other than acquiring information about the amount of water he could plan on being able to tap into for irrigating the grass and gardens intended for the property. I felt sorry for the hired firm of landscape architects whom I knew to be capable of much more in terms of offering useful approaches for water-sensitive planning and design. In the end, my lasting memory of the meeting was one of it representing the complete antithesis to the perspectives that have been laid out in the present book. No one had any idea about how the land and water might be linked on the site (chapter 1). We had no real understanding of the site from a watershed perspective (chapter 2) in order to understand what the most serious environ-

mental concerns were (chapter 3). No option strategies for development were provided (chapter 4), nor was the difficult question addressed of whether there was already enough development in the area to begin with (chapter 5). There also was no discussion about the relative strengths and weaknesses of the particular location of interest compared to those for other locations in the area (chapter 6). No information was provided, much less discussed, about what the regional conditions might be in the future (chapter 7). A water budget for the site had not been derived (chapter 8), particularly in relation to the intent to construct some sort of water-storage basin rather than a multifunctioning treatment wetland (chapter 9). And finally, the possibility of fostering environmental stewardship among future residents through encouraging watershed-supporting gardens (chapter 10) was ignored by the developer in preference for professional, out-sourced landscape maintenance. I left the meeting fearing that this was another example of sprawl with little or no attention paid to the environmental consequences of development.

PERSPECTIVES ON AQUATIC CONSEQUENCES OF SPRAWL

The following fifty perspectives to aid in understanding and managing the aquatic consequences of developmental sprawl have been distilled from the previous ten chapters.

Chapter 1: How are things linked?

- Lakes, wetlands, and rivers are not isolated systems free from terrestrial influences.
- Riparian ecotones are areas of extreme ecological significance.
- Woody debris regulates water flow to structure river geomorphology and provides important habitats to support lake biodiversity.
- Understanding the role of woody debris in aquatic systems has implications for river restoration and wildlife management.

Chapter 2: What is wrong?

- Water needs to be made more visible.
- Water-resource management is a pressing worldwide concern.
- Waterborne diseases result from antiquated water infrastructure.
- Water bodies need to be studied and managed from a landscape perspective.

- Hydrological problems cannot be solved by engineering, techno-fix solutions in the absence of addressing ethical concerns.
- Education is essential for fostering ecological consciousness and imparting environmental stewardship.
- Due to development (impervious surfaces and large pipes), we are, for the first time in history, living outside of the hydrological cycle in terms of our water sources and sinks.
- Environmental zoning and geographic information systems (GIS) prioritization of development sites and aquifer protection are essential.
- Brownfield redevelopment and integrated water management are effective means to limit the detrimental effects of sprawl.

Chapter 3: How bad is it?

- Biomonitoring can be used to gauge environmental conditions.
- Indices of biological integrity distill copious scientific information into comprehensive and comprehensible descriptions of watershed health.
- Indices facilitate communication and aid in decision making regarding the severity and progress of environmental contamination or restoration.
- Attention to mathematical naivete and subjective biases are important for development of a defensible environmental index.

Chapter 4: How can development be planned?

- Understanding and minimizing the environmental consequences of watershed development requires establishing a systematic framework from which to make assessments of progress in the various planning approaches being implemented.
- Concepts of biological health (integrity) and energy (tiger) release can be combined to create an option-strategy protocol for water-sensitive development planning.
- Such a protocol allows for decisions to be made about the levels of development permissible in relation to limiting the effects of sprawl on, for example, riparian damage, aquifer protection and recharge, wetland loss and replacement, green business sustainability, lake acidification, agriculture, drainage and stream protection, and watershed management.
- Use of this protocol enables communication among stakeholders and improves grassroots involvement in laying out strategies for managing sprawl.

Chapter 5: What is the ultimate development cap?

• Studies of the environmental implications of sprawl are hampered by lack of contextural reference from which to establish defensible development thresholds.

• Building empirical predictions from cross-system analysis moves watershed development management from a reactive to a proactive mode.

• Threshold limits to the extent of watershed development can be established in relation to maintaining desired levels of, for example, biological integrity, fishery yield, lake metabolism, coastal eutrophication, and wetland biodiversity.

• These techniques enable a primary objective prediction of future conditions to aid in building alternative development scenarios that project population growth and estimate the effects of landscape sprawl.

Chapter 6: What locations can be developed?

• Site assessment is required to determine and prioritize locations most suitable for development with the fewest possible environmental repercussions.

• GIS analysis of water vulnerability is used to estimate the watershed-scale effects of sprawl development.

• Individual site visits and development acceptability evaluations are necessary to validate the assumptions and vagaries in the watershed-scale GIS models.

• Water-sensitive variables applied in judging site development potential include vulnerability of wetlands, presence of riparian forest buffers, threats to water quality, and septic system suitability.

• Wildlife-sensitive variables applied in judging site development potential include presence of endangered species, biodiversity, and habitat fragmentation and connectivity.

• Amenity variables applied in judging site-development potential include agriculture viability, visual quality, and presence of historic or cultural resources.

• Construction and maintenance variables applied in judging site-development potential include energy and microclimate issues, projected construction costs, and wastewater treatment feasibility.

Chapter 7: What will the future look like?

• Implications of watershed development are best understood through spatially explicit comparisons.
• Alternative futures modeling generates predictions of the impacts of land-use alterations on watershed attributes that might result from various forecasted or hypothetical sprawl-development scenarios.
• This approach provides a GIS-based computer framework to incorporate ecological science into community-based decision making.
• Through visualizing and evaluating various build-out scenarios, alternative futures modeling opens up a dialogue among watershed stakeholders about development choices and their associated environmental and economic repercussions if implemented.

Chapter 8: How can damage be fixed?

• One of the most serious consequences of sprawl development is a marked decline in water quality due to contaminated stormwater runoff.
• It may be possible to protect water resources from pollution by adoption of a suite of modified land-development provisions such as enabling density zoning and land-use combinations, creating stream buffers, limiting impervious cover, constructing biking and walking paths, infill zoning, limiting street widths and curbs, encouraging use of porous surface materials, limiting parking, building vegetated biofiltration swales, treating hot spots of contamination, labeling inlet drains, and limiting site clearing, grading, and disturbance during construction.
• Effective stormwater management involves partnering with public works departments in designing, building, and maintaining best management practives (BMPs).
• Stormwater infrastructure projects needn't look natural but should always engender a civic quality, allowing people to engage the site and experience its water.
• Innovative design needs to be supported by affirmative policy and active maintenance.
• Regarding site development from a perspective of derived predevelopment and postdevelopment water budgets helps in the design of effective stormwater treatment systems.

Chapter 9: Can public parks help?

- Sustainable design, presently in a state of tokenism or faddism, can, if developed further, promote wise land stewardship and reduce the environmental effects of sprawl.
- The reality of sustainable design as practiced by the profession of landscape architecture has yet to live up to its self-congratulatory, green rhetoric.
- An exception to this generalization is the creation of treatment wetland parks that fuse art and science toward sustaining local nature at the same time as inspiring stewardship for distant areas through education.
- Such functional art projects range from those in which pieces of art are inserted into the park to those in which the park itself is the piece of art, there being no correct balance between the mix of design artifice and naturalness.

Chapter 10: What about private and public waterside areas?

- Watershed stewardship as a counter to watershed development begins with landscape architecture at home and in the neighborhood.
- Private waterfront buffer gardens can provide some of the ecological benefits of riparian forests in terms of enhancing wildlife habitat, controlling erosion, and improving water quality, along with the added benefits to homeowners of increasing backyard aesthetics as well as reducing maintenance requirements.
- Creation of public waterside greenways can be both ecologically and sociologically important ways to reclaim neglected areas for the support of local nature and neighborhood culture.
- Participatory encouragement and widespread acceptance of such projects depends upon effectively and enthusiastically communicating the underlying concepts and beneficial goals in an accessible, user-friendly format.

Chapter Twelve

Application

Master Planning for Protecting and Restoring an Urban Wild and River

The morning following the large rainstorm provided insight into just how hydrologically sensitive the Alewife watershed was in relation to its development. Leaving my apartment, I went down to the basement and spent an hour raising my soggy sports equipment up from the recently impounded waters there. Then, going outside for a morning walk revealed that many of my neighbors were likewise suffering from flooding, the sound of basement pumps filling the air along with the sight of unattractive-looking water shooting out from hoses into the water-filled streets. The normally placid Alewife Brook had overflowed its banks and had swollen to at least quadruple its normal width. Autos attempting to make their way along the fringing Alewife Parkway were pushing a two-foot-high bow wave of water as they struggled forward. Later, when I learned more about the hydrological history of the area, the only surprise seemed to be that such flooding did not occur more frequently. Several years later—this time after I had moved beyond the ever-expanding floodplain—I went for a jog after another such "storm of the century." As I negotiated around the still-bubbling stormwater discharges, washed-out bridges, and autos stalled in the floodwaters, I thought back to what I had learnt about how this particular watershed had once functioned prior to all the development. How could the economic pressures for further housing and commercial space be balanced against the environmental requirements for more stormwater storage in the area? And at another occasion, during an early morning walk to return a rented video, I crossed over Alewife Brook atop the same historic bridge that the British had used during their retreat from the incident of the "shot heard 'round the world" in the town of Concord. Traffic had not yet reached its rush-hour peak, and as I looked down from the bridge into the concrete-channeled Alewife Brook, I was surprised to see, for the first time in my

life from such a perspective, a great blue heron lift its head upward at my star-
tled gasp. Then, slowly flapping its wings, the majestic bird rose and fled to a
more secluded location. The powerful sense of awe of this encounter with
urban wildlife was in many ways more memorable than the many other obser-
vations of wildlife made in remote wilderness areas. Again and again it was
those memories of the heron looking up at me and of the cars stranded in the
floodwaters that I kept alive in my mind while I worked on the master plan for
my neighborhood greenspace of the Alewife Reservation and Greenway.

INTRODUCTION

The Alewife Brook area, part of the Mystic River Watershed, is Boston's most
polluted and flood-prone drainage basin. Situated at the periphery of the four
communities of Cambridge, Arlington, Belmont, and Somerville in the northwest corner of the greater metropolitan region, the Alewife Brook area has
become a marginalized, abused, and often forgotten landscape, a microcosm
of urban planning and design at its very worst. A history of massive hydrological manipulation of what once was referred to as the "Great Swamp" has
left a mere sliver of greenspace surrounded by a network of strangling roads,
infringing homes, and threatening suburban and industrial development. The
conflicting visions for use of the neglected neighborhoods, industrial brownfields, degraded waterscapes, and forgotten parklands provide a wonderful
opportunity for tackling the challenges and complexities involved with undertaking restorative redevelopment in an overdeveloped watershed.

This final chapter outlines elements of water-sensitive planning and design
that were incorporated into the master plan for the region of the Alewife
Reservation and Greenway (TBG 2003). Frequent reference will be made to
many of the perspectives covered in chapters 1 through 10 in order to show
how these can be applied to understanding and managing the effects of sprawl
upon a single, nonglamorous location that is illustrative of many watersheds
that are environmentally stressed due to development. It is particularly interesting to note in this regard the difference in tone and long-term objectives
between the ecological goals of this master plan and the much more limited
landscape architecture objectives of the master plan outlined in chapter 10.
This difference is a result of the heightened environmental sensitivity of the
Alewife Reservation and Greenway compared to that of the nearby Charles
River and is also due to an increased ecological consciousness that has per-
meated many planning departments and other public agencies.

Many place names are mentioned in the subsequent text, and these can easily be found and followed by consulting the master plan maps that are avail-

able at http://www.friendsofalewifereservation.org. My purpose, however, in presenting the detail below is to provide an example of how to communicate the perspectives described in the earlier chapters to the general public when writing such a master plan. In other words, this is the type and tone of information that will be useful for anyone charged with the task of fleshing out the skeleton of a master plan for any developed watershed.

Master Plan Justification: Context for Preserving Urban Wetlands, River Corridors, and Wild Spaces

The Alewife Reservation and Alewife Brook represent two important ecological habitat types—an urban wetland wild and an urban river corridor.

Wetlands

Wetlands combine the beauty of aesthetic form and ecological function in ways that few other landforms can match and provide at least four important roles (chapter 6):

Hydrology Modifiers.   Wetlands are "wet lands" and as such are tightly coupled with the hydrological cycle. Wetlands operate like giant sponges in that they slow down and absorb excess stormwater runoff, then gradually release the stored water over a prolonged period. This reduces peak flows downstream and lessens the chances of flooding. By reducing the velocity of floodwaters, sediments are precipitated and the threat of downstream erosion scouring is therefore lessened.

Contaminant Sinks.   Wetlands operate like landscape kidneys in that they retain and remove environmental contaminants through the use of a variety of transformations involving physical, chemical, and biological processes (chapter 9). In some cases, concentrations of contaminants can be reduced by more than 90 percent following water passage through a wetland.

Wildlife Centers.   In some watersheds, the most important role of wetlands may be their ability to structure and maintain biological integrity. The complex physical form and variable water depths of wetlands allow for the development of emergent, submerged, and floating vegetation, which in turn attracts a wide variety of animals for spawning, nesting, breeding, feeding, predator refuge, and nursery-rearing purposes. Also, wetlands are the most botanically productive habitats on earth, and as a result they support an exceptionally high number of animals. And although wetlands constitute only 5 percent of the total land surface area, over a third of all rare and endangered animal species are found there (chapter 6).

Human Amenities. Wetlands, long regarded pejoratively as "wastelands," are now recognized as providing a great number of benefits to humans. Wetlands are among the most beautiful of all landscapes and supply valued visual enjoyment and an area for varied recreational activities (chapter 9). Often being situated between residential and industrial sites, wetlands provide a wild buffer to ameliorate the stresses of increasingly urbanized lifestyles. Because early natives and colonists often settled close to wetlands due to their role as food sources, these regions often harbor a rich cultural heritage. And wetlands offer a myriad of opportunities for formalized natural history study.

River Corridors

River corridors can be the most attractive elements of urban landscapes and can provide at least four important roles (chapters 6 and 10):

Water Quality and Quantity Regulators. One of the most important functions of riparian (shoreline) forests is in filtering surface runoff and protecting downstream aquatic environments from nonpoint-source contamination. Rivers convey stormwater pulses away from sensitive areas, and their floodplains act to slow down and further treat the water during its transport.

Landscape Transformers. Rivers do not carve up the landscape in threatening, haphazard fashion. Instead, the geomorphology of rivers obeys a series of key principles that determine both the amplitude and length of meanders as well as the sequencing of pools and riffles and the occurrence of other instream landforms (chapter 1). Natural rivers are characterized by a dynamic equilibrium wherein the amount of bankside sediment being eroded in one area is balanced by that being deposited in another area.

Wildlife Connectivity. Riverways bounded by riparian forests operate as highway corridors for the relatively safe movement of animals between isolated patches of preferable habitat in a landscape that is increasingly becoming fragmented through human development. Because of this, in many regions riverways serve as important refugia for animals and support a biodiversity much greater than that found in nearby terrestrial, upland regions.

Human Greenways. Riverfronts operate as focal points for human activity —industrial, residential, and recreational. Consequently, riverfront areas, particularly confluences between streams, are often among the most important archeological sites found in any region. People are drawn to rivers for the emotional release and solace offered by flowing waters. And recreationalists are attracted to greenway parks because they frequently offer the longest trail systems uninterrupted by motorized road crossings.

Urban Wilds

Urbanization and residential sprawl consume an inordinate amount of the landscape and can exact a hard-to-measure toll on the well-being of city dwellers. In the face of increasing development pressures, urban wilds offer a respite and are integral in educating and developing an environmental consciousness in children who may not have easy access to more natural, rural ecologies (chapter 2). Most importantly, urban wilds challenge the erroneous belief in a nonoverlapping dualism of "nature" and "culture." By providing a glimpse of the vestiges of natural systems in the city, urban wilds can offer feelings of remoteness and connectivity to an earlier time. And of course, ecologically, such areas serve as important island oases for sustaining wildlife biodiversity surrounded by an inhospitable sea of roads and buildings.

Background and Purpose of Master Plan

The Massachusetts state government's Metropolitan District Commission (MDC) (whose name has been recently changed to the Department of Conservation and Recreation but will be referred to by the old and historic moniker in this chapter) is a major property owner in the Alewife area, having management control of the majority of the greenspace located there, including the 115-acre Alewife Reservation and the 2.5-mile Alewife Brook and adjacent greenway. The recognized historical, recreational, and environmental significance of this area, together with its current neglected and degraded state, motivated the MDC to develop a master plan for the habitat enhancement and ecological restoration of the Alewife Reservation and Greenway (TBG 2003).

In particular, the purpose of the master plan was to address the following key principles of ecological restoration deemed necessary by the MDC for this area:

- Suggest recommendations that will preserve and protect the present aquatic and riparian (shoreline) resources from threats of further degradation.
- Present designs to restore, wherever possible, the natural structure and functions of ecological integrity in ways that are self-sustaining through time.

• Situate all planning recommendations for the reservation and the greenway within a larger watershed or landscape context.
• Advance approaches that will mitigate or buffer agents of future degradation through the use of natural techniques of environmental repair.

Vision Statement, Goals, and Objectives

The Alewife Reservation and Greenway is situated at a precise location, both physically as well as conceptually, to function as an important nexus in both the ecology of its natural inhabitants and the lives of its nearby human residents (France 2002f). Above all, the Alewife area is about *connections*—connections of hydrological systems into a common gathering place (with a consequent problem of flooding); connections of wildlife to a seminatural area that is one of the largest urban wilds in the Boston area and therefore serves as an important oasis for sustaining biodiversity; connections of people, physically, to a gathering place of high visibility and central location within a regional network of recreation trails; and also connections of people, conceptually in time, to the last remnant of the Great Swamp, an area with an extremely rich historical legacy of early settlement and industrial development for this region of Boston.

Based on the MDC planning aspirations to preserve, maintain, and enhance open spaces and ecological resources while reconnecting people to these areas as much as possible, and also based on active solicitation of other suggestions from the public, four overall master planning goals were annunciated, each comprised of three to four major objectives (TBG 2003). It is important to recognize that although described individually below, many of these objectives for restoring and enhancing the Alewife Reservation and Greenway are overlapping in nature, such that by addressing one of them, others will simultaneously benefit.

Goal 1: Improve Water Quality and Restore Natural Hydrology

Major Objectives

• Protect existing and increase the future storage capacity of stormwater runoff to reduce threats of flooding.
• Decrease pollution from discharges of combined sewer outfalls (CSO) that overflow during times of storms.
• Decrease nonpoint sources of pollution from stormwater runoff by implementing traditional and innovative best management practices (BMPs).
• Reestablish a more stable and natural stream geomorphology.

Goal 2: Protect and Enhance Wildlife Habitat

Major Objectives

- Improve migratory and spawning habitat for anadromous (ocean-running) fish, especially the alewife—the namesake species for the entire region.
- Enhance and expand aquatic and riparian habitat for avian and mammal species.
- Protect and expand ecological connections to neighboring properties and nearby open spaces with a larger landscape perspective.
- Manage the study area to enhance species and habitat diversity (e.g., favor native species over invasives, and ensure protection of existing uplands).

Goal 3: Improve Recreational, Educational, and Cultural Opportunities

Major Objectives

- Facilitate public use of the reservation and linear greenway.
- Increase valuation of reservation by users and other stakeholders.
- Interpret ecological and cultural history from the time of the Great Swamp to today's relict wetland ecosystem.

Goal 4: Provide for Maintenance That Minimizes Costs and Maximizes Effectiveness

Major Objectives

- Create a low-maintenance and long-term self-sustaining landscape.
- Facilitate a citizen-based monitoring and stewardship program.
- Identify sources for funding and partnerships for implementing the master plan.

The master plan presents a comprehensive set of planning and design recommendations for restoring and enhancing the Alewife Reservation and Alewife Greenway. Both short-term and long-term solutions are proposed to set this process in motion. It is important to interpret the actions described as setting the foundations for moving toward establishing a sustainable future where humans and wildlife can harmoniously coexist in an urban wetland/river corridor landscape. In other words, the master plan should be regarded as a flexible prescription for watershed stewardship that is subject to revision depending on future conditions and circumstances and whose evolution and ultimate success will depend on the continued and dedicated efforts

of government and concerned citizens. At such a time as these recommendations are implemented, it is hoped that the result will be creation of an ecologically and socially vibrant urban wild and greenway—a restored link in
Charles Eliot's century-old vision of a continuous ringed park system
throughout the suburbs of metropolitan Boston (France 2002f).

History of the Study Area

Cultural

The Alewife area is steeped in a rich cultural history (France 2002f; TBG
2003). In precolonial times, the area was inhabited by Pawtuckeog Amerindi-
ans. Archeological evidence has revealed that a permanent winter camp was
established at the confluence of the Menotomy River (now the Alewife Brook)
with the larger Mystic River. And in the spring of each year, these Native
Americans would establish seasonal camps along the shores of Spy and Little
Ponds as well as on the natural high point situated near the present-day
Alewife subway station (later to be referred to by the European settlers as
"Black Island"). The Native Americans were drawn to this area at a time when
it was still a vibrant tidal marsh for purposes of catching the annual spawning
migration runs of alewife (*Alosa psuedoharengus*) and blueback herring
(*Alosa aestivalis*). In-stream fishing weirs along the Alewife Brook were used
to gather the abundant fishes, which were then dried, smoked, and stored for
later use as a major winter food staple. High points in or around the marsh
were used as hunting camps for parties pursuing the abundant waterfowl that
the wetland supported. It was along the Alewife Brook that Squaw Sachem, a
local tribal leader, deeded to the colonists those lands that would later become
the towns of Charlestown, Cambridge, and Watertown, in return for a small
annual gift of corn and title to her wigwam site overlooking Mystic Lake.

Given the proximity of the Alewife area to the developing towns of Boston
and Charlestown, and the rich upland soils found around the perimeter of the
tidal marsh, the study area was used from the earliest days of European settlement in the Bay Colony region. Soon to be referred to by the colonists as the
Great Swamp, the first inroads into the area occurred for establishment of the
common grazing land known as Black Island. With the growth in population
of Newtowne (now Cambridge), more and more of the marsh was ditched and
drained, first for pastureland and later for orchards. The last vegetable farm
persisted until the early 1950s. The first cartways penetrated the Great Swamp
in the seventeenth century, linking Cambridge with Concord. Later, the bridge
where what is now Massachusetts Avenue crosses the Alewife Brook from
Cambridge to Arlington was used by the British during their retreat from the
historic skirmishes at Concord and Lexington.

Industrial

In a period when wetlands were commonly regarded as wastelands, the area of the Great Swamp was looked upon by the colonists as an attractive location for siting those industrial activities whose presence was deemed undesirable in close proximity to the inhabitants of the developing town. The operation of tanneries, slaughterhouses, glue factories, and transportation staging areas along the banks of the Alewife Brook was integral to supporting the cattle drives and markets that took place nearby at Porter Square. During the early nineteenth century, the ice harvesting industry at Fresh and Spy Ponds became one of the first international business ventures of the newly independent country, the ice being shipped around the world. It was, however, a product of the last ice age—the thick deposits of alluvial clay underneath the Great Swamp would inspire the industry that would do the most to transform the entire Alewife landscape. From the middle of the nineteenth century through to the first decades of the twentieth century, numerous clay pits were dug into the Great Swamp to extract the valuable building material. Today, Yates, Jerry, and Blair Ponds are remnants of this period, whereas similar clay pits have since disappeared beneath the Danehy Park landfill and the Rindge Towers apartment blocks. Along with the clay industry came roads and rail lines, ovens and warehouses, and housing developments and suburban infrastructure that would together serve to accelerate the eventual destruction of the Great Swamp.

During the twentieth century, the Alewife area continued to be treated with the same disregard to environmental integrity that it had been since colonial times. Residential sprawl, ironworks, waste dump sites, chemical manufacturing plants, office buildings, the Fresh Pond Shopping Mall, a drive-in theater, automobile shops, landfills, gas stations, entertainment clubs, and other activities have all left their scars upon the once natural landscape. Together, these actions are those to be expected for such a marginalized "edge city" where environmentally harmful activities are pushed to the outer fringes of inhabited areas. During the last few decades of the twentieth century, the Alewife area became host to one of the most contentious environmental debates to ever occur in the Commonwealth of Massachusetts. The widening of the Route 2 Highway and the extension of the Red Line subway pitted groups of state and city planners and concerned citizens against one another and brought new attention to an area that had all but been forgotten. Today, as the remaining greenspaces dwindle within the Alewife area, heightened debates have begun about how to maintain the last sliver of the Great Swamp that still exists within the MDC's Alewife Reservation and how best to go about protecting it and the Alewife Greenway from further degradation due to continued threats from development and pollution.

Environmental

The trade-offs between the cultural development and the environment of the Alewife area have been felt hardest in relation to the consequent manipulations that have occurred to the waterscape. The gradual encroachment of first colonial farms followed by industrial development and then suburban sprawl have all whittled away the Great Swamp through ditching, diking, draining, and dredging. Even so, during the middle of the nineteenth century, in the area that is today the Alewife Reservation, it was still possible to see a diverse bird fauna. By the start of the twentieth century, however, the wetland was regarded by most as being nothing more than a dumpsite for animal waste and garbage. One of the first substantive hydrological changes occurred toward the end of the nineteenth century when the connection of Alewife Brook to Fresh Pond was severed in order to preserve the water quality of the latter, which had become the drinking water supply reservoir for the city of Cambridge. In time, the Alewife Brook and several other inflowing tributaries would disappear under concrete and be all but lost to memory. The most serious hydrological alterations occurred in the first decade of the twentieth century when the Craddock Dam was built on the Mystic River in Medford, thereby preventing tidal flows (and spawning fish) from moving upstream. What had once been a dynamic tidally influenced marsh now became a freshwater wetland where the stagnant water bred mosquitoes and led to fears of potential malarial outbreaks. This led to a massive excavation project in 1909–1912, when the formerly meandering Alewife Brook was straightened, deepened, channelized, and widened, all in an effort to further drain the Great Swamp. During the 1930s, in an effort to claim yet more land from the wetland, the Little River was moved to its new and more conveniently located channel and its old course filled in.

The legacy of these hydrological changes has been a loss of over 90 percent of the surface area of the Great Swamp. This has had its most serious consequence for humans in terms of the resulting flooding. The remaining portion of the wetland, located within the Alewife Reservation and squeezed between the Route 2 Highway and several buildings to the north and the office developments and subway station to the south, is today simply incapable of absorbing all the stormwater runoff that enters into the system. The flooding situation has increased in severity due to the continual development that has occurred within the watershed, paving over more and more land and thereby decreasing the potential for the rain to infiltrate into the ground and slowly make its way to the Alewife Brook. Presently, plans are being discussed to consider converting a portion of the reservation into a constructed treatment wetland in order to increase the capacity for flood storage and contaminant removal (TBG 2003).

Planning and Management

The Alewife area has been the object of many studies and resulting plans both for development and for open-space preservation in the face of that development. The area has received international attention and is studied as an example of postwar American urban planning and design at its worst. In 1995, in a special issue of a local newspaper, an editorial referred to the Alewife area as a place where earth and water, culture and nature, suburb and city collide, becoming a case history in the complexities of land-use planning that have been chronically unresolved. And in 2002, a report published on the history of the Great Swamp concluded with the belief that seldom has an area been both so trashed and so valiantly defended.

In the last years of the nineteenth century, the visionary landscape architect Charles Eliot planned the Alewife Brook Parkway as one link in his ranging network of river carriageway parks winding their way through the suburbs of Boston. The Alewife Reservation, which has existed as such since the early twentieth century, was not purchased with the intent of being an open-space jewel but really exists as a by-product of Eliot's desire to connect the Mystic River with Fresh Pond. Starting in the mid-1970s, spurred by the growing controversies about the widening of Route 2 and the Red Line extension and continuing unrelentingly until the present time, plan after plan has been made about how to best manage, develop, or preserve the Alewife area. Topics have included industrial revitalization, sustainable development, wildlife preservation, stormwater management, transportation planning, open-space management, brownfield redevelopment, office building construction, and river corridor park design. With particular reference to the MDC managed land, notable studies include two open-space plans for the Alewife Reservation in 1978 and 1985, a restoration plan for segments of the Alewife Brook Parkway in 1996, and a master plan for Blair Pond in 1999. The master plan (TBG 2003) built upon this excellent work as well as integrated many other technical studies that have been conducted over the years to create the most comprehensive plan yet produced for this important urban greenspace.

Plan Development

The master plan was developed through a three-phase planning process: Inventory of Resources, Opportunities and Options, and Planning and Design Recommendations (TBG 2003). At all stages, the process relied upon iterative inputs obtained from a concerned citizenry of neighbors, abutters, local officials, and interest groups garnered through both public meetings and solicited comments.

Summary of Phase I: Inventory of Resources

As a first step in the development of a master plan, it is essential to obtain a comprehensive, spatially explicit inventory of the conditions of the physical, biological, and cultural resources in the study area. Once such a resource inventory was established, this information was used to identify the opportunities and options in Phase II.

The Inventory of Resources (TBG 2003) was assessed by a detailed program of site visits, research of previously published documents, collation of additional relevant data from archives and libraries, and consideration of public input. Elements that were specifically examined included the physical resources of topography, geology, soils, hydrology, and geomorphology; the biological resources of fishes, terrestrial flora and fauna species, habitat types, invasive species, rare or endangered species of special concern, and ecosystem functions; and the cultural and socioeconomic resources of historical sites, open-space recreation areas, existing land uses, contaminated sites, utilities, and location of stakeholders and concerned citizenry.

A series of comprehensive maps was produced identifying those locations in the Alewife Reservation and Greenway that are particularly significant in terms of a diversity of resources. Some of these findings will be reviewed in the location-specific discussions of site conditions and suggested recommendations covered subsequently. Below is a very brief summary of some of the more salient findings considered from a general perspective (France 2002f).

Physical Resources

The study area is a low-lying remnant of the Great Swamp, having elevation rises of no more than ten feet, a longitudinal change in elevation along its entire length of less than half a foot, and an average elevation of only several feet above sea level. Following the retreat of the glaciers and formation of the nearby kettle lakes of Fresh and Spy Ponds, the soils deposited were those characteristic of poorly drained glacial outwash plains. Most of these soils have been disturbed as a result of the major intrusions into the Great Swamp. Hydrologically, the area is composed of a series of wetlands, marshes, ponds (both natural and human-created), rivers, and streams. Much of the entire area lies within the hundred-year floodplain with saturated soils located at depths from only one to nine feet below the ground surface. Flooding has been a persistent and serious problem for nearby residents, exacerbated by the fact that more than sixty storm drains and CSOs empty into the ponds and streams in the area, sometimes transporting raw sewage into home basements (this is similar to the problem once faced by the nearby Charles River, as outlined in chapter 2). Large expanses of shorelines have become degraded due to erosion, invasive species colonization, indiscriminate and inappropriate riparian development, and channel engineering modification.

Biological Resources

Although once supporting thriving populations of a diversity of fishes, today the Alewife Brook watershed is largely depauperate of all except those species most tolerant of pollution and habitat degradation. For example, preliminary surveys of benthic macroinvertebrates (France, unpubl. data) were conducted to create an index of biotic integrity (see chapter 3). Sadly, only a few alewife and blueback herring seem able to make their way into the system to spawn, while the most commonly observed species is the nonnative carp (*Cyprinus carpio*). The Alewife Reservation and Greenway land administered by the MDC is made up of a mosaic of small natural and human-created habitat types. The aquatic resources include ponds, streams, and wetlands (shallow marshes, woodland swamps, shrub swamps, wet meadows, drainage ditches, and proposed stormwater treatment basins). The terrestrial resources include closed-canopy woodlands, open-canopy mixed shrub woodlands, grasslands, parklands and lawns, parkway edges of sidewalks and scattered trees, athletic fields, paved roads and parking lots and other impervious surfaces, bikeways and pedestrian paths, and buildings. The Alewife Reservation and Greenway are home to numerous species of plants and vertebrate and invertebrate animals, including more than two hundred species of plants, eighty species of birds, fifteen species of mammals, and four species of reptiles. The most serious nuisance invasive plants are Japanese knotweed (*Polygonum vaccinifolium*) and the common reed (*Phragmites australis*). There are no official records of federal- or state-listed rare, endangered, or protected species in the study area, though there have been public sightings of some raptors of special concern. The most important "ecological services" provided to the surrounding communities by the study area include flood-storage capacity, stormwater treatment and contaminant removal, microclimate mediation, wildlife habitat, and a corridor of ecological connectivity from the Charles River to the Mystic River and Boston Harbor.

Cultural and Socioeconomic Resources

The Alewife study area provides a rich tapestry chronicling the settlement and development of the New England coastal landscape with many sites of historical interest and significance. The Alewife Reservation is the largest open space for recreation in the city of Cambridge, blessed by an ideal situation in relation to regional bike and pedestrian paths, proximity to the subway transit station, nearby playing fields and residential developments, and easy access from a system of roads and parking lots. The study area is surrounded by a diversity of land uses including commercial shopping districts, industrial and corporate centers, residential communities of predominantly high density, and some public open space. More than fifty contaminated or waste disposal sites are located within the study boundaries or on the study area periphery. The Alewife Brook Greenway serves as a utility corridor containing gas line easements, telephone lines, and sewer and storm drain pipes. More than a dozen citizen interest groups are focused on the Alewife study area, sometimes sharing common concerns, sometimes positioned at cross purposes to one another. Prevalent issues of these groups include, but are not restricted to, flooding abatement and water-quality improvement, sustaining biological diversity within the reservation, developing educational opportunities for local schools, and monitoring and influencing current and proposed future development projects in the area.

Summary of Phase II: Opportunities and Options

An option-strategy protocol (France, unpubl. data) as in chapter 4 was used as the foundation upon which to itemize and delineate a wide range of issues and ideas that were explored in terms of how their implementation would influence design and decision criteria for addressing the goals and objectives of the master plan. Some of these concepts will be reviewed in the location-specific discussions of site conditions and suggested recommendations in the next section. Below is a brief summary of some of the more significant opportunities and options considered from a general perspective.

Goal 1: Improve Water Quality and Restore Natural Hydrology. Efforts should be made by all towns to decrease pollution (especially fecal coliform bacteria) from CSO discharges by eliminating cross-contamination and illicit connections to storm drains. In addition, nonpoint sources of pollution carried by stormwater runoff from lawns and parking lots need to be addressed through implementation of low-impact development (LID) techniques such as replacing curbs, gutters, inlets, and drains wherever possible with infiltration swales (chapter 8). Attempts should be made to increase the detention time within existing wetlands and to use phytoremediation techniques to remove contaminants (chapter 9). Replacement of concrete, trapezoidal channels and buried streams with more stable and natural stream geomorphology through stabilization of streambanks with bioengineering procedures will reduce erosion and contaminant transport. Consideration of development caps on impervious surfaces (chapter 5) will increase infiltration and enhance the flood-storage capacity of the study area (chapter 8).

Goal 2: Protect and Enhance Wildlife Habitat. Attention should be paid to establishing a network of diverse habitats, especially in terms of acquiring and protecting all abutting wetlands and upland areas, to enhance habitat for migrating bird species. Provision is needed for more wild, ecologically sensitive areas within the reservation with low human use. Attempts should be made to enhance, wherever possible, ecological connections within the study area and in relation to surrounding natural areas (chapter 6). The further spread of invasive plants and animal species (both terrestrial and aquatic) must be curtailed. Improvements need to be implemented to facilitate anadromous fish passage and to create new spawning habitats.

Goal 3: Improve Recreational, Educational, and Cultural Opportunities. Efforts should be made to facilitate and improve the public use of the reservation and greenway by implementation of such approaches as better defining the MDC parkland boundaries; enhancing vistas though creative plantings and site designs; screening abutting areas for privacy and unwanted views; integrating the study area lands into the regional open-space network; developing appropriate areas for water access to encourage boating and fishing; tackling the delicate but essential task of reclaiming MDC parkland for public use from private encroachments; and optimizing access, parking, and pedestrian/vehicular circulation (chapter 10). The latter efforts could be established through improved linkages to the surrounding trail systems, formalization of a hierarchy of trails within the study area that provides for safety and develops from several strategically placed entry nodes, and creation of viewing platforms to minimize intrusion into ecologically sensitive areas (chapter 10).

Goal 4: Provide for Maintenance That Minimizes Costs and Maximizes Effectiveness. There is a recognized need to work with abutters, concerned citizens, and interest groups to establish a creative and self-sustaining long-term plan to perpetuate the goals of the master plan. Efforts need to be made to encourage and enhance citizen-based monitoring and management programs to ensure that progress is made toward actualizing the objectives of the master plan. Approaches to raise the ecological literacy (chapter 2) through fostering communication are of obvious importance in accomplishing this task (chapters 3 and 10). Creative means need to be explored for obtaining ongoing funding for restoration and maintenance that will maximize environmental involvement and stewardship of surrounding industries and businesses.

The Opportunities and Options phase of the master plan developed two alternatives differing in their attitudes toward balancing human and ecological concerns. A series of detailed maps was produced that specifically identified and contrasted the two proposals as part of the overall working process of soliciting public input in creation of the present planning document. The two working alternatives are summarized below. It is important to note that the master plan incorporates a blend of elements from both of these early alternatives that were deemed by the public, the MDC administrators, and the planning team as being the most desirable and achievable options for implementation (TBG 2003). Plans exist to merge these alternatives with those that have begun to be developed for the wider watershed (France, unpubl. data) into models of future development scenarios (as in chapter 7).

Alternative 1. The main emphasis of this alternative would be directed toward fostering ecological restoration, with the connection of wildlife and habitats (chapter 6) being the key result over cultural benefits. This would be brought about by restricting access to ecological resource areas through minimizing recreational features such as pathways. Overall, the protection, restoration, and creation of a diverse mosaic of habitat types would be given high priority, and the entire study area, both the reservation and the greenway, would be managed as a valuable natural resource area (wetlands, forested upland areas, riparian buffer zones, wildflower meadows) with important ecological functions. Flood-storage capacity would be increased by converting several riparian recreational areas into new wetland systems (chapter 9). Land acquisitions, agreements about conservation easements, etc., would be emphasized.

Alternative 2. The main emphasis of this alternative would be directed toward developing recreation, with the connection of people to use of the study area as a park dominating over ecological benefits (as the other MDC master plan described in chapter 10). This would be brought about by developing an extensive path system and making all areas accessible for people. Habitat restoration would still take place, but the budget would be considerably less and therefore the possibilities more limited than for Alternative 1. Priority would therefore be given for allocation of most of the resources to provide for people benefits such that the greenway would be managed as a landscaped park rather than as a wildlife corridor (chapter 10).

MASTER PLAN RECOMMENDATIONS

General Recommendation Summary by Category

The site improvements and amenities described in the master plan are closely linked to one another in their function and were designed to reflect the goals of improving connections for water, wildlife, and people. The basic design criteria of the master plan (TBG 2003) adopted from the option-strategy protocol exercise were to:

- Incorporate innovative stormwater management techniques into the infrastructure design.
- Create a network of wildlife habitat and plant communities using native species.
- Concentrate primary pathways along the Alewife Brook and Greenway, leaving the Alewife Reservation for passive recreation with minimized disturbance in sensitive wildlife habitat areas.
- Include educational components to highlight natural and cultural processes through innovative design and exposed infrastructure.
- Integrate educational, interpretive, and directional elements with public art.
- Use sustainable and recycled materials where possible.

The master plan (TBG 2003) details hydrological and hydraulic improvements by increasing flood-storage volume through dredging, wetland creation, and removing channel obstructions; decreasing sedimentation and increasing water quality by enhancing buffer areas; and incorporating innovative LID techniques to treat stormwater runoff (chapters 6, 7, 8, 9 and 10).

The restoration and enhancement of wildlife habitats will be accomplished by increasing the area and connectivity of wetlands and riparian and upland forests, improving soil conditions in association with removing exotic plant species, replacing lawn areas with either shoreline plantings or upland meadows, and creating stormwater treatment areas that double as biodiversity centers (chapters 6, 8, 9 and 10).

Circulation and access improvements (chapter 10) in the master plan involved the design of gateways and entrances to the Alewife Reservation and Greenway at strategic locations and careful attention to the issues of parking, public transportation, and pedestrian circulation patterns and connectivity including bridges, overlooks, and crossings in addition to the nature of path surfaces as well as landscape furnishings such as benches, lights, bike racks, etc.

As in chapter 10, the master plan considered opportunities to educate visitors about the history of the Alewife area to be of major importance. The three major themes that served as the basis for developing interpretive features included past (industrial and agricultural), present, and future land use; changes to the natural system and ecology of the area; and Native American settlement history and use of the Great Swamp.

In addition to issues addressing safety and security and delineating and screening the private-public property interface (chapter 10), the master plan

(TBG 2003) indicated two other elements that were important to meeting the goals:

- Using both permanent and temporary installations of public art as an element of education and for creating visual connections between spaces and habitats that are not immediately apparent to a visitor.
- Providing as many opportunities as possible to allow visitors to experience the water in new ways.

Recommendations by Study Area

The following discussion of study areas is arranged in hydrologic order, moving from the westernmost headwater areas near Little Pond, through the Alewife Reservation and past the subway station, and then along the course of the Alewife Brook until it terminates at the Mystic River, which in turn flows eastward into Boston Harbor. Two independent surveys of existing conditions (France, unpubl. data) based on large woody debris (LWD) and a macroinvertebrate index of biotic integrity (IBI) are adopted from chapters 1 and 3, respectively. Many of the points raised in the recommendation sections below are those discussed in chapters 6, 8, 9 and 10.

Little Pond

Existing Conditions and Key Challenges (France 2002f). Much of the shoreline of Little Pond (the westernmost source for much of the water that flows through the Alewife Brook) has been modified, and few aquatic plants are present. More than a dozen stormwater outfalls enter the pond, including a large box-culvert that receives a major portion of the runoff from the city of Belmont. The former MDC ice rink area located to the north of the pond is important for flood storage but is presently targeted for recreation development. Although Little Pond is reported to sustain some of the few spawning populations of herring in the area, fishing for all warm-water species seems to have decreased in recent years, possibly due to declines in water quality. The IBI indicated a "stressed" system, and the abundance of LWD was moderate. Trees and shrubs dominate about a third of the shoreline, the rest being occupied by residential yard and lawn encroachments. The bordering lands are important for harboring a variety of avian and mammalian wildlife. Due to the encroachments, no trails circumnavigate Little Pond, though the site does serve as a gateway to the reservation from several access points. No important cultural resources exist in the area.

Recommendations (TBG 2003)

- Reclaim all encroachments and restore the riparian buffer and shoreline around Little Pond.
- Determine sediment depths and explore the feasibility of dredging Little Pond.
- Create predator-free islands in the pond that could serve as avian nesting habitat.
- Convert mowed grass south of the pond into low-maintenance meadow communities to increase the diversity of habitat types and reduce goose feeding.
- Install paths, benches, and overlooks at strategic locations to allow for better access to the reservation and pond edge.
- Use porous pavement to create a new ecologically sensitive parking lot.

North Side of Little River and the Alewife Reservation

Existing Conditions and Key Challenges (France 2002f). This entire portion of Alewife Reservation is situated within the hundred-year floodplain, and much of it is classified as wetland habitat. Several storm drains from the office property of Arthur D. Little (ADL) enter the river. The banks of the Little River (the major tributary to the Alewife Brook) are heavily vegetated with trees and shrubs that provide shade over the water. Aquatic habitat structure is limited to woody debris, and numerous carp are present. Several groves of closed-canopy woodlands exist in the area to the west of the ADL buildings, whereas scattered trees are found to the east of the ADL parking lot. Important wildlife habitats include the wetlands and uplands located in the abutting private lands to the northwest of the reservation, some targeted for future development. The contiguous open space of the reservation is broken by the large parcel of developed private land (Acorn Park) that stretches from very near the bank of the river north to the Route 2 Highway and has a long history of flooding. Additional abutting land that serves flood-storage and wildlife-sustaining roles is privately owned and situated on the north side of Route 2 in Arlington. A dirt trail runs from the Route 2 access road to the MDC-leased ADL parking lot and then soon disappears near where the property fence comes down to the riverbank. The only cultural site in the area is the former location of the last vegetable farm located near Acorn Park Drive.

Recommendations (TBG 2003)

- Determine the depth of unconsolidated sediment in the Little River and Perch Pond, explore the feasibility of dredging to increase channel depth and flood-storage capacity, and introduce appropriate substrate to sustain invertebrate species fed on by fish.

- Stabilize eroding streambanks with native vegetation using bioengineering techniques.
- Restore wetlands on the former ADL parking lot, including open water, marsh, and an upland island, and connect these restored wetlands to the existing wetlands.
- Expand the drainage ditches that connect the ADL wetland with the Little River to provide a larger open-water area that can be used by a variety of species.
- Identify and certify vernal ponds (seasonal pools that are free of fish) near Little Pond to protect this valuable habitat, especially for amphibians.
- Increase opportunities for people to connect with the water by removing fences and building paths, bridges, and a boardwalk to create a circular-loop trail system that, at the same time, will avoid the largest contiguous areas of wildlife habitat.
- Provide an ecologically sensitive parking area near the old ADL site that can serve as a boat launch into an open-water area connected to the Little River.
- Place subtle educational and interpretive signage in key locations explaining the function of wetland systems and their history in the Alewife area.

South Side of Little River and the Alewife Reservation

Existing Conditions and Key Challenges (France 2002f).   Most of this section of the Alewife Reservation lies within the hundred-year floodplain and is consequently classified as wetland habitat. A number of major combined sewer outfalls discharge into the Little River from the south (Cambridge) that seriously degrade the water quality, as does Wellington Brook (another small feeder stream) that enters the western portion of the reservation from Blair Pond. The substrate of the Little River is difficult to judge, as the water is always very murky. LWD is negligible. Encroachments exist from the apartment complex located near Perch Pond. The southern banks of Little River are heavily vegetated by a variety of colonizing shrubs and contain patches of canopied woodlands. Disturbed land in the form of a mosaic of hummocks and a flood-protecting berm exist in this area as a result of piled fill from construction of the rail line. This is the largest contiguous stretch of land in the reservation and, as a result, supports a diversity of wildlife. The entire southern edge of the reservation is bordered by a large sand and gravel pathway that runs west from the subway station to Blanchard Road in Belmont. A network of unplanned and overgrown dirt trails leads off this major pathway and penetrate the reservation south of Little River without, however, the option for circulation. An important access point exists at Perch Pond, where a trail makes a dangerous crossing of the rail line to reach Blair Pond immediately south of the reservation. Notable cultural resources include the former location of one of the most important farms in the area, now occupied by the Hills Estates apartment complex, the old ice industry rail line running along the southern edge of the reservation, and the historic Black Island upland area that served as a Native American hunting camp and as the colonial grazing common, now mostly covered by an industrial building.

Recommendations (TBG 2003)

- Stabilize the eroding banks at Wellington Brook through bioengineering techniques and enhanced forested riparian buffer to reduce sediment input into the stream system.
- Create a new stormwater treatment wetland that will also benefit the surrounding wetlands through increased infiltration and temporarily rising groundwater levels.
- Create a major gateway to the reservation at the Alewife subway station, incorporating a proposed bridge over the brook that will connect to a planned bicycle path and a public gathering area featuring interpretive and educational elements.
- Install a circulation system throughout the reservation to provide access to key features and allow for pedestrian loops of various lengths, along which interpretive/educational signage (including real-time water-quality monitoring boards) will be placed at strategic locations.

Alewife Subway Station Area

Existing Conditions and Key Challenges (France 2002f). This section of the Alewife Reservation occurs within the hundred-year floodplain and is classified as wetland habitat. The culvert under Route 2 just downstream from the confluence of Little River with Alewife Brook serves as a major flow constriction that maintains the wetlands in the reservation. Alewife Brook, which emerges from its buried pipe to join Little River near the subway station, contributes contaminated stormwater runoff. Portions of Alewife Brook and Little River near the subway station have been armored to prevent further erosion from the storm runoff surges that occur in the area. Yates Pond is infested by both common reed and Japanese knotweed, has a "poor" IBI rating, and is entirely surrounded by transportation infrastructure, appearing to have lost its hydrological connection to Alewife Brook. Runoff from the subway station parking garage is funneled into Yates Pond. Due to the presence of the subway station, the Minuteman Bicycle Trail, and the nearby recreation fields in both

Arlington and Cambridge, this area is the most important access point to the MDC parklands. The only landscaped portion is the small section where the Minuteman Bicycle Trail passes through the reservation along the Route 2 access road. A paved sidewalk runs along the edge of the subway station access road that overlooks Yates Pond. Yates Pond, a former ice harvesting site, is the only important cultural resource in the area.

Recommendations (TBG 2003)

- Remove invasive species and establish native plantings that can be used to help improve the ability of the area to treat stormwater runoff from the tiered parking lot at the subway station.
- Provide access along Yates Pond with a boardwalk parallel to the sidewalk, providing a safer connection to the nearby path.
- Install interpretive signage and educational features about the clay industry at Yates Pond and about the water quality in the Alewife Brook.

Alewife Brook between Route 2 Rotary and Henderson Bridge

Existing Conditions and Key Challenges (France 2002f).   This section of the Alewife Brook contains more than a dozen stormwater outfalls and flows within a concrete trapezoidal channel that is bordered by a chain-link fence and trees and shrubs, including Japanese knotweed. Aquatic habitat structure is poor given the absence of in-stream plants and the presence of trash, although the abutting so-called cattail marsh (now colonized by common reed) is home to many birds. Residences along the Arlington side of the channel experience frequent and severe flooding, exacerbated by the constriction of the bridge at Massachusetts Avenue. Some encroachments exist in this area. This is a major gateway into the Alewife Reservation and Greenway where the well-utilized Minuteman Bicycle Trail crosses from Cambridge to Arlington on its way to Lexington. A low-use dirt trail, often overgrown with grasses, winds around the cattail marsh and runs alongside the western side of the brook to the landscaped Bicentennial Park situated at Massachusetts Avenue. The eastern border of the Alewife Parkway is fringed with trees, residences, a strip of parkland, and a paved sidewalk. The only cultural structure of note is the Massachusetts Avenue Bridge over which the British forces retreated following the skirmishes at Concord and Lexington during the colonial war.

The section of the Alewife Brook after Massachusetts Avenue continues to flow within a concrete trapezoidal channel into which twenty stormwater outfalls discharge and is bordered by a chain-link fence, trees, and invasive shrubs. Aquatic habitat structure continues to be poor due to absence of in-stream vegetation and LWD and the presence of trash. In addition to a small landscaped continuation of Bicentennial Park beside Massachusetts Avenue, the western side of the brook is accessed by a small dirt path located beside a new hotel and Arlington residences. The eastern border of the parkway is tree lined and includes a paved sidewalk where a few encroachments exist. Cultural resources of note include the historic Cambridge Alms House, in the northern part of the city on the eastern edge of the parkway, and an inflow, which is all that remains of Tannery Brook where industry developed and where a fishing weir had been used by both colonists and Native Americans.

Recommendations (TBG 2003)

- Restore the cattail marsh as an ecologically valuable wetland by investigating the feasibility of excavation to increase flood-storage capacity, by creating a riparian buffer to increase biodiversity and contribute to the treatment of incoming stormwater, and by creating a natural channel connection from the marsh to the Alewife Brook, which would provide potential spawning habitat for fish.
- Investigate the feasibility of removing the concrete lining of the Alewife Brook stream bed and banks and restoring a reforested, sinuous natural channel of varying depth and bed composition that will provide beneficial habitat for aquatic biota and birds as well as reduce peak summer temperatures.
- Selectively remove exotic species in riparian areas and replace with native plant communities.
- Incorporate biofiltration swales into the park design to treat stormwater runoff from the Alewife Brook Parkway, which currently discharges contaminated runoff directly into the brook.
- Replace areas of mown turf grass along the parkway and brook with a low-maintenance, tall-fescue grass mix as well as seeding selected areas as meadows to diversify the habitat.
- Remove the fence along Alewife Brook to allow for better visual access, as it will no longer be needed following naturalization of the banks, which will eliminate the safety hazard of the current steep, concrete banks.
- Enhance circulation along both sides of the Alewife Brook and create a link to the Minuteman Bicycle Trail.
- Improve the Massachusetts Avenue–Alewife Brook Parkway intersection to serve as a gateway to the Alewife Greenway.
- Prune vegetation at bridges to allow for scenic views along the restored river corridor.
- Improve the character of the parkway by roadside plantings and new lights.
- Incorporate Bicentennial Park and Massachusetts Avenue Bridge history into an interpretive program that will also highlight the nearby location of the Native American fishing weir.

• Reclaim MDC land from encroachments to implement the above recommendations.

Alewife Brook between Henderson Bridge and Broadway Avenue

Existing Conditions and Key Challenges (France 2002f). This section of the Alewife Brook contains twenty stormwater outfalls and flows within a fenced, rectangular concrete channel squeezed between St. Paul's Cemetery and the Alewife Parkway. In-stream habitat structure such as LWD for sustaining aquatic resources is almost nonexistent, and the marcroinvertebrate IBI rating is "poor." This is the narrowest portion of the entire greenway with encroachments on either side. The narrow, tree-lined banks of the brook give way to the cemetery on the Arlington side and an eroded paved sidewalk on the Cambridge side that actually overhangs the brook with no trees to shade the water. Views of this section from either the Henderson or Broadway Bridges of the open space of the cemetery are attractive. There are no cultural resources of note.

Recommendations (TBG 2003)

• As for the immediate upstream section, investigate the feasibility of replacing the concrete channel bed with a naturalized form that will have all the aforementioned ecological benefits accruing from such action.
• Install in-stream habitat structures such as woody debris to increase biodiversity and improve water quality.
• Develop stands of riparian vegetation to provide shade and reduce midsummer peak temperatures.
• Construct a path along the brook and attempt to separate as much as possible pedestrians and cyclists from automobiles through strategic plantings.

Alewife Brook between Broadway Avenue and the Mystic Valley Parkway

Existing Conditions and Key Challenges (France 2002f). This section of the Alewife Brook is a natural channel composed of mostly unconsolidated muck with a few locations where bankside destabilization appears imminent. Two dozen storm drains discharge into this section of the brook, which continues to be fenced along its entire length. In-stream habitat structure is formed by LWD, and spawning herring have been observed near the confluence of the Mystic River. The IBI rating is "favorable." Most of the western (Arlington) bank is covered by a dense stand of Japanese knotweed alongside which a dirt pathway runs and into which some encroachments intrude. The eastern (Cambridge) bank is also covered by knotweed except in the Dilboy Field area, where recreational infrastructure and a parking lot front onto the water, severing the dirt riverside pathway in the process. A wide section of parkland exists here, and several encroachments are located across the tree-lined Alewife Parkway. The confluence represents a major gateway to the Alewife Greenway in that it communicates with recreational trails of the Mystic Valley Parkway on either side of the Mystic River that runs from the lake headwaters to Boston Harbor. Two sites of cultural importance are found here: the permanent overwintering campsite of Native Americans at the confluence, and the putative location of another Native American village site across from Dilboy Field that has important historical significance.

Recommendations (TBG 2003)

- Stabilize eroding streambanks with native vegetation, which will reduce sedimentation and thus support a higher aquatic biodiversity
- Plant riparian vegetation to reduce summer temperatures and to provide a supply of woody debris to the brook as well as the avian habitat.
- Create a wildflower meadow south of the baseball field to increase habitat diversity.
- Retrofit the parking lots at Dilboy Stadium with LID techniques to retain and treat runoff from the asphalt surfaces before it enters the brook.
- Install a contiguous pathway for pedestrians and bicyclists.
- Improve the Broadway–Alewife Brook Parkway intersection to serve as a gateway to the Alewife Greenway.
- Create a Gateway Park at the intersection of the Alewife Brook with the Mystic River, which will incorporate park amenities, play features, paths, stream access, and interpretive features about the Native American fishing camps in the area.
- Expand the existing playground north of Broadway to incorporate water play structures to provide water experience for both fun and learning.
- Install a viewing area with streamside benches, and provide boat access at the Dilboy parking lot.
- Improve existing active recreational facilities at the stadium area.

Recommendations Outside the Study Area

Given that the master plan pertains to the reservation and the greenway—a study area that comprises less than 4 percent of the total Alewife watershed—it is naive to think that the MDC land can be successfully managed in isolation, uncoupled from actions taking place simultaneously within the surrounding cityscape (France 2002f). In particular, future plans to develop both the abutting properties as well as the more distant, but still closely ecologically linked, Alewife Industrial Quadrangle area need to be carefully considered in light of their potential impacts to the restored reservation and the downstream greenway. In short, now that a master plan exists for the MDC land, it is important to go back and review, extract, and promulgate the more promising elements from the earlier plans developed for the surrounding area. The various alternative urban planning initiatives should then be examined from a futures scenario perspective (chapter 7) in terms of their merit for sustaining and protecting the investments of the restored Alewife Reservation and Greenway in a context of the watershed and its landscape ecology, regional trail network, and education curricula.

Watershed Planning (Targeting and Sustaining Master Planning Goal 1)

It is essential to place site-specific, restorative designs in both a larger landscape and a larger management context, in this case dealing where the two meet—the watershed. Watersheds are important to urban communities because they help to foster a sense of place in a developed cityscape and because their waters aid in providing much-needed solace in daily lives. Importantly from an environmental perspective, watersheds are the most appropriate units in which to effectively manage water resources in the urban landscape. Following years of benign neglect at best and purposeful detrimental human activity at worst, even if all the recommendations of the master plan are immediately implemented, it is difficult to imagine that the Alewife Reservation and Brook-Greenway will be able to maintain its rejuvenated health in isolation of required changes within the watershed. A cardinal need therefore exists to place the Alewife Reservation and Brook-Greenway back into its landscape and to develop an effective and comprehensive watershed management plan that will prevent, or at least reduce, the severity of the problems that necessitated the restoration efforts in the first place. To tackle issues of watershed restorative redevelopment necessitates embracing a vision that is best approached in small steps in order to ensure the greatest likelihood of success (chapter 2).

The elements that need to be addressed in developing a plan for the Alewife watershed and that are adapted from other studies include:

Land-Use Planning

- Determination of an impervious cover model for the entire watershed (chapter 5).
- Examination of land-use management techniques and predictions from alternative futures development scenarios (chapter 7) for the entire watershed.

Land Conservation

- Identification and prioritization for protection of all water-sensitive development and infiltration sites for the entire watershed (chapter 2).

- Prioritization for protection and possible acquisition of all undeveloped lands adjacent to the potential sites for creation of wetlands (chapter 9) or detention basins to increase flood-storage capacity.

Aquatic Buffers

- Examination of protective buffer-strip creation potential, design, and planting schemes for headwater streams and ponds (chapter 10).

Better Site Design and Stormwater BMPs

- Development of guidance directives for reducing stormwater runoff by encouraging a "start at the source" BMP effort by individual homeowners (chapters 8 and 10).
- Prioritized site assessment of the potential for retrofitting LID stormwater BMPs such as "green parking lots" into the existing urban framework (chapter 8).
- Discouragement of underground stormwater detention basins now used by developers as a means to achieve a no-net discharge of runoff from their sites due to the inadequacy of such systems for concomitantly sustaining wildlife compared to wetland treatment parks (chapter 9).

Erosion and Sediment Control

- Development of guidance directives for reducing erosion effects by all property owners.
- Prioritized site-exploration assessment of the potential for retrofitting erosion control BMPs into the existing urban framework (chapters 8 and 10).

Nonstormwater Discharges

- Investigation of structural and nonstructural controls for limiting lawn and wastewater discharges and for uncoupling illicit connections with an accompanying management plan and detailed implementation strategy and budget.

Watershed Stewardship Programs

- Outline for program of fostering choices for public and private stewardship to sustain watershed management (chapter 2).

Landscape Ecology Planning (Targeting and Sustaining Master Planning Goal 2)

One measure of the ecological health of a landscape is the overall connectivity of the natural open spaces that are present (chapter 6). The network of green corridors connecting "island" habitat patches throughout a fragmented landscape creates a mosaic of attractive and inhospitable locales for wildlife. Land-use planning all too often occurs at the scale of individual development sites with little understanding about the implications of those projects upon the larger, ecological context of the landscape or region. There is a serious need to shift land-use planning from its reactive mode—merely responding to existing environmental constraints—to a more proactive mode whereby green open spaces are prioritized first and human developments fitted into, not against, the ecological landscape (see chapters 2 and 6). The Alewife Reservation and Greenway are urban wilds within a sea of suburban sprawl and generally unrestrained development. The long-term viability of healthy populations of terrestrial animals located within the reservation and greenway needs to be considered from a landscape perspective in terms of undertaking planning efforts that will (a) maintain a resident population of a sufficient size to ensure genetic diversity, and (b) facilitate the genetic exchange with other, distant populations.

Several elements that need to be addressed in developing a landscape ecology plan (detailed in chapter 6) for the Alewife area include:

Habitat Patches

- Prioritization for protection and possible acquisition of all undeveloped and vacant lands adjacent to the reservation and the greenway as potential sites for increasing the size of the contiguous wildlife habitat.
- Identification and characterization (e.g., overall size and ability to sustain populations, ratio of interior to edge dimensions, habitat diversity and edge structure, resilience to disturbance, and recolonization potential) of isolated habitat patches proximal to the reservation and greenway.
- Prioritization for protection of those patches deemed most beneficial for augmenting and sustaining wildlife within the MDC managed lands.

Corridors and Connectivity

- Identification and characterization (e.g., corridor width and length dimensions, gap isolation between patches, "stepping stone" connectivity of patches) of those areas that can be connected to the reservation and greenway through creation of wildlife corridors.

- Prioritization for protection of those locations deemed most suitable for creating wildlife corridors to the MDC-managed lands (e.g., the existing corridor provided by the Mystic River to the Mystic Lakes; the potential to create a further corridor along the Mystic River to Boston Harbor; a potential corridor through the future-developed Alewife Industrial Quadrangle that will link the Alewife Reservation via Blair Pond and Rafferty Park to the Fresh Pond Reservation; and the potential corridor from Little Pond to Spy Pond underneath Route 2).

Regional Trail Network and Education Curricula Planning (Targeting and Sustaining Master Planning Goal 3)

Outdoor recreation has become as popular within cities as it has always been in the countryside. One reason for this urban increase is due to the accelerated construction of greenways and regional trail networks. Today, greenways, in addition to providing a recreational amenity, have taken on a multifaceted role for wildlife habitat and water-quality improvement, environmental education, and improving social conditions (chapter 10). In terms of public circulation and pedestrian and cycling use, it is of course essential to connect the newly designed trail systems within the Alewife Reservation and Greenway to the larger network of trails throughout the surrounding region. Opportunities for such interlinking exist with the Minuteman Bicycle Trail, which runs from Davis Square in Somerville past the reservation and northwest to Lexington; with the Mystic River Greenway, which runs from the confluence of the Alewife Brook north to the Mystic Lakes; and with the Mass Central Bicycle Trail, which will run west from the Alewife subway station into the city of Blemont and beyond. The potential also exists for establishing several new trails that would communicate with the MDC lands of this study. Perhaps the most exciting such possibility would be a greenway that which might run alongside a newly daylighted (opened-up) Alewife Brook from the subway station south to connect with the Fresh Pond Reservation.

IMPLEMENTATION

The recommendations of the master plan for restoring the Alewife Reservation and Greenway were prioritized to several preidentified sites both of high visibility and in obvious need of major repair to establish even basic ecological functioning (TBG 2003). There are seven key components of the master plan designed to facilitate its implementation, the last four of which from France (2002f) will be elaborated on in more detail:

1. Schedule in terms of a five-year itemized action plan that carries the intentions of the master planning stage through the design development stage and to the construction documents stage.
2. Comprehensive budget for all intended improvement strategies.
3. Required permits and legal documents for the proposed work in environmentally sensitive areas such as wetlands, endangered species habitats, historic and archeological sites, and locations with hazardous materials being present.
4. Imaginative examination of the diversity of potential funding sources to accomplish the recommendations.
5. Resolution of encroachments from unauthorized abutters that have illegally extended their properties.
6. Creation of a manual that specifically explains the maintenance and management guidelines needed to protect the investment of the restored landscape.
7. System to encourage community involvement and foster stewardship.

Possible Funding Strategies

Open-space and parkland plans amount to little unless supported by adequate funding resources to implement the recommendations. Given the present climate of governmental financial constraint, it is unrealistic to suppose that the restoration and enhancement of the Alewife Reservation and Greenway can be accomplished solely by support garnered from within the MDC. It therefore becomes critical to creatively explore all avenues of outside funding in order to actualize the goals of the master plan (France 2002f).

Public Sector Sources

State and Federal Grant Programs.   An entire suite of options exists for targeted solicitation of funding to support wildlife habitat restoration, flood mitigation, and recreational greenway development. Opportunities for local funding sources include the city councils, parks/recreation departments, and planning agencies; the public works and environmental services departments involved with stormwater and wastewater management; departments dealing with alternative transportation, tourism, and economic development; the district school boards and local public arts programs; and the local conservation commissions. State agencies that support the sort of recommendations made in the master plan include agencies whose mandates are managing state parks, establishing wetland mitigation banks, and restoring fish and game populations as well as transportation planning, river management, and environmental and public health concerns. Federal funding opportunities include the Army Corps of Engineers, the Environmental Protection Agency, the Federal Emergency Management Agency, the Fish and Wildlife Service, and the National Marine Fisheries Service. For example, the Friends of the Alewife Reservation have already proven successful in obtaining funding from several sources, and two other opportunities are currently being explored with the U.S. Army Corps of Engineers, which has identified several sites for potential wetland restoration within the Alewife area. Also, the Mystic River Watershed Association has applied for state money to initiate a program of stormwater source control for area residents.

Public Agency Joint Ventures.   Which agencies stand to benefit from implementation of the recommendations in the Alewife Reservation and Greenway master plan? Many of the local, state, and federal agencies listed above should also be approached to formalize working partnerships that are mutually beneficial to both the MDC and their respective public service mandates. One such current initiative is the cooperative planning between the MDC and the City of Cambridge's Department of Public Works for investigating use of a portion of the reservation for creating a stormwater management wetland (as in chapter 8) that would also support wildlife as well as become a public amenity.

Joint Development Techniques.   Joint development involves obtaining funding from private real estate developers in conjunction with establishment of public facilities as a means to create new tax revenues and other benefits through public-private partnerships. Typical approaches include incentive zoning for developers in return for landscaping, trail construction, or donations of abutting land as open-space easements (one national success story in this regard that serves as a good model is the Ballona Wetlands Foundation in Los Angeles). Such procedures are not, however, without controversy and have been tentatively explored for several sites within the study area.

Public Finance.   Some of the most successful past and present wetland and river corridor restoration projects in the country (e.g., the Las Vegas Wash) have achieved this status as a result of obtaining a large funding base through local voters approving a special tax to manage the specific project. Also, one other approach that is being used elsewhere in the country involves establishment of a stormwater tax in which residents and businesses are charged in relation to the amount of runoff that leaves their properties. Adoption of such a program for the Alewife watershed could help sustain the improvements that might be funded by a combination of any of the options discussed above.

Private Sector Sources

Foundation and Individual Grants.   Companies and individuals can donate some of their wealth under federal and state tax laws through establishment of semi-independent foundations run by a board of trustees and paid staff. Given the relative wealth of residents and corporations within the greater Alewife area, creation of such an entity could provide much-needed support for both the restoration and the maintenance recommendations of the master plan. Over 90 percent of all charitable contributions nationwide come from individuals. For some potential donors, planned giving and estate bequests for supporting land trusts are options that are appealing and worth exploring for the Alewife area.

Special Events and Fund-raisers.   A wealth of opportunities exists, limited only by the imagination, for creating public interest and financial support for ongoing restoration and enhancement efforts within the Alewife Reservation and Greenway. A recent event organized by the Friends of the Alewife Reservation in which the Massachusetts environmental secretary began the special statewide Biodiversity Days campaign from the banks of the Alewife Brook was a wonderful initiative that brought wide attention and some funding to the area. Similar opportunities exist for engaging other high-ranking government officials and private celebrities as a means for raising both the visibility and support for the Alewife Reservation and Brook-Greenway. The highly successful Mystic River Run, in which joggers follow the spawning run of alewife upstream to an environmental fair at the race's finish line, serves as another wonderful, easily adaptable model for mobilizing public support through recreation and education.

Encroaching Business Contributions.   Leverage for raising funds to implement the master plan will be easiest from those organizations whose physical site or infrastructure lies within the MDC public lands, yet whose removal would be very problematic. Obvious candidates that should be approached for contributions in this light include several institutions situated along the greenway.

Abutting Business Contributions.   The Alewife Reservation and the Alewife Greenway are both fringed by a large number of abutters including apartment complexes, retail businesses, and commercial office spaces. These institutions should be approached within a framework of soliciting sponsorship for restoration improvements to be undertaken along the particular section of the MDC lands to which they are adjacent. The strategy employed would be to establish an "adopt a wetland/greenway" program where site improvements in the immediate area would be accredited to the sponsoring group in a newsletter or some other form of public notification.

Neighborhood Business Contributions. Restoration of the Alewife Reservation and Greenway will provide numerous economic benefits to the area: property values and expenditures by residents will increase, corporate relocation will grow, and commercial opportunities will develop along with the rising intrinsic values of the valuable greenspace. Attempts should be made to engage those businesses that are situated within walking distance of the MDC lands. Here, though the "sell" might be harder than for abutting businesses, the potential still exists to encourage good corporate citizenship through supporting the overall neighborhood improvements that will be ensue through implementation of the master plan recommendations.

Encroachment Resolution

One of the most delicate yet important implementation procedures of the master plan for the Alewife Reservation and Greenway involves resolving confusions about land ownership and reclaiming properties (commercial, industrial, and residential) that have over the years extended into the MDC parkland (France 2002f). Such encroachments range from minor intrusions such as gardens and temporary storage of yard or construction waste, to intermediate intrusions such as vehicle parking lots and fences to the water's edge, to major intrusions such as construction of buildings and cemeteries. The framework for resolving encroachment issues includes surveying property lines to determine ownership and identify possible violations and to notify and negotiate with abutting property owners who have been informed and educated about the overall mission of the MDC Alewife Reservation and Greenway (chapter 10).

Maintenance and Management

Urban wilds and greenways are long-term investments that need a sincere commitment to developing, implementing, and supporting a comprehensive maintenance and management plan. Establishment of such objectives must be regarded as being integral components and not afterthoughts to the desired success of any master plan (France 2002f).

Maintenance

The Alewife Reservation and Greenway will require long-term investments in both routine and remedial maintenance. Routine maintenance involves establishing a recurring program of tending the landscape and includes such activities as invasive-plant control, trash collection, and minor repairs to infrastructure. Remedial maintenance involves repairing seriously damaged infrastructure and natural systems and includes such activities as streambank stabilization, fixing a pedestrian bridge following a major flood, or replacing signage destroyed by vandalism.

Management

The question of who should manage the system is important; such options include existing state and local authorities, nonprofit groups, partnering with private-sector investors, or creation of a special new entity to assume the ongoing tasks. What is essential, however, is that the entire Alewife system, from Little Pond through the reservation and along the greenway to the confluence with the Mystic River, should be managed as a single entity to ensure uniformity of the vision and programming of the management decisions. The five key components that have frequently been identified as being essential to open-space management programs include:

- Consideration of user safety and risks
- Patrol and emergency procedures
- Administration, programming, and events
- Stewardship and enhancement
- Funding for ongoing activities

Community Input and Stewardship

Planning is a vital component of open-space and parkland management, but it is all for naught unless there is a will to take action (France 2002f). Often the plans that work best are those supported by a mobilized community of concerned individuals, organizations, corporations, and institutions. Public-private partnerships can provide the best opportunities to ensure implementation success by combining community spirit, entrepreneurial drive, volunteerism, good corporate citizenship, financial resources, professional expertise, and long-term commitment. Above all, it is important to grow a sense of community ownership and stewardship to help produce tangible results in implementing the recommendations of the master plan and therefore restoring and enhancing the quality of the Alewife Reservation and Greenway.

Volunteer Efforts

Restoration.   All truly sustainable, and therefore successful, environmental restoration projects are as much about restoring degraded relationships between humans and nature as they are about simply repairing degraded physical landscapes. All efforts should be made to engage the local community in the actual physical act of restoring the Alewife Reservation and Greenway rather than relying only upon outside professional practitioners. The track record for ensuring ongoing maintenance of restoration projects that have been supported by such direct public involvement is much higher than that of projects in which the residents had no hands-on engagement in the planting and simple earth-working activities.

Stewardship. Public involvement is the key to any successful planning effort. Failure to raise this public involvement generates "orphan" open spaces and parklands that persist in a healthy and sustainable state only within the pages of planning documents and not the real world. The involvement of concerned individuals for periodic trash cleanup and removal of colonizing invasive plants will be essential to ensure that the recommendations of the master plan become achievable.

Organizations

Education. Commitment to restore and enhance the Alewife Reservation and Greenway will be facilitated by public investment in the area and its issues through creation of interpretative programs for both schoolchildren and adults. Distilling and translating technical information (chapter 3) in the form of brochures, reports, slide shows, videos, and models into nonstructural elements such as school programs and guided tours will continue to help inform the public about the goals of the master plan (chapter 10).

Coalition Building. At present, more than a dozen public advocacy groups have focused interests on various attributes pertinent to the long-term well-being of the Alewife Reservation and Greenway. Unfortunately, these voices of concern have been diluted by their very diversity. The entire Alewife area would benefit from a coalition of this cacophony into an effective, unified voice through which to lobby for greater outside attention and funding. The best option might be to increase an affiliation with the established Mystic River Watershed Association and to use this foundation as the basis from which to mobilize efforts pertaining to the Alewife subwatershed.

Literature Cited

Abbott, R. M. 1999. Ecological integrity and the green business hypothesis: A tiger by the tale. Unpublished manuscript.

———. 2005. Into the great wide open: Rethinking design in an era of economic, social, and environmental change. Pp. 29–42 in R. L. France, ed., *Facilitating watershed management: Fostering awareness and stewardship.* Rowman & Littlefield.

Abbott, R., and M. Holland. 2006. *Where we live: Chasing the dream of urban sustainability.* Green Frigate Books.

Ahern, J., Robert France, Michael Hough, Jon Burley, Wood Turner, Stephen Schmidt, et al. 2002. Ecology across the curriculum: Conceptual issues, learning objectives, and implementation models. Pp. 397–414 in B. Johnson and K. Hill, *Ecology and design: Frameworks for learning.* Island Press.

Andrus, C. W., B. A. Long, and H. A. Froehlich. 1988. Woody debris and its contribution to pool formation in a coastal stream 50 years after logging. *Canadian Journal of Fisheries Aquatic Sciences* 45: 2080–2086.

Angermeier, P. L., and J. R. Karr. 1984. Relationships between woody debris and fish habitat in a small warmwater stream. *American Fisheries Society Transactions* 113: 716–726.

Anon. 1996. Greenscaping. *USDA Natural Resources Conservation Service.* Milford, NH.

———. 1997. Protecting and enhancing shorelands for wildlife. *University of New Hampshire Cooperative Extension.*

———. 1998. Lawns and landscapes in your watershed. *Massachusetts Department of Environmental Protection.* Boston, MA.

————. 1999. Comprehensive shoreland protection act RSA 483-B. *New Hampshire Department of Environmental Services.* Concord, NH.

————. 2000. Preservation of scenic areas and viewsheds. *New Hampshire Office of State Planning.* Concord, NH.

————. 2002. ASLA awards. *Landscape Architecture Magazine* (November): 66.

Apfelbaum, S. 2005. Stormwater management: A primer and guidelines for future programming and innovative demonstration projects. Pp. 321–333 in R. L. France, ed., *Facilitating watershed management: Fostering awareness and stewardship.* Rowman & Littlefield.

Arendt, R. G. 1996. *Conservation design for subdivisions: A practical guide to creating open space networks.* Island Press.

ASLA (American Society of Landscape Architects). 1993a. Taking up the challenge. *Land* 35: 5.

————. 1993b. Environmental ethics: Elective only? *Land* 35: 2.

Bachelard, G. 1999. *Water and dreams: An essay on the imagination of matter.* Dallas Inst. Human. Cult. Dallas, TX.

Baker, J. P., D. W. Hulse, S. V. Gregory, D. White, J. Van Sickle, P. A. Berger, et al. 2004. Alternative futures for the Willamette River Basin, Oregon. *Ecological Applications* 14: 313–324.

Baker, J. P., and D. H. Landers. 2004. Alternative-futures analysis for the Willamette River Basin, Oregon. *Ecological Applications* 14: 311–312.

Batty, M. 1998. From environment and planning B to planning and design: Traditions, transitions, translations, transformations. *Environmental Planning B: Planning and Design* 1998: 1–9.

Bays, J., J. Cormier, N. Pouder, B. Bear, and R. France. 2002. Moving from single-purpose treatment wetlands toward multifunction designed wetland parks. Pp. 357–358 in R. L. France, ed., *Handbook of water sensitive planning and design.* Lewis Publishers.

Beatley, T. 1994. *Ethical land use: Principles of policy and planning.* John Hopkins University Press.

Benjamin, T. 2002. Natural resource stewardship planning and design: Fresh Pond Reservation (Massachusetts). Pp. 407–429 in R. L. France, ed., *Handbook of water sensitive planning and design.* Lewis Publishers.

Berger, P. A., and J. P. Bolte. 2004. Evaluating the impact of policy options on agricultural landscapes: An alternative-futures approach. *Ecological Applications* 14: 342–454.

Berris, C. 1995. Scenic, recreational, and tourism values and resources. Chap. 6 in *Sustainable ecosystem management in Clayoquot Sound: Government of British Columbia Report 5.*

Bilby, R. E., and G. E. Likens. 1980. Importance of organic debris dams in the structure and function of stream ecosystems. *Ecology* 61: 1107–1113.

Bilby, R. E., and J. W. Ward. 1989. Changes in characteristics and function of woody debris with increasing size of streams in western Washington. *American Fisheries Society Transactions* 118: 368–378.

Blau, D. 2002. Watershed management plans: Bridging from science to policy to operations (San Francisco, California). Pp. 459–475 in R. L. France, ed., *Handbook of water sensitive planning and design*. Lewis Publishers.

Bowers, R., J. Irion, B. Keyer, and L. Weaner. 1998. Guidelines for ecologically sound residential landscapes. *Association of Professional Landscape Designers*. Chicago, IL.

Bragg, D. C., and J. L. Kershner. 1997. Evaluating the long-term consequences of forest management and stream cleaning on coarse woody debris in small riparian systems of the central Rocky Mountains. *Fish Habitat Relationships Technical Bulletin 21*.

Brukilacchio, L., and J. Hill. 2005. Taking it to the streets: Watershed awareness efforts merge with public art. Pp. 197–214 in R. L. France, ed., *Facilitating watershed management: Fostering awareness and stewardship*. Rowman & Littlefield.

Buikema, A. L., and E. F. Benfield. 1979. Use of macroinvertebrate life history information in toxicity tests. *Journal of Fisheries Research Board of Canada* 36: 321–328.

Bullard, K. 2005. Riparian pocket parks as a means for physically and conceptually connecting people to urban waters. Pp. 309–317 in R. L. France, ed., *Facilitating watershed management: Fostering awareness and stewardship*. Rowman & Littlefield.

Cairns, J. 1975. Quantification of biological integrity. Pp. 171–187 in R. K. Ballentine and L. J. Guarria, eds., *The integrity of water*. U.S. Environmental Protection Agency.

Calkins, M. 2001. Leeding the way: A look at the way landscape architects are using the LEED Green Building Rating System. *Landscape Architecture Magazine* (May): 36–44.

Campbell, C. S., and M. H. Ogden. 1999. *Constructed wetlands in the sustainable landscape*. John Wiley and Sons.

Cantwell, M. 2002. The effect of spatial location in land-water interactions: A comparison of two modeling approaches to support watershed planning (Newfoundland, Canada). Pp. 577–599 in R. L. France, ed., *Handbook of water sensitive planning and design*. Lewis Publishers.

Carlson, J. Y., C. W. Andrus, and H. A. Froehlich. 1990. Woody debris, channel features, and macroinvertebrates of streams with logged and undisturbed riparian timber in northeastern Oregon, U.S.A. *Canadian Journal of Fisheries Aquatic Sciences* 47: 1103–1111.

CEQ (Council on Environmental Quality). 1975. *Planning for environmental indices*. National Academy of Science.

Christensen, D. L., R. W. Nero, and P. F. Olesiok. 1996. Impacts of lakeshore residential development on coarse woody debris in north temperate lakes. *Ecological Applications* 6: 1143–1149.

Cohen, R. 1998. *The Massachusetts Riverways Program.* www.riverways.org.

Coiner, C. J., J. Wu, and S. Polasky. 2001. Economic and environmental implications of alternative landscape designs in the Walnut Creek Watershed of Iowa. *Ecological Economics* 38: 119–139.

Colby, M. 1990. *Environmental management in development: The evolution of paradigms.* John Wiley and Sons.

Cole, J. J., B. L. Peierls, N. F. Caraco, and M. L. Pace. 1993. Nitrogen loading of rivers as a human-driven process. Pp. 128–143 in W. McDonnell and S. Pickett, eds., *Humans as components of ecosystems.* Springer-Verlag.

CPB (Chesapeake Bay Program). 1998. *Integrating build-out analysis and water quality modeling to predict the environmental impacts of alternative development scenarios.* U.S. Environmental Protection Agency.

———. 2001. Better backyard: A citizens' resource guide to beneficial landscaping and habitat restoration in the Chesapeake Bay watershed. U.S. Environmental Protection Agency.

CRJ (Carol R. Johnson Associates). 1998. *Upper Charles River Reservation master plan.* Metropolitan District Commission, Boston, MA.

Damon, B., and A. H. Mavor. 2005. Combining art and science: The Living Water Garden in Chengdu, China. Pp. 293–306 in R. L. France, ed., *Facilitating watershed management: Fostering awareness and stewardship.* Rowman & Littlefield.

Davenport, T. E. 2003. *The watershed project management guide.* Lewis Publishers.

Del Giorgio, P. A., and R. H. Peters. 1993. Balance between phytoplankton production and plankton respiration in lakes. *Canadian Journal of Fisheries and Aquatic Science* 50: 282–289.

Dillon, P. J., K. H. Nichols, W. D. Scheider, N. D. Yan, and J. S. Jeffries. 1986. *Lakeshore capacity study: Trophic status report.* Ontario Ministry of Municipal Affairs.

Doenges, J. M., C. P. Allan, R. J. Jontos, and C. A. Lieber. 1990. *Carrying capacity of public water supply watersheds: A literature review of impacts on water quality from residential development.* Connecticut Department of Environmental Resources Bulletin 11. Hartford, CT.

Dole, D., and E. Niemi. 2004. Future water allocation and in-stream values in the Willamette River Basin: A basin-wide analysis. *Ecological Applications* 14: 355–367.

Dramstad, W. E., J. D. Olson, and R. T. T. Forman. 1996. *Landscape ecology principles in landscape architecture and land-use planning.* Island Press.

Dreiseitl, H., D. Grau, and K. H. Ludwig. 2001. *Waterscapes: Planning, building and designing with water.* Birkhauser Press.

Dudley, T., and N. H. Anderson. 1982. A survey of invertebrates associated with wood debris in aquatic habitats. *Melandria* 39: 1–22.

Ekbo, G. 1950. *Landscape for living.* Architectural Record.

Elliott, S. T. 1986. Reduction of a dolly varden population and macrobenthos after removal of logging debris. *American Fisheries Society Transactions* 115: 392–400.

EPA. 1975. *The integrity of water.* U.S. Environmental Protection Agency.

———. 2001. *Our built and natural environments: A technical review of the interactions between land use, transportation, and environmental quality.* U.S. Environmental Protection Agency.

———. 2004. *Protecting water resources with smart growth.* U.S. Environmental Protection Agency.

Everett, R. A., and G. M. Ruiz. 1993. Coarse woody debris as a refuge from predation in aquatic communities: An experimental test. *Oecologia* 93: 475–486.

FAO (Food and Agriculture Organization). 1976. *Indices for measuring response of aquatic ecological systems to various human influences.* FAO Fisheries Technical Paper No. 151.

Felkner, J. S., and M. W. Binford. 2002. Modeling a soil moisture index using geographic information systems in a developing country context (Thailand). Pp. 513–540 in R. L. France, ed., *Handbook of water sensitive planning and design.* Lewis Publishers.

Ferguson, B. 2005. *Porous pavements.* CRC Press.

Ferguson, B., D. Nichols, and S. Weinberg. 2000. Water quality land development provisions. Paper presented at the Water Sensitive Planning and Design Symposium, Harvard School of Design.

Findlay, C. S., and J. Houlahan. 1997. Anthropogenic correlates of species richness in southeastern Ontario wetlands. *Conservation Biology* 11: 1000–1009.

Fisher, L. 1990. Thermodynamics and ecosystem integrity. Pp. 131–152 in C. Edwards and H. Regier, eds., *An ecosystem approach to the integrity of the Great Lakes in turbulent times.* Great Lakes Fishery Commission.

FISRWG (Federal Interagency Stream Restoration Working Group). 1998. *Stream corridor restoration: Principles, processes, and practices.* Federal Interagency Stream Restoration Working Group.

Flink, C. 1993. *Greenways: A practical guide to planning, design, and management.* Island Press.

———. 2002. Greenways as green infrastructure in the new millennium. Pp. 395–405 in R. L. France, ed., 2002. *Handbook of water sensitive planning and design.* Lewis Publishers.

Fontaine, T. D., and D. J. Stewart. 1990. Trophic dynamics and ecosystem integrity in the Great Lakes: Past, present, and possibilities. Pp. 153–168 in C. Edwards and H. Regier, eds., *An ecosystem approach to the integrity of the Great Lakes in turbulent times.* Great Lakes Fishery Commission.

Forbes, S. A. 1887. The lake as a microcosm. *Bulletin of Illinois Natural History Survey* 15: 537–550.

Forman, R. T. T. 1997. *Land mosaics: The ecology of landscapes and regions.* Cambridge University Press.

Forman, R. T. T., D. Sperling, J. A. Bissonette, A. P. Clevenger, C. D. Cutshall, V. H. Dale, et al. 2003. *Road ecology: Science and solutions.* Island Press.

Foster, D. R., G. Motzkin, and B. Slater. 1998. Land-use history as long-term broad-scale disturbance: Regional forest dynamics in central New England. *Ecosystems* 1: 96–119.

France, R. L. 1986. Current status of methods of toxicological research on freshwater crayfish. *Canadian Technical Report Fisheries and Aquatic Science* 1414: 45.

———. 1990. Theoretical framework for developing and operationalizing an index of zoobenthos community integrity: Application to biomonitoring with zoobenthos communities in the Great Lakes. Pp. 169–193 in C. Edwards and H. Regier, eds., *An ecosystem approach to the integrity of the Great Lakes in turbulent times.* Great Lakes Fishery Commission.

———. 1992a. Gaian integrity: A clarion precept for global preservation. *The Trumpeter* 9: 159–164.

———. 1992b. Use of sequential sampling of amphipod abundance to classify the biotic integrity of acid-sensitive lakes. *Environmental Management* 16: 157–166.

———. 1992c. Garbage in paradise. *Nature* 355: 504.

———. 1993. The Lake Hazen Trough: A late-winter oasis in a polar desert. *Biological Conservation* 63: 149–151.

———. 1997a. The importance of beaver lodges in structuring littoral communities in boreal headwater lakes. *Canadian Journal of Zoology* 75: 1009–1013.

———. 1997b. Potential for soil erosion from decreased litterfall due to riparian clearcutting: Implications for boreal forestry and warm- and cool-water fisheries. *Journal of Soil and Water Conservation* 52: 452–455.

———. 2000. Smoky mirrors and unreflected vampires: From eco-revelation to eco-relevance in landscape design. *Harvard Design Magazine* 10: 36–40.

———, ed. 2002a. *Handbook of water sensitive planning and design.* Lewis Publishers.

———. 2002b. Janus planning: Using computer tools to look backard and forward simultaneously. P. 576 in R. L. France, ed., *Handbook of water sensitive planning and design*. Lewis Publishers.

———. 2002c. Factors influencing sediment transport from logging roads near boreal trout lakes (Ontario, Canada). Pp. 635–645 in R. L. France, ed., *Handbook of water sensitive planning and design*. Lewis Publishers.

———. 2002d. Buffer strips: More than green eyelashes? P. 378 in R. L. France, ed., *Handbook of water sensitive planning and design*. Lewis Publishers.

———. 2002e. Corridors that integrate natural, societal, and social elements. P. 430 in R. L. France, ed., *Handbook of water sensitive planning and design*. Lewis Publishers.

———. 2002f. Preliminary master planning document for the Alewife Watershed. Unpublished document.

———. 2003a. *Deep immersion: The experience of water*. Green Frigate Books.

———. 2003b. *Profitably soaked: Thoreau's engagement with water*. Green Frigate Books.

———. 2003c. *Wetland design: Practices and principles for landscape architecture and land-use planning*. W. W. Norton.

———. 2003d. Green world, gray heart? The promise and reality of landscape architecture in sustaining nature. *Harvard Design Magazine* 13 (Spring/Summer): 30–36.

———, ed., 2005. *Facilitating watershed management: Fostering awareness and stewardship*. Rowman & Littlefield.

———, ed. 2006. *Healing natures, repairing relationships: New perspectives on restoring ecological spaces and consciousness*. Rowman & Littlefield.

France, R. L., and J. Blais. 1998. Lead concentrations and stable isotopic evidence for transpolar contamination of plants in the Canadian High Arctic. *Ambio* 27: 506–508.

France, R. L., H. Culbert, and R. Peters. 1996. Decreased carbon and nutrient input to boreal lakes from particulate organic matter following riparian clear-cutting. *Environmental Management* 20: 579–583.

France, R. L., J. S. Felkner, M. Flaxman, and R. Rempel. 2002. Spatial analysis of applying Ontario's timber management guidelines: GIS analysis for riparian areas of concern. Pp. 601–613 in R. L. France, ed., *Handbook of water sensitive planning and design*. Lewis Publishers.

France, R. L., and D. F. Fletcher. 2005. Watermarks: Imprinting water(shed) awareness through environmental literature and art. Pp. 103–121 in R. L. France, ed., *Facilitating watershed management: Fostering awareness and stewardship*. Rowman & Littlefield.

France, R. L., and R. H. Peters. 1995. Predictive model of the effects on lake metabolism of decreased airborne litterfall through riparian deforestation. *Conservation Biology* 9: 1578–1586.

France, R. L., and C. Rigg. 1998. Examination of the "founder effect" in biodiversity research: Patterns and imbalances in the published literature. *Diversity and Distributions* 4: 77–86.

France, R. L., and T. C. Weiskel. 1997. Water and ecological integrity: Some basic conceptual and measurement problems. *Harvard Seminar Environmental Ethics.* http://ecoethics.net/bib/1997/enca-009.htm.

Francis, M. 2003. *Village Homes: A community by design.* Island Press.

Freemark, K. 1995. Assessing effects of agriculture on terrestrial wildlife: Developing a hierarchical approach for the U.S. EPA. *Landscape and Urban Planning* 31: 99–115.

———. 1999. Managing agricultural development. Unpublished note.

———. 2000. Modeling effects of alternative landscape design and management on water quality and biodiversity in Midwest agricultural watersheds. Paper presented at the Water Sensitive Planning and Design Symposium, Harvard School of Design.

Frey, D. G. 1975. Biological integrity of water: An historical approach. Pp. 127–140 in R. K. Ballentine and L. J. Guarria, eds., *The integrity of water.* U.S. Environmental Protection Agency.

Fuller, J. L., D. R. Foster, J. S. McLachlan, and N. Drake. 1998. Impact of human activity on regional forest compositon and dynamics in central New England. *Ecosystems* 1: 76–95.

Gewertz, K. 2005. Third rock blues: Peter Raven warns of planetary catastrophe. *Harvard University Gazette* 19: 7–8.

Glekson, A. 1971. *The ecological basis of planning.* John Wiley and Sons.

Goldman, C. R. 1993. The conservation of two large lakes. *Verth Verein Limnology* 25: 388–391.

Goldsmith, E. 1988. Gaia: Some implications for theoretical ecology. *The Ecologist* 18:64–74.

Golodetz, A. D., and D. R. Foster. 1997. History and importance of land use and protection in the North Quabbin region of Massachusetts (USA). *Conservation Biology* 11: 227–235.

Hacker, A. L., and B. E. Coblentz. 1993. Habitat selection by mountain beavers recolonizing Oregon coast range clearcuts. *Journal of Wildlife Management* 57: 847–853.

Hackl, D. 1983. The redesign of an urban riverside landscape. *Garten Landscape* 83(2): 103–106.

Haddon, W. 1970. On the escape of tigers: An ecologic note. *Technology Review* 6: 45–48.

Hagan, S. 2003. Five reasons. *Harvard Design Magazine* 13 (Spring/Summer): 4–11.

Hakanson, L., and R. H. Peters. 1995. *Predictive limnology: Methods for predictive modelling.* SPB Academic Publications.

Harries, M., and L. Heder. 2005. The touch of water: Artists working with water and communities. Pp. 259–277 in R. L. France, ed., *Facilitating watershed management: Fostering awareness and stewardship.* Rowman & Littlefield.

Heathcote, I. W. 1998. *Integrated watershed management: Principles and practices.* John Wiley and Sons.

Henderson, C. L., C. J. Dindorf, and F. J. Rozumalski. 2003. *Lakescaping for wildlife and water quality.* Minnesota Department of Natural Resources.

Herricks, E. E., and J. C. Cairns. 1982. Biological monitoring. Part III: Receiving system methodology based on community structure. *Water Resources* 16: 141–153.

Herson-Jones, L. M., Heraty, M., and Jordan, B. 1995. *Riparian buffer strategies for urban watersheds.* Metropolitan Washington Council Governments.

Hilderbrand, R. H., A. D. Lemby, C. A. Dolloff, and K. H. Harpster. 1997. *Design considerations for large woody debris placement.* Department of Fisheries and Wildlife Sciences, Utah State University Publication 84322–5210.

Holling, C. S. 1978. *Adaptive environmental assessment and management.* John Wiley and Sons.

Holling, C. S., and M. A. Goldberg. 1970. Ecology and planning. *Journal of the American Institute of Planners* 35: 221–230.

Horner, R. A., J. J. Skupien, E. H. Livingston, and H. E. Shaver. 1994. *Fundamentals of urban runoff management: Technical and institutional issues.* U.S. Environmental Protection Agency.

House, R. A., and P. L. Boehne. 1986. Effects of instream structures on salmonid habitat and populations in Tobe Creek, Oregon. *North American Journal Fisheries Management* 6: 38–46.

Hubbard, B. M. 1998. *Conscious evolution: Awakening the power of our social potential.* New World Library.

Hulse, D., A. Branscomb, and S. Payne. 2004. Envisioning alternatives: Using citizen guidance to map future land and water use. *Ecological Applications* 14: 325–341.

Hulse, D., J. Eilers, K. Freemark, C. Hummon, and D. White. 2000. Planning alternative future landscapes in Oregon: Evaluating effects on water quality and biodiversity. *Landscape Journal* 19: 1–19.

Hulse, D. W., and S. V. Gregory. 2001. Alternative futures as an integrative framework for riparian restoration of large rivers. Pp. 195–212 in V. H. Dale and R. A. Haeuber, eds., *Applying ecological principles to land management.* Springer.

Hutchinson, N. J. 2002. Limnology, plumbing and planning: Evaluation of nutrient-based limits to shoreline development in Precambrian Shield watersheds. Pp. 647–682 in R. L. France, ed., *Handbook of water sensitive planning and design.* Lewis Publishers.

Hutchinson, N. J., B. P. Neary, and P. J. Dillon. 1991. Validation and use of Ontario's trophic status model for establishing lake development guidelines. *Lake and Reservoir Management* 7: 13–23.

Illich, I. 1986. *H₂0 and the waters of forgetfulness.* Marion Boyars.

Ingle-Sidorowicz, H. M. 1982. Beaver increase in Ontario: Result of changing environment. *Mammalia* 46: 533–552.

Jackson, J. H., and V. H. Resh. 1988. Sequential decision plans in monitoring benthic macroinvertebrates: Cost savings, classification accuracy, and development of plans. *Canadian Journal of Fisheries and Aquatic Sciences* 45: 280–286.

Johnson, B., and K. Hill. 2002. *Ecology and design: Frameworks for learning.* Island Press.

Johnson, C. A., and R. J. Naiman. 1987. Boundary dynamics at the aquatic-terrestrial interface: The influence of beaver and geomorphology. *Landscape Ecology* 1: 47–57.

———. 1990. Browse selection by beaver: Effects on riparian forest composition. *Canadian Journal of Forest Research* 20: 1036–1043.

Jones, R., and C. Clark. 1987. Impact of watershed urbanization on stream insect communities. *Water Resources Bulletin* 15: 176–184.

Kain, R., ed. 1981. *Planning for conservation.* St. Martin's.

Kalff, J. 1996. Robert Henry Peters, 1946–1996. *Canadian Journal of Fisheries and Aquatic Science* 53: 1692–1694.

Karr, J. R. 1981. Assessment of biotic integrity using fish communities. *Fisheries* 6: 21–27.

Karr, J. R., and E. W. Chu. 1999. *Restoring life in running waters: Better biological monitoring.* Island Press.

Kay, J. J. 1990. A non-equilibrium thermodynamic framework for discussing ecosystem integrity. Pp. 239–256 in C. Edwards and H. Regier, eds., *An ecosystem approach to the integrity of the Great Lakes in turbulent times.* Great Lakes Fishery Commission.

Keller, E. A., and F. J. Swanson. 1979. Effects of large organic material on channel form and fluvial processes. *Earth Surface Processes* 4: 361–380.

Kennedy, P. 1993. *Preparing for the twenty-first century.* Random House.

Kingsmill, S. 1997. *Naturally kept shorelines.* Ontario Cottage Association.

Korth, R. 1999. *What is a shoreline buffer?* www.co.lincoln.wi.us/html.

Landwehr, J. M., and R. A. Deininger. 1976. A comparison of several water quality indexes. *Journal of Water Pollution Control Federation* 48: 954–958.

Lazar, A., D. Peterson, and R. Calvo. 2000. *The Florida Keys carrying capacity study.* Urban Land Institute.

Lehmukl, D. M. 1979. Environmental disturbance and life histories: Principles and examples. *Journal of Fisheries Research Board of Canada* 36: 329–334.

Lehtinen, R. M., N. D. Mundahl, and J. C. Madejczyk. 1997. Autumn use of woody snags in backwater and channel border habitats of a large river. *Environmental Biology Fishes* 49: 7–19.

Leopold, A. 1947. *A Sand County almanac with essays on conservation from Round River.* Ballantine.

Leopold, L. B. 1994. *A view of the river.* Harvard University Press.

Levin, S. A., and K. D. Kimball. 1984. New perspectives in ecotoxicology. *Environmental Management* 8: 375–442.

Likens, G. E. 1984. Beyond the shoreline: A watershed-ecosystem perspective. *Verhun International Verein Limnology* 22: 1–22.

Linehan, J. R., and M. Gross. 1998. Back to the future, back to basics: The social ecology of landscapes and the future of landscape planning. *Landscape and Urban Planning* 42: 207–223.

Lyle, J. 1985. *Design for human ecosystems: Landscape, land use, and natural resources.* Island Press.

MacDonald, John D. 1962. *A flash of green.* Fawcett Gold Medal.

Manning, O. D. 1997. Design imperatives for river landscapes. *Landscape Research* 22:67–94.

Marsh, W. M. 1998. *Landscape planning environmental applications.* John Wiley and Sons.

McDonough, W., and M. Braungart. 2002. *Cradle to cradle: Remaking the way we make things.* North Point Press.

McHarg, I. 1969. *Design with nature.* Natural History Press.

McLahlan, A. J. 1970. Submerged trees as a substrate for benthic fauna in the recently created Lake Kariba (Central Africa). *Journal of Applied Ecology* 7: 253–266.

Meeuwig, J. J., and R. H. Peters. 1996. Circumventing phosphorus in lake management: A comparison of chlorophyll a predictions from land-use and phosphorus-loading models. *Canadian Journal of Fisheries and Aquatic Science* 53: 1795–1806.

Merchant, C. 2004. *Reinventing Eden: The fate of nature in Western culture.* Routledge.

Meyer, S. 2005. WatershedAtlas.com: Educating the public. Pp. 93–100 in R. L. France, ed., *Facilitating watershed management: Fostering awareness and stewardship.* Rowman & Littlefield.

Michaels, S. 1999. Of life and combined option-strategy protocol. Unpublished note.

Miller, D. L., J. Karr, and R. Steedman. 1988. Regional application of an index of biotic integrity for use in water resource management. *Fisheries* 13: 12–20.

Mitchell, F. 2002. Shoreline buffers: Protecting water quality and biological diversity (New Hampshire). Pp. 361–378 in R. L. France, ed., *Handbook of water sensitive planning and design.* Lewis Publishers.

Montgomery, S. 1997. Lawns: An un-American obsession. *The Boston Globe,* August 25.

Monzyk, F. R., W. E. Kelso, and D. A. Rutherford. 1997. Characteristics of woody cover used by brown madtoms and pirate perch in coastal plain streams. *American Fisheries Society Transactions* 126: 665–675.

Moring, J. R., M. T. Negus, R. D. McCullough, and S. W. Henke. 1990. Large concentrations of submerged pulpwood logs as fish attraction structures in a reservoir. *Bulletin Marine Science* 44: 609–615.

Moring, J. R., J. Rooling, and B. Sante. 1986. Ecological importance of submerged pulpwood logs in a Maine reservoir. *Transactions American Fisheries Society* 115: 335–342.

Mozingo, L. A. 1997. The aesthetics of ecological design: Seeing science as culture. *Landscape Journal* 35 (Spring): 46–59.

Mueller, A. 1998. *The aquifer recharge management model: Evaluating the impacts of urban development on groundwater resources.* MLA thesis. Harvard School of Design.

Mueller, A., R. L. France, and C. Steinitz. 2002. Aquifer recharge management model: Evaluating the impacts of urban development on groundwater resources (Galilee, Israel). Pp. 615–634 in R. L. France, ed., *Handbook of water sensitive planning and design.* Lewis Publishers.

Murcott, G., J. Cooper, and H. Beck. 2002. *Glenn Murcutt: A singular architectural practise; 2002 laureate of the Pritzker Architecture Prize.* Images Publications.

Naiman, R. J., J. J. Magnuson, D. M. McKnight, and J. A. Stanford. 1995. *The freshwater imperative: A research agenda.* Island Press.

Naiman, R. J., D. M. McDowell, and B. S. Farr. 1984. The influence of beaver (*Castor canadensis*) on the production dynamics of aquatic insects. *Verhun International Verein Limnology* 22: 1801–1810.

Nassauer, J., R. C. Corry, and R. M. Cruse. 2002. Alternative future landscape scenarios: A means to consider agricultural policy. *MJA Journal* 57: 45–53.

Negus, M. T. 1987. The influence of submerged pulpwood on feeding and condition of fishes in a reservoir. *Hydrobiologia* 148: 63–72.

Newbury, R., M. Gaboury, and C. Watson. 1995. *Field manual of urban stream restoration.* U.S. Environmental Protection Agency.

Nichols, D., B. Ferguson, and S. Weinberg. 1997. *Land development provi-*

sions to protect Georgia water quality. Georgia Department of Natural Resources, Environmental Protection Division.

North, P. 2005. Elevating wetland consciousness: Environmental education and art. Pp. 281–290 in R. L. France, ed., *Facilitating watershed management: Fostering awareness and stewardship.* Rowman & Littlefield.

Noss, R. F., M. A. O'Connell, and D. D. Murphy. 1998. *The science of conservation planning: Habitat conservation under the Endangered Species Act.* Island Press.

Novak, M. 1976. *The beaver in Ontario.* Special Publication, Ontario Ministry Natural Resources.

NRDC. 2002. *Paving our way to water shortages: How sprawl aggravates the effects of drought.* National Resources Defense Council.

O'Brien, J., and D. Driscoll. 2000. Charles River Greenway. Paper presented at the Water Sensitive Planning and Design Symposium, Harvard School of Design.

O'Connor, N. A. 1991. The effects of habitat complexity on the macroinvertebrates colonizing wood surfaces in a lowland stream. *Oecologia* 85: 504–512.

O'Neill, R. V., T. Williams, and B. Shuler. 1997. Monitoring environmental quality at the landscape scale. *Bioscience* 47: 513–519.

Orr, D. W. 1992. *Ecological literacy: Education and the transition to a postmodern world.* SUNY Press.

———. 1994. *Earth in mind: On education, environment, and the human prospect.* Island Press.

Pace, M. L., and P. A. del Giorgio. 1996. In memorium: Dr. Robert H. Peters. *Marine Ecology Progress Series* 142: 1.

Palmer, J. A. 1998. *Environmental education in the 21st century: Theory, practice, progress and promise.* Routledge.

Palmer, P. J. 1993. *To know as we are known: Education as a spiritual journey.* Harper.

Patchett, J. 1999. Letter from the chair. *ASLA Professional Interest Group on Water Conservatoin Newsletter.* American Society of Landscape Architects.

Patrick, R. 1975. Identifying integrity through ecosystem study. Pp. 155–164 in R. K. Ballentine and L. J. Guarria, eds., *The integrity of water.* U.S. Environmental Protection Agency.

Peck, S. 1998. *Planning for biodiversity: Issues and examples.* Island Press.

Peters, R. H. 1986. The role of prediction in limnology. *Limnology and Oceanography* 31: 1143–1159.

———. 1991. *A critique for ecology.* Cambridge University Press.

Pinkham, R. 1999. *Daylighting: New life for buried streams.* Rocky Mountain Institute.

Plant, M. 1998. *Education for the environment: Stimulating practice.* Peter Francis.

Pollan, M. 1991. *Second nature: A gardener's education.* Delta.

Poole, K. 2005. Watershed management as urban design: The civic hydrology of Bellevue, Washington. Pp. 337–349 in R. L. France, ed., *Facilitating watershed management: Fostering awareness and stewardship.* Rowman & Littlefield.

PRCWA (Parker River Clean Watershed Association). 1999. *Waterfront gardens: A guide to planting a landscaped buffer to protect your river, stream, wetland, or pond.* PRCWA Byfield.

Purdum, G. E. 1997. A model for identifying the vulnerability of streams and rivers to land use-induced changes. *Landscape Research* 22: 209–224.

Rapport, D. J. 1989. What constitutes ecosystem health? *Perspectives in Biology and Medicine* 33: 1143–1159.

Regier, H. A., and R. L. France. 1990. Perspectives on the meaning of ecosystem integrity in 1975. Pp. 1–16 in C. Edwards and H. Regier, eds., *An ecosystem approach to the integrity of the Great Lakes in turbulent times.* Great Lakes Fishery Commission.

Richman, T. 2005. Innovation diffusion and water-sensitive design. Pp. 45–51 in R. L. France, ed., *Facilitating watershed management: Fostering awareness and stewardship.* Rowman & Littlefield.

Richman, T., J. Worth, P. Dawe, J. Aldrich, and B. Ferguson. 1999. *Start at the source: Design guidance manual for stormwater quality protection.* Bay Area Stormwater Management Agencies.

Rigler, F. H., and R. H. Peters. 1995. *Science and limnology: Excellence in ecology,* vol. 6. Ecology Institute.

Riley, A. L. 1998. *Restoring streams in cities: A guide for planners, policymakers, and citizens.* Island Press.

Robinson, E. G., and R. L. Beschta. 1990. Characteristics of coarse woody debris for several coastal streams of southeast Alaska, USA. *Canadian Journal of Fisheries Aquatic Sciences* 47: 1684–1693.

Rodiek, J. E., and F. R. Steiner. 1998. Special issue: Landscape architecture research and education. *Landscape and Urban Planning* 42: 73–302.

Rogers, P., T. Ford, R. Forman, and T. Weishel. 2000. Horizon issues in water resources management. Paper presented at the Water Sensitive Planning and Design Symposium, Harvard School of Design.

Roolf, B., and B. Lambright. 2000. Helping homeowners to plant buffers: Waterfront gardens. Paper presented at the Water Sensitive Planning and Design Symposium, Harvard School of Design.

Rosenberg, D., D. Schindler, and R. Nero. 1981. Recent trends in environmental impact assessment. *Canadian Journal of Fisheries and Aquatic Sciences* 38: 591–624.

Ryder, B. A., and K. Swoope. 1997. Learning about riparian rehabitation: Assessing natural resource and landscape architecture student teams. *Journal Natural Resources Life Science Education* 26: 115–119.

Ryder, R. A., and C. J. Edwards. 1985. *A conceptual approach for the application of biological indicators of ecosystem quality in the Great Lakes Basin.* International Joint Commission, Windsor, Ontario.

Salvesen, D. 1994. *Wetlands: Mitigating and regulating development impacts.* The Urban Land Institute.

Santelmann, M., D. Hulse, and D. White. 2001. Applying ecological principles to land-use decision making in agricultural watersheds. Pp. 226–252 in V. H. Dale and R. A. Haeuber, eds., *Applying ecological principles to land management.* Springer.

Scarfo, R. 1989. Stewardship and the profession of landscape architecture. *Landscape Journal* 8: 60–68.

Schaeffer, D. J., E. E. Herricks, and H. W. Kerster. 1988. Ecosystem health: 1. Measuring ecosystem health. *Environmental Management* 12: 445–455.

Schearer, A. W. 2005. Approaching scenario-based studies: Three perceptions about the future and considerations for landscape planning. *Environment and Planning B: Planning and Design* 32: 67–87.

Schloss, J. 2002. GIS watershed mapping: Developing and implementing a watershed natural resources inventory (New Hampshire). Pp. 557–599 in R. L. France, ed., *Handbook of water sensitive planning and design.* Lewis Publishers.

Schloss, J., P. Zandbergen, M. Bavinger, and R. France. 2002. Multiple objectives in watershed management through use of GIS analysis. Pp. 685–686 in R. L. France, ed., *Handbook of water sensitive planning and design.* Lewis Publishers.

Schueler, T. 1995. *Site planning for urban stream protection.* Center Watershed Protection.

Schueler, T. R., and H. K. Holland, eds. 2000. *The practice of watershed protection.* Center for Watershed Protection, Ellicot City, MD.

Schwenk, T. 1989. *Water: The element of life.* Rudolf Steiner Press.

Serafin, R. 1990. Rehabilitating Great Lakes integrity in times of surprise. Pp. 37–44 in C. Edwards and H. Regier, eds., *An ecosystem approach to the integrity of the Great Lakes in turbulent times.* Great Lakes Fishery Commission.

Short, F. T., and D. M. Burdick. 1996. Quantifying eelgrass habitat loss in relation to housing development and nitrogen loading in Waquoit Bay, Massachusetts. *Estuaries* 19: 730–739.

Short, F. T., D. M. Burdick, S. Granger, and S. W. Nixon. 1996. Long-term decline in eelgrass, *Zostera marina* L., linked to increased housing development. *Seagrass Biology Proceedings* 3 (1996): 291–298.

Smith, G. A., and D. R. Williams. 1999. *Ecological education in action: On weaving education, culture, and the environment.* SUNY Press.

Spirn, A. W. 1995. Constructing nature: The legacy of Frederick Law Olmsted. Pp. 91–113 in W. Cronon, ed., *Uncommon ground: Rethinking the human place in nature.* W. W. Norton.

Steedman, R. J. 1988. Modification and assessment of an index of biotic integrity to quantify stream quality in southern Ontario. *Canadian Journal of Fisheries and Aquatic Science* 45: 492–501.

———. 2005. Buzzwords and benchmarks: Ecosystem health as a management goal. Pp. 17–24 in R. L. France, ed., *Facilitating watershed management: Fostering awareness and stewardship.* Rowman & Littlefield.

Steedman, R. J., and H. A. Regier. 1990. Ecological basis for and understanding of ecosystem integrity in the Great Lakes Basin. Pp. 257–272 in C. J. Edwards and H. A. Regier, eds., *An ecosystem approach to the integrity of the Great Lakes in turbulent times.* Great Lakes Fishery Commission.

Steinitz, C. 1990. A framework for theory applicable to the education of landscape architects (and other design professionals). *Landscape Journal* 9: 136–143.

———. 1998. Private course material, Harvard Graduate School of Design.

———. 2000. A case study with water at its core: Alternative futures for the region of Beit She'an, Jenin and northern Jordan. Paper presented at the Water Sensitive Planning and Design Symposium, Harvard School of Design.

———. 2002. On teaching ecologic principles to designers. Pp. 231–244 in B. Johnson and K. Hill, eds., *Ecology and design: Frameworks for learning.* Island Press.

Steinitz, C., H. Arias, S. Bassett, M. Flaxman, T. Goode, T. Maddock, et al. 2003. *Alternative futures for changing landscapes: The upper San Pedro River Basin in Arizona and Sonora.* Island Press.

Steinitz, C., M. Binford, P. Cote, et al. 1996. *Biodiversity and landscape planning: Alternative futures for the region of Camp Pendelton, California.* Harvard Graduate School of Design.

Steinitz, C., R. Peiser, et al. 2001. *Nature and humanity in harmony: Alternative futures for the West Lake, Hangzhou, China.* Harvard Graduate School of Design.

Steinitz, C., A. Rachamimoff, M. Flaxman, et al. 1999. *Coexistence, cooperation, partnership: Alternative futures for the region of Beit She'an Jenin and northern Jordan.* Harvard Graduate School of Design.

Swanson, F. J., M. D. Bryant, G. W. Lienkaemper, and J. R. Sedell. 1984. *Organic debris in small streams: Prince of Wales Island, southeast Alaska.* USDA Forest Service.

Takei, J., and M. P. Keane. 2001. *Sakuteiki: Visions of the Japanese garden; A modern translation of Japan's gardening classic.* Tuttle.

TBG (The Bioengineering Group). 2003. *Alewife Reservation & Alewife Brook master plan.* Metropolitan District Commission, Boston, MA.

Thayer, R. 1994. *Gray world, green heart: Technology, nature, and the sustainable landscape.* John Wiley and Sons.

Thomas, W. A. 1972. Indicators of environmental quality: An overview. Pp. 1–5 in *Indicators of environmental quality.* Plenum.

Thompson, J. W. 2005. Land matters. *Landscape Architecture* (February): 1.

Thompson, W., and K. Sorvig. 2000. *Sustainable landscape construction: A guide to green building outdoors.* Island Press.

Time. 2002. Special issue: How to save the earth. *Time* 160(9) (August 26).

Triska, F. J., and K. Cromack. 1979. The role of wood debris in forests and streams. Pp. 171–190 in R. H. Waring, ed., *Forests: Fresh perspectives from ecosystem analysis.* Oregon University Press.

Truett, J. B., A. K. Johnson, W. D. Rowe, K. D. Feigner, and L. J. Manning. 1975. Development of water quality management indices. *Water Quality Research Bulletin* 51: 436–448.

USDA. 1998. *Stream corridor restoration: Principles, processes, and practices.* U.S. Department of Agriculture.

USDH. 2003. *The practice of low impact development.* U.S. Department of Housing.

Valiela, I., T. Cummins, and B. Shearer. 1992. Couplings of watersheds and coastal waters: Sources and consequences of nutrient enrichment in Waquoit Bay, Massachusetts. *Estuaries* 15: 443–457.

Vallentyne, J. R. 1978. Facing the long-term: An inquiry into opportunity to improve the climate for research with reference to limnology in Canada. *Journal of Fisheries Research Board of Canada* 35: 350–369.

Van Sickle, J., J. Baker, A. Herlihy, P. Bayley, S. Gregory, P. Haggerty, et al. 2004. Projecting the biological condition of streams under alternative scenarios of human land use. *Ecological Applications* 14: 368–380.

Vogele, L. E., and W. C. Rainwaer. 1975. Use of brush shelters as cover by spawning black basses (*Micropterus*) in Bull Shoals Reservoir. *Transactions of the American Fisheries Society* 2: 264–269.

Wenk, W. 2000. Policy, system, site: Continuities in ecological planning and design. Paper presented at the Water Sensitive Planning and Design Symposium, Harvard School of Design.

Wilson, E. O. 1984. *Biophilia.* Harvard University Press.

Winterbottom, D. 2005. Applying the theory: Design/build models for water harvesting and watershed awareness. Pp. 231–251 in R. L. France, ed., *Facilitating watershed management: Fostering awareness and stewardship.* Rowman & Littlefield.

Woodward, J. 2000. *Waterstained landscapes: Seeing and shaping regionally distinctive places.* Johns Hopkins University Press.

Zimmerman, R. 2000. Water resource planning for environmental zoning: Sustaining resources through growth management. Paper presented at the Water Sensitive Planning and Design Symposium, Harvard School of Design.

Zucker, L. 1999. Reforming agricultural drainage to protect rural streams. Unpublished note.

Zucker, L., A. Weekes, M. Vian, and J. D. Dorsey. 2002. Treating rivers as systems to meet multiple objectives. Pp. 431–444 in R. L. France, ed., *Handbook of water sensitive planning and design.* Lewis Publishers.

About the Author

Robert L. France is an adjunct associate professor of landscape ecology at Harvard University's Graduate School of Design. He has conducted research from the high arctic to the tropics and has published hundreds of articles on a wide variety of environmental topics. Dr. France is the author or editor of the technical books *Handbook of Water Sensitive Planning and Design, Wetland Design: Principles and Practices for Landscape Architects and Land-Use Planners, Facilitating Watershed Management: Fostering Awareness and Stewardship,* and *Healing Natures, Repairing Relationships: New Perspectives on Restoring Ecological Spaces and Consciousness,* the latter two titles published by Rowman & Littlefield. He is also author or editor of the popular books *Deep Immersion: The Experience of Water, Profitably Soaked: Thoreau's Experience of Water, Reflecting Heaven: Thoreau on Water, Wetlands of Mass Destruction: Ancient Presage for Contemporary Ecocide in Southern Iraq,* and *Ultreia! Onwards!: Progress of the Pilgrim.*

Index

agriculture: drainage and rural stream protection, 55–56; irrigation agriculture, 15; management frameworks for development, 54–55, 100–103; potential of a site for agricultural development, 86

Alewife Reservation and Greenway, 160–161; Alewife Brook between Broadway Avenue and the Mystic Valley Parkway, 182–183; Alewife Brook between Henderson Bridge and Broadway Avenue, 182; Alewife Brook between Route 2 Rotary and Henderson Bridge, 180–182; and the Alewife Industrial Quadrangle area, 183; Alewife subway station area, 179–180; biological resources of, 171; community input and stewardship, 192–193; cultural and socioeconomic resources of, 171–172; cultural history of, 166; encroachment resolution and, 191; environmental history of, 168; industrial history of, 167; Little Pond, 176–177; maintenance and management of, 191–193; and the Metropolitan District Commission (MDC), 163–164; north side of Little River and the Alewife Reservation, 177–178; physical resources of, 170–171; planning and management of, 169; south side of Little River and the Alewife Reservation, 178–179. *See also* Alewife Reservation and Greenway, master plan for

Alewife Reservation and Greenway, master plan for: background and purpose of the master plan, 163–164; funding strategies, 188–191; general recommendations by category, 174–176; implementation of the master plan, 187–188; master plan development, phase I: inventory of resources, 169–172; master plan development, phase II: opportunities and options (goals and alternatives), 172–174; master plan development, phase III (*see* recommendations by study area; recommendations outside the study area); master plan justification, 161–163; recommendations by study area, 176–183; recommendations outside the study area, 183–187; vision statement, goals, and objectives, 164–166

215